The
Future-Proof Lawyer:
Leveraging Automation and Innovation for Long-Term Growth

Jasmine Gavigan

The Future-Proof Lawyer:

Leveraging Automation and Innovation for Long-Term Growth

Edition: First

Publication Date: October 2024

Author: Jasmine Gavigan

Independently Published

Copyright © 2024 Jasmine Gavigan

All rights reserved. No part of this book may be reproduced, distributed, or transmitted in any form or by any means, including photocopying, recording, or other electronic or mechanical methods, without the prior written permission of the author, except in the case of brief quotations embodied in critical reviews and certain other non-commercial uses permitted by copyright law. For permission requests, contact the author at jasminegavigan@gmail.com.

ISBN: 9798340485236

Hardcover

Adapt or get left behind.

This book equips modern legal professionals with the tools and strategies needed to thrive in a rapidly changing industry, where innovation and automation are no longer optional but essential. As automation, artificial intelligence, and digital transformation reshape the delivery of legal services, the question is no longer if you will adapt - but how.

The **Future-Proof Lawyer** is your definitive guide to thriving in this new era. Whether you're a seasoned attorney or just beginning your legal career, this book provides the tools, strategies, and insights needed to stay ahead in a rapidly evolving industry. Discover how to:

1. **Leverage Workflow Automation** to streamline your practice, reduce errors, and enhance client satisfaction.
2. **Embrace Productized Services** that offer predictable, scalable, and efficient solutions for client service.
3. **Navigate the Challenges of Legal Tech** by understanding the opportunities and ethical considerations of AI, machine learning, and other emerging technologies.
4. **Build a Future-Ready Practice** by fostering a culture of continuous improvement, innovation, and client-centered service.

Filled with real-world examples, case studies, and actionable advice, The **Future-Proof Lawyer** empowers you not just to survive but to *lead* in the age of legal automation. This book is not merely about keeping up with change—it's about spearheading it.

The future is now.

The legal industry is poised to undergo a transformation unlike any other in its history. As clients demand more efficiency, transparency, and value, law firms and legal professionals must adapt to meet these expectations or risk being left behind.

The Future-Proof Lawyer: Leveraging Automation and Innovation for Long-Term Growth provides a roadmap for navigating this transformation. Drawing on the latest developments in legal technology, this book guides you through the process of integrating automation and innovation into your practice.

You will learn how to:

- **Implement Cutting-Edge Automation Tools**: Understand the technologies reshaping the legal landscape, from AI-driven document review to automated compliance monitoring.
- **Transform Your Legal Services**: Explore the shift from traditional billable hours to productized legal services that deliver more value to clients while creating new revenue streams for your practice.
- **Stay Competitive in a Global Market**: Discover how to leverage technology to offer cross-border legal services, expand into emerging markets, and build a practice that can adapt to global legal trends.
- **Overcome Barriers to Innovation**: Learn how to foster a culture that embraces change, encourages experimentation, and continuously improves.

Authored by a legal professional with firsthand experience in implementing these transformative practices, The **Future-Proof Lawyer** is an essential resource for anyone looking to stay competitive and lead in the next chapter of legal services.

The Author

Jasmine Gavigan combines nearly two decades of legal expertise with a visionary approach to technology. Starting her career as an intellectual property legal assistant, she developed a hands-on, solutions-driven approach to transforming how legal services are delivered. Whether working with global corporations or agile startups, Jasmine has consistently redefined workflows in today's tech-driven legal landscape.

As the founder of WorkCart, a no-code platform revolutionizing service businesses, Jasmine has firsthand experience designing automated systems that simplify even the most complex processes. Her work with top-tier law firms and in-house legal teams gives her a unique perspective on the intersection of legal practice and technology, allowing her to create strategies that are both efficient and scalable.

Taking a mid-career break from legal services, Jasmine became an early employee at Canadian e-commerce platform Shopify, where she honed her business consulting skills and gained valuable insights into e-commerce and technology. These experiences now shape her approach to legal innovation, applying the same strategies used to deliver products to global customers to providing legal services for global clients.

This is not the book an average lawyer would write. Jasmine's expertise in automation and legal service innovation offers a practical, tech-forward roadmap for transforming outdated processes into streamlined, value-driven systems that save time and deliver results. Whether you're looking to optimize operations or explore new business models, Jasmine's guidance is your key to navigating the future of legal practice.

Jasmine Gavigan

Contents

Preface 7
Introduction: The Case for Automation in Law 8
Chapter 1: The Evolution of Legal Services 11
Chapter 2: Understanding Workflow Automation 31
Chapter 3: The Problem with the Billable Hour 59
Chapter 4: The Rise of Productized Services 74
Chapter 5: Designing Workflow Automation for Legal Services 92
Chapter 6: Building a Productized Legal Service 101
Chapter 7: Automation Tech Stack 121
Chapter 8: Implementing Workflow Automation in a Law Firm 143
Chapter 9: Overcoming Barriers to Innovation 152
Chapter 10: The Economic Impact of Automation 171
Chapter 11: Case Studies of Successful Legal Automation 181
Chapter 12: The Future of Legal Services 185
       Future-Proof: Imagining of Legal Services in 2050 185
       Becoming Future-Proof Lawyers 187
Chapter 13: Ethical Considerations in Legal Automation 199
Chapter 14: Marketing and Selling Productized Legal Services 217
       Playbook: Marketing and Selling Productized Services 234
Chapter 15: Measuring Success and Scaling Automation 239
       Playbook: Scaling Workflow Automation 258
Chapter 17: Building a Culture of Continuous Improvement 264
Chapter 18: Legal Automation and the Global Market 282
Appendix A: Glossary 294
Appendix B: Resources 299
Appendix C: Tools 304

Preface

This book is designed as both a guide and a resource for legal professionals seeking to navigate the integration of automation and innovation into their legal service business. Each chapter addresses specific areas of legal work that are ripe for transformation, providing practical strategies, tools, and case studies to illustrate how automation can enhance efficiency and service delivery.

While the chapters are organized by topic, you may find that some concepts—such as workflow automation or productized legal services—are covered in more than one section. This is intentional, as these themes are integral to multiple facets of modern legal practice. I encourage you to approach the book both as a reference you can return to for specific insights and as a broader exploration of how automation can reshape your work.

Whether you are looking to adopt new technology, improve your firm's efficiency, or simply better understand the potential of legal innovation, this book offers a flexible structure to support your learning. Feel free to read sequentially or skip to the sections most relevant to you. And, as with the evolving landscape of law, remember that revisiting concepts in different contexts can deepen your understanding and broaden your perspective.

Introduction: The Case for Automation in Law

The Need for Innovation in Legal Services

The legal industry, like many others, is at a crossroads where the traditional methods of delivering services are being challenged by technological advancements and changing client expectations. Clients today demand more transparency, predictability, and efficiency in their legal services.

As the intersection between people and technology continues to evolve, standardized processes, workflow automation, and productized services are increasingly shaping the future of legal practice. Workflow automation involves the use of technology to automate routine and repetitive tasks, freeing up lawyers to focus on more complex and value-added work. This not only increases efficiency but also reduces the likelihood of human error, resulting in more consistent and reliable outcomes for clients.

Productized services take workflow automation a step further by transforming legal services into standardized, repeatable offerings that are delivered at a fixed price. This model shifts the focus from time spent to value delivered, aligning the lawyer's incentives with the client's goals. For example, rather than billing hourly for contract reviews, a law firm might offer a flat-fee service for reviewing and drafting standard contracts. This approach provides clients with greater cost certainty and allows law firms to scale their services more effectively.

The shift towards automation and productization is not just about adopting new technologies; it's about fundamentally rethinking the way legal services are delivered. It requires a move away from the traditional mindset of valuing time over results and towards a model that prioritizes efficiency, innovation, and client satisfaction.

The Argument for Automation and Productized Services

As the legal industry continues to evolve, those who embrace automation and productized services will be ideally positioned to meet the demands of a rapidly changing market. Workflow automation can drastically reduce the time spent on routine tasks, such as document review, legal research, and case management. By automating these processes, law firms can reduce costs and increase efficiency, while delivering services more quickly and accurately.

Productized services allow law firms to diversify their offerings and tap into new revenue streams. By creating standardized services that can be easily replicated, firms can serve more clients, often without a corresponding increase in overhead. This scalability is particularly important in an increasingly competitive legal market, where clients are more cost-conscious and have higher expectations for service delivery.

The adoption of automation and productized services also addresses some of the critical challenges facing the legal profession today, such as burnout, inefficiency, and the rising cost of legal services. By reducing reliance on the billable hour and shifting towards a more value-driven approach, law firms can create a more sustainable and rewarding work environment for their lawyers, while also making legal services more accessible and delivering better outcomes for their clients.

Challenging The Billable Hour

It's no secret. For decades, the billable hour has stood as the bedrock of legal practice. Yet, it has also fostered inefficiencies, overwork, and a fundamental misalignment between the interests of lawyers and their clients. By prioritizing time spent over results achieved, this model creates an unintended incentive where delays may benefit lawyers financially, even as clients demand timely, cost-effective solutions.

As these flaws become increasingly evident to both sides, the legal profession faces an urgent call for innovation. Workflow automation and productized services present a powerful alternative, shifting the focus from hours worked to value delivered. These advancements promise not only greater efficiency and profitability for law firms but also more transparent, client-centered outcomes.

Setting the Stage for the Book

This book argues that the future of effective legal services lies in embracing workflow automation and productized services. Throughout the following chapters, we will explore the history of the legal profession, examine the limitations of the current model, and provide practical guidance on how to implement innovative approaches in your law firm or legal service business. By the end of this book, you will have a clear understanding of how automation and productization can transform your legal practice, enabling you to deliver more value to your clients while also achieving greater efficiency and profitability.

The journey begins with understanding where we came from—the origins of the billable hour and its impact on the legal profession. From there, we will delve into the technologies and strategies that can help you navigate the future of law with confidence and clarity. Whether you are in-house, a solo practitioner, or part of a large firm, this book will provide the tools and insights you need to thrive in a rapidly changing legal landscape.

Chapter 1: The Evolution of Legal Services

History of the Legal Industry

The legal profession is one of the oldest and most venerable in the world, with roots that can be traced back to ancient civilizations[1]. However, the modern legal industry as we know it began to take shape in the medieval period, particularly in England, where the foundations of contemporary legal practice were laid.

Origins of the Legal Profession in England

The origins of the legal profession in England are closely tied to the development of common law, which began to take shape in the 12th century under King Henry II. This period saw the establishment of royal courts and the growing use of judicial decisions to create precedents, forming the foundation of what would become the English common law system. As legal processes became more formalized and complex, the need for specialized knowledge arose, giving rise to professional advocates who could argue cases before the King's courts.[2]

By the 13th century, these advocates began to organize themselves into guild-like associations, leading to the establishment of the Inns of Court in London. The Inns of Court became the primary institutions for legal education and training, serving as both professional associations and educational establishments. The four Inns—Lincoln's Inn, Inner

---

[1] Bonner, Robert J. (1927). Lawyers and Litigants in Ancient Athens: The Genesis of the Legal Profession. New York: Benjamin Blom
[2] Brundage, James A. (1994). "The Rise of the Professional Jurist in the Thirteenth Century." Syracuse Journal of International Law and Commerce

Temple, Middle Temple, and Gray's Inn—were responsible for the training and admission of barristers, the advocates who argued cases in court.[3]

During this time, the legal profession was divided into two main branches: barristers and solicitors. Barristers were the specialists who appeared in court, while solicitors handled the broader aspects of legal work, including preparing cases and advising clients. This division of labor laid the groundwork for the professional structures that continue to define the legal industry today.

Early Modern Period Legal Practice

As the English legal system evolved, so did the role of lawyers. By the 16th century, the legal profession had become more formalized, with the introduction of written records and the establishment of legal precedent as a guiding principle. Lawyers were increasingly seen as essential intermediaries between the law and the public, and their expertise became more highly valued.

The growth of commerce and trade during the early modern period also played a significant role in the development of the legal profession. As commercial activity expanded, so did the demand for legal services to resolve disputes, draft contracts, and protect property rights. This period saw the rise of the attorney, a legal practitioner who combined the roles of solicitor and barrister, particularly in smaller towns and rural areas where the formal distinction between the two was less pronounced.

The increasing complexity of legal work led to the development of specialized areas of practice. Lawyers began to focus on specific fields such as property law, contract law, and criminal law, reflecting the growing diversity of legal needs. This specialization contributed to the professionalization of the legal industry and established the foundations for modern legal practice.

---

[3] Webster, James C. (1911). "Inns of Court". In Chisholm, Hugh (ed.). Encyclopædia Britannica. Vol. 14 (11th ed.). Cambridge University Press,

The Industrial Revolution and the Expansion of Legal Services

The Industrial Revolution of the 18th and 19th centuries brought about profound economic and social changes that further shaped the legal profession.[4] The rapid expansion of industry and commerce created new legal challenges, such as labor disputes, corporate governance, and intellectual property rights. The legal profession responded by developing new areas of expertise to address these emerging issues.

During this period, the legal profession became more accessible to a broader segment of society. Legal services were no longer the exclusive domain of the wealthy elite; as the middle class expanded, so too did the demand for legal representation and advice. This democratization of legal services led to the growth of law firms and the proliferation of solicitors, who provided legal services to individuals and businesses alike.

The rise of large, urban law firms in the 19th century marked a pivotal shift in the legal profession's structure. Many of these firms were family-run enterprises, with senior partners passing the business down through generations, ensuring continuity and prestige. This growth was driven by the increasing complexity of legal work, particularly with the demands of industrialization, corporate governance, and evolving commercial transactions.[5] To manage the multifaceted aspects of major cases, these firms required teams of specialized lawyers, leading to the creation of more formal, hierarchical structures within the profession. During this time, the role of legal secretaries and clerks became vital, as they handled administrative tasks that enhanced efficiency and allowed lawyers to focus on more substantive legal matters.[6] These changes laid the groundwork for the modern, large-scale law firms we recognize today.

---

[4] Deakin, Simon, and Frank Wilkinson. The Law of the Labour Market: Industrialization, Employment, and Legal Evolution. Oxford University Press, 2005.
[5] Gordon, Robert W. "The American Legal Profession, 1870–2000." In The Cambridge History of Law in America, edited by Michael Grossberg and Christopher Tomlins, Vol. 3,. Cambridge University Press, 2008
[6] Friedman, Lawrence M. "The Legal Profession: At Work." In A History of American Law, 4th ed., New York: Oxford University Press, 2019

Professionalization and Regulation in the 20th Century

The 20th century brought further changes to the legal profession, particularly in the areas of professionalization and regulation. In many countries, the legal profession became subject to stricter oversight and regulation by professional bodies. In England and Wales, for example, the Law Society and the Bar Council were established to regulate solicitors and barristers, respectively. These organizations set standards for legal education, professional conduct, and the admission of new members to the profession.

The professionalization of the legal industry also extended to the United States, where the American Bar Association (ABA) played a central role in shaping the standards and practices of the legal profession. The ABA's establishment of the Model Rules of Professional Conduct in 1983 provided a comprehensive framework for ethical legal practice, influencing the regulation of the profession across the country.

During the 20th century, the legal profession also became more diversified, with the admission of women and minority groups into the profession, although significant barriers to entry and advancement remained. The increased diversity of the legal profession brought new perspectives and approaches to legal practice, enriching the profession as a whole.

The Globalization of Legal Services

As the 20th century progressed, the legal profession began to adapt to the forces of globalization. The expansion of international trade, the rise of multinational corporations, and the increasing interconnectedness of economies created new opportunities and challenges for lawyers. Global law firms emerged, offering cross-border legal services and advising clients on complex international transactions and disputes.

The globalization of legal services also led to the harmonization of certain legal standards and practices across jurisdictions. International organizations, such as the United Nations and the World Trade Organization, developed treaties and agreements that influenced national legal systems and created new areas of legal practice, such as international arbitration and trade law.

At the same time, the legal profession faced new pressures, including the need to stay abreast of rapidly changing laws and regulations in multiple jurisdictions. The rise of international legal networks and alliances allowed law firms to collaborate across borders, sharing knowledge and resources to better serve their clients in a globalized world.

The Need for a Paradigm Shift

The historical development of the legal industry has been characterized by continuous adaptation to societal, economic, and technological changes. However, despite these changes, certain aspects of legal practice, such as the billable hour model, have remained remarkably resilient. This book argues that the emergence of the billable hour as the dominant billing method has had profound implications for the legal profession, shaping the way lawyers work and how legal services are delivered. Yet, as the legal industry enters a new era of technological innovation and globalization, there is a growing recognition that the traditional approaches to legal practice may no longer be sustainable.

This historical overview sets the stage for a deeper exploration of how the billable hour came to dominate the legal profession and why it is now facing significant challenges. As we look to the future, it is clear that a fundamental business model change is needed—one that embraces new models of legal service delivery, such as workflow automation and productized services. These innovations have the potential to address many of the limitations of the traditional model, creating a more efficient, client-centered, and sustainable legal industry.

Emergence of the Billable Hour

The billable hour, now a ubiquitous feature of legal practice, did not always dominate the profession. Its emergence as the primary method of billing for legal services is a relatively recent development, dating back to the mid-20th century. Understanding how the billable hour became the dominant billing method requires examining the broader context of legal practice during this period, as well as the economic and cultural forces that propelled its adoption.

The Pre-Billable Hour Era: Fixed Fees and Retainers

Before the widespread adoption of the billable hour, legal services were typically billed through fixed fees, retainers, or contingency fees. Fixed fees were common for routine legal services, such as drafting wills, handling property transactions, or processing simple legal documents. Retainers were often used for ongoing legal representation, with clients paying a lump sum upfront for a lawyer's availability and services over a set period.[7]

Contingency fees, where a lawyer's payment was contingent upon winning a case, were primarily used in personal injury and other types of litigation where the client might not be able to afford legal representation otherwise. These billing methods placed the focus on the value of the service provided rather than the time spent delivering it.

This approach had its benefits, particularly for clients, who appreciated the predictability of costs. However, it also had limitations, especially as legal matters grew more complex and unpredictable. Fixed fees could undervalue the work required for particularly challenging cases, while retainers sometimes failed to reflect the actual amount of work performed. This lack of alignment between effort and compensation created inefficiencies and dissatisfaction on both sides of the lawyer-client relationship.

The Post-War Boom and the Rise of the Billable Hour

The shift towards the billable hour began in earnest after World War II, during a period of significant economic expansion in the United States. The post-war boom led to an increase in corporate activity, mergers and acquisitions, and regulatory oversight, all of which created new and more complex demands for legal services. Law firms, particularly those serving corporate clients, faced growing pressure to demonstrate the value of their work in a quantifiable way.

It was during this time that the billable hour started to gain traction as a billing method. The model offered a straightforward and ostensibly fair way to charge for legal services: clients paid for the actual time lawyers spent on their cases. This approach appealed to both lawyers

---

[7] Friedman, Lawrence M. A History of American Law. 4th ed., Oxford University Press, 2019

and clients, particularly in complex, open-ended matters where the amount of work required could not be easily predicted.

The billable hour's rise to prominence can be traced back to the 1950s, particularly in the U.S. legal market. This period marked a significant transformation in the structure and management of law firms, as the growth of large corporate firms in cities like New York, Chicago, and Los Angeles necessitated greater efficiency and accountability.[8] A pivotal moment occurred in 1958, when the American Bar Association (ABA) published its influential pamphlet "*The 1958 Lawyer and His 1938 Dollar*".[9] This pamphlet encouraged lawyers to move away from fixed fees and adopt time-based billing to better align their practices with the profit-driven efficiencies seen in manufacturing. By promoting the billable hour as a transparent and fair way to track lawyer productivity, the ABA set the stage for it to become the dominant billing method in the legal profession.

One of the most influential developments was the adoption of timekeeping practices within law firms. Partners and associates began to track the hours spent on client work meticulously, breaking down their time into six-minute increments. This practice allowed firms to bill clients more accurately and to demonstrate the volume of work being done. It also provided a basis for assessing the productivity of lawyers within the firm, as billable hours became a key metric for evaluating performance.

Institutionalization and Standardization

By the 1960s, the billable hour had become the dominant billing method in the legal profession, particularly among large firms serving corporate clients. Several factors contributed to this shift:

- **Economic Incentives:** The billable hour provided a clear and direct way for law firms to increase revenue. As firms grew in size, they needed a standardized method to bill clients and allocate resources. The billable hour allowed firms to charge clients based on the exact amount of work performed, which

---

[8] ABA Journal Article: Cassens Weiss, Debra. "Accounting 'Rogue Outliers' Seek to Change Billable Hour." ABA Journal, July 31, 2013
[9] American Bar Association. The 1958 Lawyer and His 1938 Dollar. ABA Special Committee on Economics of Law Practice, 1958

seemed to align effort with compensation more directly than flat fees or retainers.
- **Client Demand:** Corporate clients, dealing with increasingly complex legal issues, began to demand more transparency and accountability from their legal advisors. The billable hour allowed clients to see precisely how much time was spent on their matters, which, in theory, justified the fees they were being charged.
- **Management and Control:** As law firms expanded, managing partner productivity and firm profitability became more critical. The billable hour provided a straightforward metric for assessing individual lawyer performance. Associates' career progression often became closely tied to their ability to meet or exceed billable hour targets, which were set by firm management as a way to ensure firm profitability.
- **Technological Advancements:** The introduction of time-tracking tools and other office technologies in the 1960s and 1970s further entrenched the billable hour. These technologies made it easier for lawyers to track their time accurately and for firms to generate detailed invoices for clients. As time-tracking became more precise, the billable hour became even more embedded in the fabric of legal practice.
- **Legal Industry Culture:** The legal profession's conservative and risk-averse nature also played a role in the widespread adoption of the billable hour. As more firms adopted the model, it became the industry standard, and any deviation from this norm was viewed with skepticism. The billable hour was seen as a reliable, objective measure of work, which made it difficult for alternative billing models to gain traction.

The Billable Hour's Entrenchment in Legal Practice

By the late 20th century, the billable hour had become almost synonymous with legal practice, particularly in the United States. It was during this period that the model's influence extended beyond large corporate firms to smaller firms and even solo practitioners. The model was viewed as the "gold standard" for legal billing, and most law firms organized their business operations around it.

Law firm profitability became increasingly tied to the number of billable hours generated, leading to the establishment of minimum billable hour requirements for associates. These requirements, often ranging from 1,800 to 2,200 hours per year, became a key factor in law firm economics, influencing everything from hiring practices to lawyer compensation.[10]

However, as the billable hour became more entrenched, its limitations also became more apparent. Critics argued that it incentivized inefficiency, as lawyers could increase their revenue by spending more time on tasks rather than completing them quickly and effectively. In addition, the focus on billable hours created a high-pressure work environment, contributing to stress, burnout, and a culture of overwork within the legal profession.

The billable hour also had significant implications for client relationships. While the model provided transparency, it also led to escalating legal costs, often creating tension between lawyers and their clients. Clients, particularly those in corporate settings, began to push back against rising legal fees, seeking alternative billing arrangements that offered more predictability and value.

Early Attempts at Innovation

As the legal profession evolved throughout the 20th century, so did the awareness of the limitations and challenges posed by the traditional billable hour model. In response, various movements and technological advancements emerged, aiming to innovate the practice of law and address some of its inherent inefficiencies. While these early attempts at innovation were groundbreaking in their own right, many struggled to gain widespread acceptance, often due to cultural and institutional resistance within the profession.

The Legal Aid Movement

One of the earliest and most significant attempts at innovation within the legal profession was the the Legal Aid movement. This movement began in the late 19th century, driven by the growing recognition that access to legal representation should not be limited to the wealthy elite. The aim was to provide affordable or even free legal services to

---

[10] National Association for Law Placement (NALP). "Billable Hours Requirements at Law Firms." NALP Bulletin, May 2006.
This report highlights the billable hour requirements at law firms, showing that most firms set targets ranging from 1,800 to 2,200 hours per year. The data indicates that about 24% of firms required 1,800 hours, while 21% required 1,900 hours, with 2,000-hour requirements being more common in larger cities like Chicago and Miami.

those who could not afford to pay for them, particularly the working class and low income individuals.[11]

The Legal Aid movement gained momentum in the United States during the early 20th century, with the establishment of the Legal Aid Society in New York City in 1876. The Society sought to ensure that everyone, regardless of income, had access to justice. Over the following decades, similar organizations were established across the country, providing essential legal services in areas such as housing, employment, and family law.

In the 1960s, the movement received a significant boost with the creation of the Office of Economic Opportunity (OEO) under President Lyndon B. Johnson's War on Poverty. The OEO established federally funded legal services programs, which expanded access to legal aid across the United States. This initiative represented a major innovation in the legal profession, as it formalized the provision of legal services to underserved populations and laid the groundwork for the modern legal aid system.

However, despite its noble intentions, the Legal Aid movement faced significant challenges. Funding was often inconsistent, and legal aid organizations struggled to meet the overwhelming demand for their services. Many within the legal profession viewed legal aid as a second-tier practice, with lower prestige and financial rewards compared to private practice. This perception contributed to the movement's struggle to attract top talent and secure the resources needed to sustain its operations.

The Legal Aid movement represented a critical early attempt to innovate within the legal profession, challenging the traditional notion that legal services were a luxury only the wealthy could afford. It also highlighted the need for alternative models of legal service delivery, a theme that would reemerge in later efforts to innovate the profession.

The Rise of Legal Technology: LexisNexis and Beyond

Another significant early attempt at innovation within the legal profession was the introduction of legal technology, particularly the

---

[11] Batlan, Felice, and Marianne Vasara-Aaltonen, eds. Histories of Legal Aid: A Comparative and International Perspective. Palgrave Macmillan, 2022

development of legal research databases like LexisNexis. In the pre-digital era, legal research was an arduous and time-consuming process, involving manual searches through vast volumes of case law, statutes, and legal commentaries, sometimes located off-site or in different cities. This labor-intensive work was often billed by the hour, contributing to the inefficiencies and high costs associated with legal services.

In 1973, LexisNexis revolutionized legal research by launching one of the first computerized legal research databases.[12] Lexis, initially developed by Mead Data Central, allowed lawyers to search through a vast repository of legal documents electronically, drastically reducing the time required to find relevant case law and statutes. This innovation represented a major leap forward in the efficiency and effectiveness of legal research.

LexisNexis provided lawyers with the ability to conduct keyword searches, access case law from multiple jurisdictions, and retrieve legal documents instantly. This was a significant departure from the traditional method of leafing through physical law books, and it offered a glimpse of the potential for technology to transform legal practice.

However, the adoption of LexisNexis and similar technologies was not without resistance.[13] Many lawyers, particularly those who had built their careers on traditional research methods, were initially skeptical of computerized legal research. There was a fear that reliance on technology might lead to the erosion of fundamental legal skills or that it would reduce the billable hours that could be charged for research. The high cost of accessing these early databases was also a barrier for smaller firms and solo practitioners.

Despite these challenges, the success of LexisNexis paved the way for further technological innovations in the legal profession. Over the following decades, legal technology continued to evolve, with the development of more advanced research tools, case management software, and document automation systems. These technologies promised to increase efficiency, reduce costs, and improve the

---

[12] Miller, Stephen. "For Future Reference, a Pioneer in Online Reading." The Wall Street Journal, January 12, 2012
[13] Bues, Micha-Manuel, and Matthaei, Emilio. LegalTech on the Rise: Technology Changes Legal Work Behaviours, But Does Not Replace Its Profession. Springer, 2017.

accuracy of legal work, but they also challenged the traditional business models and practices of law firms.

The Introduction of Alternative Fee Arrangements

In the 1980s and 1990s, as dissatisfaction with the billable hour grew among both clients and lawyers, the legal profession began to experiment with alternative fee arrangements (AFAs).[14] AFAs represented a significant attempt to innovate legal billing practices, offering alternatives to the traditional time-based billing model.

Several types of AFAs were introduced, including:

- **Flat Fees:** Clients were charged a single, predetermined fee for a specific legal service, regardless of the time spent. This model provided cost certainty for clients and incentivized lawyers to work efficiently.
- **Contingency Fees:** Lawyers were compensated only if they won the case, typically receiving a percentage of the settlement or judgment. While already common in personal injury and some types of litigation, contingency fees began to be explored in other areas of law.
- **Success Fees:** Similar to contingency fees, success fees involved a bonus paid to the lawyer if a specific outcome was achieved, on top of a reduced hourly rate or flat fee.
- **Retainers with Performance Incentives:** Clients paid an upfront retainer, with additional payments based on the achievement of specific milestones or outcomes.

AFAs were seen as a way to align the interests of lawyers and clients more closely, moving away from the incentives of the billable hour that rewarded time spent over results achieved. They also offered clients greater predictability and control over legal costs, which was particularly appealing in an era of increasing economic uncertainty.

However, the widespread adoption of AFAs faced significant hurdles. Many law firms were reluctant to move away from the billable hour, which had become deeply ingrained in their business models and profit structures. Partners, particularly in large firms, were concerned about the potential financial impact of AFAs, fearing that they might

---

[14] Susskind, Richard. Tomorrow's Lawyers: An Introduction to Your Future. Oxford University Press, 2013

lead to reduced revenue or require significant changes in how legal work was valued and compensated.

Clients, while often eager to explore alternatives to the billable hour, were also cautious. There was concern that AFAs might result in lower-quality work if lawyers were incentivized to complete tasks too quickly or cut corners. Additionally, negotiating and structuring AFAs could be complex, requiring a level of trust and collaboration between lawyers and clients that was not always present.

Despite these challenges, AFAs did gain traction in certain areas of legal practice, particularly in transactional work and high-volume, routine matters where the scope of work could be more easily defined. However, the billable hour remained the dominant billing method, and AFAs were often seen as exceptions rather than the rule.

Legal Process Outsourcing (LPO) and Early Offshoring

The late 20th and early 21st centuries also saw the emergence of Legal Process Outsourcing (LPO) as another attempt to innovate within the legal profession. LPO involved the outsourcing of routine legal tasks, such as document review, legal research, and contract drafting, to third-party providers, often located in countries with lower labor costs.[15]

The concept of LPO was driven by the need to reduce the cost of legal services while maintaining quality. By outsourcing repetitive and time-consuming tasks, law firms and corporate legal departments could focus their in-house resources on higher-value work. This model also allowed firms to offer more competitive pricing to clients, particularly for large-scale projects such as litigation discovery or regulatory compliance.

India, in particular, became a hub for LPO services, thanks to its large pool of English-speaking lawyers and lower labor costs.[16] The growth of LPO was supported by advancements in communication and

---

[15] Ross, Mark. "Legal Process Outsourcing: Redefining the Legal Services Delivery Model." In Liquid Legal: Transforming Legal into a Business Savvy, Information Enabled and Performance Driven Industry, edited by Kai Jacob, Dierk Schindler, and Roger Strathausen. Springer, 2017
[16] Frumin, Ben. "The LPO Revolution." Indian Business Law Journal, April 18, 2008

information technology, which made it easier to manage and coordinate legal work across borders.

While LPO offered significant cost savings and operational efficiencies, it also faced resistance within the legal profession. Critics argued that outsourcing legal work could lead to a loss of quality control, as well as concerns about data security and confidentiality. There was also apprehension about the potential impact on jobs within the legal profession, particularly for junior lawyers who traditionally handled much of the routine work that was now being outsourced.

Despite these concerns, LPO continued to grow, particularly among large multinational corporations and global law firms. It represented a significant shift in how legal services were delivered, challenging the traditional model of legal practice and paving the way for further innovation.

The Challenges of Early Legal Innovation

The early attempts at innovation within the legal profession - from the Legal Aid movement to the rise of legal technology and alternative fee arrangements - shared a common theme: they sought to address the limitations and inefficiencies of traditional legal practice. However, these efforts often faced significant challenges, both from within the profession and from external factors.

Cultural resistance was perhaps the most significant barrier to innovation. The legal profession has long been characterized by a deep respect for tradition and precedent, with a conservative approach to change. Many lawyers were reluctant to embrace new methods or technologies that challenged the established norms of practice. This resistance was often compounded by the hierarchical structure of law firms, where senior partners, who had built their careers on traditional models, were often the gatekeepers of change.

Institutional barriers also played a role. The legal profession is highly regulated, with strict ethical standards and professional rules that can make it difficult to experiment with new approaches. For example, ethical concerns about conflicts of interest, client confidentiality, and the unauthorized practice of law often limited the scope of innovation in areas such as legal technology and outsourcing.

In addition to these factors, the economic incentives embedded in the billable hour model created a powerful disincentive to change. As long as law firm profitability was tied to the number of hours billed, there was little motivation to adopt more efficient practices that could reduce billable hours and, by extension, revenue.

Setting the Stage for a Paradigm Shift

The early attempts at innovation within the legal profession, while groundbreaking, often struggled to gain widespread acceptance. However, they laid the foundation for the more radical transformations that would come in the 21st century. As the limitations of the billable hour became increasingly apparent, and as clients demanded more value-driven services, the legal profession began to recognize the need for a paradigm shift.[17]

In the chapters that follow, we will explore how these early innovations set the stage for the adoption of workflow automation and productized services. These modern approaches represent the next step in the evolution of legal services, offering the potential to overcome many of the challenges that have long plagued the profession. By embracing these innovations, law firms can move beyond the constraints of the billable hour and towards a more efficient, client-centered, and sustainable model of legal practice.

Legal Innovation: Failing Forward

Some early attempts at innovation within the legal profession, despite their potential to transform legal practice, were largely unsuccessful in achieving widespread adoption. While these initiatives introduced new concepts and tools that could have addressed many of the profession's inefficiencies, several factors contributed to their limited impact. Chief among these were deep-seated cultural resistance and significant institutional barriers, both of which created an environment where change was slow and often stifled.

Cultural Resistance: The Weight of Tradition

One of the most formidable obstacles to innovation in the legal profession has been its deeply ingrained culture of conservatism and respect for tradition. The practice of law is historically rooted in precedent, with an emphasis on continuity and stability. This mindset, while valuable in ensuring consistency and reliability in legal

---

[17] Rethinking Law Firm Culture: Is the Push for High Billable Hours Eroding Lawyer Well-Being?" PublicLawLibrary.org, July 19, 2024

outcomes, has also fostered a resistance to change that is pervasive across the profession.

The Conservative Nature of the Legal Profession

Lawyers are trained to be risk-averse. From the earliest days of legal education, the importance of adhering to established rules, precedents, and procedures is emphasized. This conservative approach is further reinforced in the practice of law, where the consequences of errors can be severe—not only for the client but also for the lawyer's career. This inherent caution makes lawyers less inclined to experiment with new methods or technologies, particularly those that could disrupt established practices.

The profession's hierarchical structure also plays a significant role in resisting change. In many law firms, senior partners—who have spent their careers mastering and benefiting from traditional practices—hold the most influence. These senior figures often view new approaches with skepticism, preferring the methods that have reliably brought them success. This generational divide can make it difficult for innovative ideas to gain traction, as younger lawyers and associates, who may be more open to change, lack the authority to implement new practices.

The Prestige Factor

Another cultural factor is the prestige associated with traditional legal practices, particularly within large, established firms. The billable hour, for example, became a symbol of the lawyer's expertise and dedication, with high billable hours often seen as a mark of success and professional achievement. The prestige associated with long hours and detailed manual work (such as in-depth legal research) contributed to a culture where efficiency improvements and automation were viewed as shortcuts, potentially undermining the perceived value of legal work.

This prestige-driven mindset extended to other areas as well, such as the reluctance to adopt alternative fee arrangements or embrace legal aid work. Many in the profession viewed these innovations as a threat to the status quo, fearing that they could diminish the profession's stature or lead to a commoditization of legal services.

Fear of Obsolescence

The fear of obsolescence also fueled resistance to innovation. Lawyers who had built their careers on traditional methods were concerned that new technologies or alternative billing models could render their skills less valuable or even obsolete. For example, the introduction of computerized legal research tools like LexisNexis was met with anxiety by those who had spent years honing their ability to navigate vast libraries of legal texts. Similarly, the rise of legal process outsourcing (LPO) raised concerns about job security, particularly for junior lawyers who traditionally performed the routine tasks now being outsourced.

This fear was not unfounded. The rapid pace of technological change has disrupted numerous industries, and the legal profession is not immune to these forces. However, rather than embracing innovation as an opportunity to enhance their work and provide greater value to clients, many in the profession saw it as a threat to their established roles and livelihoods.

Institutional Barriers: Regulation and Professional Norms

In addition to cultural resistance, institutional barriers also played a significant role in the failure of early attempts at innovation. The legal profession is one of the most heavily regulated industries, with strict ethical standards and professional norms that govern how legal services are delivered. While these regulations are designed to protect clients and ensure the integrity of the profession, they can also stifle innovation and limit the adoption of new practices.

Regulatory Constraints

Legal practice is governed by a complex web of regulations and ethical rules, which vary by jurisdiction but generally include strict guidelines on client confidentiality, conflicts of interest, and the unauthorized practice of law. These regulations are enforced by professional bodies, such as the American Bar Association (ABA) in the United States and the Law Society in the United Kingdom, which have the authority to discipline lawyers who violate ethical standards

While these regulations are essential for maintaining the integrity of the legal profession, they can also create obstacles for innovation. For example, the ethical rules surrounding client confidentiality made it difficult for early adopters of legal technology to convince their colleagues to embrace new tools that stored sensitive client data electronically.[18] Concerns about data security and the potential for breaches created significant hesitation, even as technology offered solutions that could improve efficiency and accuracy.

Similarly, the rules governing the unauthorized practice of law created challenges for innovations like legal process outsourcing.[19] Many jurisdictions have strict definitions of what constitutes the practice of law, and these definitions often include activities such as legal research and document preparation. This made it difficult for law firms to outsource these tasks to non-lawyers, particularly in foreign jurisdictions where legal qualifications might differ. The fear of violating ethical rules and facing sanctions deterred many firms from exploring outsourcing as a viable option.

The Billable Hour as an Institutional Norm

The billable hour, while not a formal regulation, became an institutional norm that was deeply embedded in the business models of law firms. As the primary method of billing, it shaped everything from firm management practices to lawyer compensation structures. Firms organized their operations around maximizing billable hours, with partner profits and associate promotions often tied directly to the number of hours billed.[20]

This institutionalization of the billable hour created a powerful disincentive to adopt alternative billing models, such as flat fees or success-based fees. Even when clients expressed a desire for more predictable and value-based pricing, many firms were reluctant to move away from the billable hour, fearing that it would lead to reduced revenue or require a significant restructuring of their business models.

Additionally, the emphasis on billable hours reinforced a short-term focus on maximizing immediate revenue rather than investing in long-term innovations that could improve efficiency and client satisfaction. This short-termism made it difficult for firms to justify the upfront costs of adopting new technologies or exploring alternative service delivery

---

[18] Wright, Steven A. Ethics, Law and Technology Adoption: Navigating Technology Adoption Challenges. Macadamia Solutions LLC, 2024
[19] Pandey, Shashi Shekhar. The Law and Practice of Legal Process Outsourcing. South Asian ed., CCH India, 2008
[20] American Bar Association. ABA Commission on Billable Hours Report. American Bar Association, 2002

models, even when these innovations had the potential to generate greater value over time.

Lack of Incentives for Innovation

Institutional resistance was further compounded by a lack of incentives for innovation within the legal profession. Unlike in other industries, where innovation is often rewarded through market competition or investor funding, the legal profession has traditionally operated within a relatively insular and stable market. The demand for legal services has historically been strong, and the barriers to entry for new competitors have been high, particularly for large corporate clients.

This lack of competitive pressure meant that many law firms had little motivation to innovate. As long as the traditional models were profitable and clients continued to pay for services, there was little reason to invest in new approaches that might disrupt the status quo. Additionally, the partnership structure of many law firms, where profits are distributed among partners based on the firm's annual revenue,[21] created a disincentive to invest in innovations that might reduce short-term profitability, even if they offered long-term benefits.

The Inertia of Success

One of the most significant reasons for the failure of early innovations in the legal profession is the inertia created by success. The billable hour, traditional legal research methods, and established billing models have all contributed to the success of law firms for decades. This success creates a sense of complacency, where the risks of changing established practices seem to outweigh the potential benefits.

Law firms that thrive under the traditional model are often the least likely to embrace change. The attitude of "if it isn't broke, don't fix it" prevails, particularly among large, well-established firms that dominate the market. Even when the limitations of the traditional model become apparent, the perceived risks of innovation—whether financial, ethical, or reputational—are often seen as too great to justify abandoning the tried-and-true methods.

---

[21] Maister, David H. Managing the Professional Service Firm. Free Press, 1993

This inertia is particularly strong in firms that cater to corporate clients, where the complexity and high stakes of legal work make experimentation seem risky. The fear of losing clients, damaging the firm's reputation, or compromising legal outcomes leads many firms to stick with the familiar, even as they acknowledge the need for change.

The Challenges of Innovation in Law

The early attempts at innovation within the legal profession were marked by bold ideas and promising technologies, but their impact has been limited by a combination of cultural resistance, institutional barriers, and the inertia of established success. The legal profession's conservative nature, its strict regulatory environment, and the deep entrenchment of the billable hour model created a challenging environment for change.

Hopefully, these early efforts have not been not in vain. They have laid the groundwork for future innovations and highlighted the areas where change is most needed. As the legal profession continued to evolve, the lessons learned from these early attempts at innovation will inform the development of new approaches that could overcome these barriers and create a more efficient, client-centered legal industry.

In the following chapters, we will explore how these lessons have been applied in the modern era, with the rise of workflow automation and productized services offering new solutions to the challenges that have long plagued the legal profession. These innovations represent the next stage in the evolution of legal services, providing a path forward for firms willing to embrace change and adapt to the demands of the 21st-century legal market.

Chapter 2: Understanding Workflow Automation

Workflow automation is a transformative approach that has revolutionized various industries by streamlining processes, reducing human error, and enhancing efficiency. In the legal sector, it offers a way to automate routine tasks, freeing up lawyers to focus on more complex and value-added work.

This chapter introduces the concept of workflow automation, tracing its origins and core principles—process standardization, scalability, and efficiency. It explores how these principles have been successfully applied in industries such as finance, healthcare, and logistics, providing a foundation for understanding how they can be adapted to legal practice.

Workflow Automation

Workflow automation refers to the use of software, technology, and algorithms to automate a sequence of tasks that would otherwise require manual input. These tasks can range from simple administrative functions, like data entry and document routing, to more complex processes, such as customer service  workflows or compliance checks. Automation can be applied to both repetitive tasks and those that require decision-making based on predefined rules.

In a typical workflow, there are multiple steps that need to be completed in a specific order. These steps often involve different people, departments, or systems. Workflow automation ensures that these steps are carried out consistently and efficiently by automating the transitions between them, minimizing delays and errors that often occur with manual processes. For example, in a law firm, the process of drafting, reviewing, and approving a contract can be automated so that once a draft is completed, it is automatically routed to the appropriate attorney for review, then sent to the client for approval, all without the need for manual tracking or follow-up.

Origins of Workflow Automation

The concept of workflow automation has its roots in the industrial revolution, where the focus on efficiency and productivity led to the development of assembly lines and mechanized production processes. However, the modern concept of workflow automation, as we understand it today, began to take shape in the mid-20th century, particularly with the advent of computer technology and software development.

One of the earliest and most influential examples of workflow automation was the introduction of assembly lines by Henry Ford in the early 1900s.[22] Ford's assembly lines revolutionized the manufacturing process by breaking down complex tasks into smaller, repeatable steps that could be performed quickly and efficiently by workers. This approach dramatically increased production speed and consistency while reducing costs, setting the stage for future innovations in process automation.

As technology advanced, the principles of automation were applied to other industries, particularly those involving complex, repetitive tasks. The introduction of mainframe computers in the 1960s and 1970s enabled businesses to automate data processing and administrative tasks on a large scale. For instance, banks began using automated systems for processing checks and managing accounts, while manufacturing companies implemented computerized control systems to monitor and manage production lines.[23]

The evolution of software in the 1980s and 1990s further expanded the possibilities of workflow automation. The development of business process management (BPM) software allowed organizations to map out their workflows digitally and automate them using computers.[24] This era also saw the rise of enterprise resource planning (ERP)

---

[22] Royston, Angela. Henry Ford and the Assembly Line. Rosen Publishing, 2015
[23] Brynjolfsson, Erik, and McAfee, Andrew. The Second Machine Age: Work, Progress, and Prosperity in a Time of Brilliant Technologies. W.W. Norton & Company, 2014
[24] Dumas, Marlon, et al. Fundamentals of Business Process Management. Springer, 2013

systems, which integrated various business processes into a single software platform, enabling more seamless and efficient operations across entire organizations.[25]

Transition to the Digital Age

The rise of the internet and digital technologies in the late 20th and early 21st centuries brought about a new wave of automation opportunities. Cloud computing, artificial intelligence (AI), and machine learning have all contributed to the growth of workflow automation by enabling more sophisticated and flexible automation solutions. These technologies have allowed businesses to automate not only routine tasks but also more complex processes that involve decision-making, data analysis, and customer interaction.

In today's digital age, workflow automation has become a critical tool for organizations looking to stay competitive in a rapidly changing market. Companies across industries are leveraging automation to improve productivity, reduce costs, and enhance customer experiences. From automated customer service chatbots to AI-powered analytics platforms, workflow automation is reshaping the way businesses operate and interact with their customers.

Core Principles of Automation

To fully understand the potential of workflow automation, it is essential to grasp the core principles that underpin its application across industries. These principles—*process standardization*, *scalability*, and *efficiency*—form the foundation of successful automation strategies.

Process Standardization

One of the key principles of workflow automation is process standardization, which involves creating uniform procedures for completing tasks and processes. Standardization is essential for automation because it ensures that the same steps are followed consistently every time, which reduces variability and errors.

---

[25] Leon, Alexis. Enterprise Resource Planning. McGraw-Hill, 2008.

In a standardized process, each task is clearly defined, and the roles and responsibilities of each participant are well-established. This clarity allows for the creation of automated workflows that can be executed with minimal human intervention. For example, in a legal setting, the process of filing a motion with the court can be standardized so that each step—from drafting the motion to submitting it electronically—is automated according to a predefined set of rules.

Standardization also makes it easier to identify opportunities for improvement. By analyzing standardized workflows, organizations can pinpoint inefficiencies, bottlenecks, and redundant steps that can be eliminated or optimized. This continuous improvement cycle is a critical aspect of successful automation.

Challenges of Standardization

While standardization is critical for automation, it can also be challenging to implement, particularly in complex or creative environments like legal practice. Lawyers often value the flexibility to approach cases and tasks in their own way, tailoring their methods to the specific needs of each client or situation. This flexibility, while valuable, can make it difficult to establish standardized processes.

However, standardization does not necessarily mean eliminating flexibility or creativity. Instead, it involves identifying the routine, repetitive aspects of legal work that can be standardized without compromising the quality or customization of services. For instance, while the drafting of a complex legal argument may require a high degree of individual input, the process of preparing a standard form contract or filing a motion with the court can be standardized and automated, freeing up time for more strategic work.

Scalability

Scalability is another fundamental principle of workflow automation. Automated workflows are designed to handle varying volumes of work without requiring significant changes to the underlying processes. This scalability is particularly important for organizations that experience fluctuations in demand or are looking to grow their operations.

With scalable automation, organizations can manage increased workloads without a corresponding increase in labor costs or time. For example, an automated document review system can handle hundreds or even thousands of documents in a fraction of the time it would take a human reviewer, allowing law firms to take on larger projects or serve more clients without compromising quality.

Scalability also enables organizations to expand their operations into new markets or service lines with minimal additional investment. Automated workflows can be replicated and adapted to new contexts, allowing businesses to maintain consistency and efficiency as they grow.

Challenges of Achieving Scalability

While scalability offers significant benefits, it can also present challenges. One of the main challenges is ensuring that automated workflows remain effective as they scale. As the volume of work increases, so too does the complexity of managing and maintaining automated systems. Organizations must invest in monitoring and maintenance to ensure that automated workflows continue to operate smoothly as they scale.

Another challenge is integrating scalable automation solutions with existing systems and processes. In many organizations, legacy systems may not be designed to handle the demands of modern, scalable automation. Upgrading or replacing these systems can be costly and time-consuming, but it is often necessary to achieve the full benefits of scalable automation.

Efficiency

Efficiency is at the heart of workflow automation. By automating routine and repetitive tasks, organizations can complete processes faster, with fewer resources and less human error. This increased efficiency translates into cost savings, higher productivity, and improved outcomes.

In many industries, efficiency gains from automation have been transformative. For instance, in the financial services industry, automation has streamlined everything from loan processing to fraud detection, reducing the time and effort required to complete these tasks while improving accuracy and compliance. Similarly, in healthcare, automation has been used to manage patient records, schedule appointments, and even assist in diagnosing and treating patients, all of which contribute to better patient care and reduced costs.

Efficiency is also closely tied to the ability to focus on higher-value work. By automating routine tasks, employees can devote more time to strategic and creative activities that require human judgment and expertise. In the legal sector, this means that lawyers can spend less time on administrative tasks and more time on complex legal analysis, client interactions, and case strategy.

Measuring and Improving Efficiency

To fully realize the benefits of automation, organizations must be able to measure and improve efficiency continuously. This involves collecting data on workflow performance, such as the time taken to complete tasks, the number of errors, and resource utilization. By analyzing this data, organizations can identify areas where efficiency can be improved and make adjustments to their automated workflows accordingly.

Continuous improvement is a key aspect of efficient automation. Even after a workflow has been automated, there is always room for refinement. For example, an automated contract review process might initially focus on identifying key terms and clauses, but over time, it could be enhanced to include more sophisticated analysis, such as identifying potential legal risks or suggesting alternative language. By iterating on automated workflows, organizations can achieve ever-greater levels of efficiency.

Challenges to Achieving Efficiency

While automation can significantly enhance efficiency, achieving and maintaining high levels of efficiency is not without challenges. One of the main challenges is ensuring that automated workflows are properly designed and implemented from the outset. Poorly designed workflows can lead to inefficiencies, such as redundant steps or bottlenecks, that undermine the benefits of automation.

Another challenge is managing the balance between efficiency and quality. While automation can speed up processes, it is important to ensure that the quality of work is not compromised. In the legal sector, this means that automated tools must be carefully calibrated to ensure that they deliver accurate and reliable results. For example, an AI-powered legal research tool must be trained on high-quality data to ensure that it provides relevant and accurate information.

Organizations must be prepared to invest in the necessary infrastructure and training to support efficient automation. This includes not only the technology itself but also the people who will be using it. Lawyers and support staff must be trained to work with automated systems effectively, and organizations must invest in ongoing maintenance and support to ensure that these systems continue to operate efficiently.

Applications in Various Industries

Workflow automation has had a profound impact across various industries, driving efficiency, reducing costs, and enabling organizations to deliver higher quality services at scale. By examining how workflow automation has transformed industries such as finance, healthcare, and logistics, we can gain valuable insights into its potential application within the legal sector. Each of these industries has leveraged automation to address unique challenges and opportunities, demonstrating the versatility and effectiveness of automation technologies.

Finance

The finance industry has been at the forefront of adopting workflow automation, driven by the need to manage complex transactions, ensure regulatory compliance, and process vast amounts of data quickly and accurately.[26] Automation has been particularly transformative in areas such as transaction processing, risk management, and customer service.

Transaction Processing

One of the most significant applications of workflow automation in finance is the automation of transaction processing. Banks and financial institutions handle millions of transactions daily, ranging from simple payments to complex securities trades. Traditionally, processing these transactions required significant manual effort, with employees responsible for entering data, verifying information, and reconciling accounts.

With the advent of automation, much of this work has been delegated to automated systems. For example, robotic process automation (RPA) bots can handle repetitive tasks such as data entry, validation, and

---

[26] Philippon, Thomas. The FinTech Revolution: How Finance and Technology Are Reshaping the World's Biggest Industry. MIT Press, 2019

reconciliation at a fraction of the time it would take a human employee. These bots can work around the clock, ensuring that transactions are processed quickly and accurately, reducing the likelihood of errors and delays.

Automation has also enabled the development of real-time payment systems, where transactions are processed and settled almost instantly. This has improved customer satisfaction by providing faster service and reducing the time it takes for funds to be available.

Risk Management

Risk management is another area where workflow automation has had a significant impact. Financial institutions are required to manage various types of risks, including credit risk, market risk, and operational risk. Traditionally, risk management involved manual analysis of large datasets, often requiring significant time and expertise.

With automation, financial institutions can use AI and machine learning algorithms to analyze vast amounts of data in real-time, identifying patterns and anomalies that could indicate potential risks. For example, AI-powered systems can monitor trading activities and flag suspicious transactions that might indicate market manipulation or fraud. Similarly, automated credit scoring systems can assess the creditworthiness of loan applicants by analyzing their financial history and other relevant data, providing instant decisions.

These automated systems not only enhance the accuracy and speed of risk management processes but also enable financial institutions to be more proactive in mitigating risks. By identifying potential issues early, they can take preventive measures, reducing the likelihood of financial losses.

Customer Service

In the finance industry, customer service has also been transformed by workflow automation. Automated customer service systems, such as chatbots and virtual assistants, can handle a wide range of customer inquiries, from checking account balances to processing loan applications. These systems use natural language processing (NLP) to understand and respond to customer queries in real-time, providing quick and accurate service without the need for human intervention.

 For instance, a customer might use a bank's chatbot to inquire about recent transactions or to apply for a new credit card. The chatbot can guide the customer through the process, answering questions and collecting the necessary information. If the inquiry is complex or requires human judgment, the system can escalate the issue to a human representative, who is provided with all the relevant information to handle the case efficiently.

By automating routine customer service tasks, financial institutions can improve response times, reduce operational costs, and free up human agents to focus on more complex or high-value interactions. This enhances overall customer satisfaction and allows banks to provide a more personalized service.

Healthcare

In the healthcare industry, workflow automation has revolutionized patient care, administrative processes, and compliance management.[27] By automating routine tasks, healthcare providers can focus more on patient outcomes and less on paperwork, leading to improved efficiency and better healthcare delivery.

Patient Records and Data Management

One of the most significant applications of workflow automation in healthcare is the management of patient records and data. Electronic Health Records (EHR) systems have replaced traditional paper-based records, allowing healthcare providers to store, access, and share patient information digitally. These systems automate the collection, storage, and retrieval of patient data, ensuring that healthcare providers have accurate and up-to-date information at their fingertips.

EHR systems also enable the automation of routine tasks such as appointment scheduling, prescription management, and billing. For example, when a doctor prescribes medication, the EHR system can automatically send the prescription to the pharmacy, update the patient's records, and generate an invoice. This reduces the

---

[27] Willcocks, Leslie P., et al. Intelligent Automation in Healthcare. Palgrave Macmillan, 2024

administrative burden on healthcare staff and ensures that patients receive timely and accurate care.

Automation has also improved the accuracy and efficiency of diagnostic processes. For instance, AI-powered diagnostic tools can analyze medical images, such as X-rays or MRIs, to detect abnormalities and assist doctors in making accurate diagnoses. These tools can process large volumes of data quickly, identifying patterns that might be missed by human observers, and providing valuable insights that inform treatment decisions.

Patient Care and Treatment Planning

Automation has also played a crucial role in enhancing patient care and treatment planning. AI and machine learning algorithms can analyze patient data to predict health outcomes, recommend personalized treatment plans, and monitor patient progress in real-time. For example, an AI system might analyze a patient's medical history, genetic information, and lifestyle factors to predict their risk of developing a chronic condition, such as diabetes or heart disease. The system can then recommend preventive measures, such as dietary changes or medication, to reduce the risk.

In addition to predictive analytics, automation is used in treatment planning for complex medical procedures. For instance, in oncology, automated systems can analyze clinical data and research to recommend personalized treatment plans for cancer patients. These plans take into account the patient's specific condition, genetic profile, and other factors, ensuring that they receive the most effective treatment.

Compliance and Reporting

Workflow automation has also transformed compliance and reporting processes in healthcare. Healthcare providers must comply with a wide range of regulations, from patient privacy laws like HIPAA in the United States to various reporting requirements for government health programs. Automation ensures that these regulations are adhered to consistently and efficiently.

For example, automated compliance systems can monitor patient records to ensure that they meet privacy standards, flagging any potential violations for review. Similarly, automated reporting tools can generate and submit required reports to regulatory bodies, reducing the administrative burden on healthcare staff and ensuring that compliance deadlines are met.

Logistics

The logistics industry has undergone a dramatic transformation due to workflow automation, particularly in the areas of supply chain management, inventory control, and transportation.[28] Automation has enabled logistics companies to handle the complexities of global supply chains more efficiently, reducing costs and improving service levels.

Supply Chain Management

Supply chain management is one of the most complex aspects of logistics, involving the coordination of suppliers, manufacturers, warehouses, and transportation providers. Workflow automation has significantly improved the efficiency of supply chain management by automating key processes such as order processing, inventory management, and supplier coordination.

For example, automated systems can process orders from customers, check inventory levels, and place orders with suppliers automatically. These systems can also track the status of orders in real-time, providing visibility into the entire supply chain and allowing logistics managers to make informed decisions. If a supplier is delayed, the system can automatically reroute orders to an alternative supplier or adjust delivery schedules to minimize disruptions.

Inventory Control

In logistics, maintaining optimal inventory levels is crucial for minimizing costs and ensuring timely delivery. Automation plays a key role in inventory control by continuously monitoring stock levels and predicting demand based on historical data and market trends. Automated inventory systems can generate purchase orders, schedule deliveries, and manage stock across multiple locations, ensuring that inventory is always at the right levels.

---

[28] Boute, Robert N., and Udenio, Maxi. AI in Logistics and Supply Chain Management. In Global Logistics and Supply Chain Strategies for the 2020s, edited by Rico Merkert and Kai Hoberg, Springer, 2023.

For instance, a large retailer might use an automated inventory system to manage stock across its network of warehouses and stores. The system can automatically redistribute inventory based on demand, ensuring that popular items are always in stock and reducing the need for last-minute orders. This not only reduces costs but also improves customer satisfaction by ensuring that products are available when needed.

Transportation and Delivery Optimization

Transportation is another area where automation has had a significant impact in logistics. Automated systems are used to optimize delivery routes, manage fleets, and track shipments in real-time. These systems use algorithms to determine the most efficient routes for delivery vehicles, taking into account factors such as traffic, weather, and delivery windows.

For example, a logistics company might use an automated route planning system to optimize the delivery of goods to multiple locations. The system can analyze traffic patterns, delivery deadlines, and vehicle capacities to determine the most efficient route for each vehicle. This reduces fuel consumption, delivery times, and costs, while also minimizing the environmental impact of transportation.

Automation is also driving innovation in last-mile delivery, the final leg of the supply chain where goods are delivered to the end customer. Companies like Amazon and UPS are experimenting with autonomous delivery vehicles and drones, which have the potential to further reduce delivery times and costs. These technologies are still in the early stages of adoption, but they represent the next frontier of automation in logistics.

Warehouse Automation

Warehouses are the backbone of the logistics industry, and automation has revolutionized how they operate. Automated warehouse management systems (WMS) coordinate all aspects of warehouse operations, from receiving and storing goods to picking and shipping orders. These systems use a combination of software, robotics, and AI to optimize the movement of goods within the warehouse, reducing the time and labor required to fulfill orders.

For example, a WMS might use robots to retrieve items from storage shelves and bring them to packing stations, where they are prepared for shipping. The system can prioritize orders based on urgency, optimize the layout of the warehouse to minimize travel time, and even predict future demand to ensure that popular items are stored in easily accessible locations.

Warehouse automation not only increases efficiency but also improves accuracy, reducing the likelihood of errors such as picking the wrong item or shipping to the wrong address. This leads to higher customer satisfaction and lower return rates, which are critical for maintaining profitability in the competitive logistics industry.

Lessons for the Legal Sector

The transformative impact of workflow automation in industries such as finance, healthcare, and logistics provides valuable lessons for the legal sector. Each of these industries has faced unique challenges, from managing large volumes of transactions and data to ensuring compliance with complex regulations. By leveraging automation, they have been able to streamline operations, reduce costs, and deliver better services to their customers.

For the legal sector, the potential of workflow automation is immense. Just as automation has optimized transaction processing in finance, improved patient care in healthcare, and streamlined supply chains in logistics, it can similarly enhance the efficiency and effectiveness of legal services. Whether it's automating routine tasks such as document review and billing, improving the accuracy of legal research through AI, or managing case workflows more effectively, the principles and technologies of automation offer the legal profession a path to greater innovation and client satisfaction.

Technology Behind Workflow Automation

Workflow automation is powered by a range of advanced technologies that enable organizations to automate complex tasks, streamline operations, and improve efficiency. These technologies—including artificial intelligence (AI), machine learning, robotic process automation (RPA), and cloud computing—are the driving forces behind modern automation solutions. By understanding how these technologies work and how they can be applied, organizations can harness their full potential to transform their operations.

<u>Artificial Intelligence (AI) and Machine Learning</u>

Artificial Intelligence (AI) is a broad field of computer science that aims to create machines capable of performing tasks that typically require human intelligence. These tasks include problem-solving, decision-making, language processing, and recognizing patterns in data. AI is at the forefront of many modern automation initiatives, enabling systems to perform complex tasks with minimal human intervention.

Machine Learning, a subset of AI, involves training algorithms to learn from data and make predictions or decisions without being explicitly programmed for specific tasks. Machine learning models can identify patterns in large datasets, allowing them to perform tasks such as predicting outcomes, classifying data, and even generating human-like text. These capabilities make machine learning an essential component of workflow automation, particularly in tasks that involve large volumes of data or require a high degree of accuracy.

Applications of AI and Machine Learning in Workflow Automation

- **Predictive Analytics**: In finance, AI-driven predictive analytics can assess credit risk by analyzing a borrower's financial history and behavior, allowing banks to make more informed lending decisions. In the legal sector, AI can be used to predict the outcome of cases based on historical data, helping lawyers to craft more effective strategies.
- **Natural Language Processing (NLP):** NLP is a branch of AI that focuses on the interaction between computers and human language. It enables machines to understand, interpret, and

generate human language. In customer service, NLP powers chatbots that can understand and respond to customer inquiries, providing quick and accurate service without the need for human intervention. In the legal industry, NLP is used in tools like contract analysis software, which can automatically identify and extract key clauses from legal documents, streamlining the review process.

- **Document Review and Analysis:** AI-powered tools are revolutionizing the way legal professionals handle document review. These tools can sift through large volumes of documents, identifying relevant information and flagging potential issues. This not only speeds up the review process but also reduces the risk of missing critical details. For example, e-discovery platforms use AI to identify relevant documents in litigation cases, significantly reducing the time and cost associated with manual document review.
- **Personalization and Recommendation Engines:** AI is also used to create personalized experiences for users. In e-commerce, recommendation engines suggest products to customers based on their past behavior and preferences. In the legal sector, AI can be used to recommend relevant legal precedents or research materials based on the specifics of a case, helping lawyers to build stronger arguments.

Benefits of AI and Machine Learning

- **Increased Accuracy:** AI systems can analyze vast amounts of data with a level of precision that is difficult for humans to match. This leads to more accurate predictions, classifications, and decisions.
- **Scalability:** AI-driven automation systems can scale easily to handle increasing volumes of data and tasks, making them ideal for organizations looking to expand their operations.
- **Continuous Improvement:** Machine learning models improve over time as they are exposed to more data, becoming more accurate and efficient. This capability allows AI-driven automation systems to evolve and adapt to changing needs.

Challenges of Implementing AI and Machine Learning

- **Data Quality:** The effectiveness of AI and machine learning models depends heavily on the quality of the data they are trained on. Poor-quality data can lead to inaccurate predictions and decisions.

- **Complexity:** Implementing AI and machine learning solutions requires specialized knowledge and expertise, which can be a barrier for some organizations.
- **Ethical Considerations:** The use of AI raises ethical concerns, particularly around issues of bias, privacy, and accountability. Organizations must ensure that their AI systems are transparent, fair, and comply with relevant regulations.

Robotic Process Automation (RPA)

Robotic Process Automation (RPA) is a technology that enables organizations to automate repetitive, rule-based tasks by using software robots, or "bots." RPA bots mimic human actions, such as entering data, processing transactions, and interacting with digital systems, but they do so much faster and with greater accuracy. RPA is particularly well-suited for tasks that involve high volumes of repetitive work and require minimal decision-making.

Applications of RPA in Workflow Automation

- **Data Entry and Processing:** One of the most common uses of RPA is automating data entry and processing tasks. For example, in the finance industry, RPA bots can automatically enter transaction data into accounting systems, reconcile accounts, and generate financial reports. This reduces the time and effort required to complete these tasks and minimizes the risk of errors.
- **Invoice Processing:** In many organizations, invoice processing is a time-consuming task that involves manually entering invoice details, verifying information, and routing invoices for approval. RPA can automate this entire process, extracting data from invoices, checking for discrepancies, and routing them for approval automatically. This not only speeds up the process but also reduces the risk of late payments and penalties.
- **Compliance Monitoring:** In regulated industries such as finance and healthcare, RPA is used to monitor compliance with regulatory requirements. Bots can automatically check transactions against compliance rules, flagging any that require further review. This ensures that organizations remain compliant while reducing the workload on compliance teams.
- **Customer Service Automation:** RPA bots are also used in customer service to handle routine tasks such as updating customer records, processing requests, and generating

reports. For example, when a customer submits a service request, an RPA bot can automatically log the request, update the customer's account, and send a confirmation email. This improves response times and frees up customer service agents to focus on more complex issues.

Benefits of RPA

- **Cost Savings:** RPA can significantly reduce operational costs by automating routine tasks, allowing organizations to reallocate resources to higher-value activities.
- **Improved Accuracy:** RPA bots follow predefined rules and processes with precision, reducing the likelihood of errors that can occur with manual tasks.
- **Quick Implementation:** RPA solutions can often be implemented relatively quickly, without the need for extensive changes to existing systems.
- **Scalability:** RPA bots can be scaled up or down to handle varying workloads, making them ideal for organizations that experience fluctuations in demand.

Challenges of Implementing RPA

- **Process Selection:** Not all processes are suitable for RPA. Organizations must carefully select processes that are rule-based, repetitive, and stable.
- **Maintenance and Management:** RPA bots require ongoing maintenance to ensure they continue to operate effectively as systems and processes change.
- **Integration with Other Technologies:** RPA works best when integrated with other automation technologies, such as AI and machine learning. Ensuring seamless integration can be complex.

Cloud Computing

Cloud Computing refers to the delivery of computing services—including servers, storage, databases, networking, software, and analytics—over the internet ("the cloud"). Cloud computing allows organizations to access and use computing resources on-demand, without the need for on-premises infrastructure. This flexibility is a key enabler of workflow automation, as it provides the scalable, on-demand resources needed to support automated systems.

Applications of Cloud Computing in Workflow Automation

- **Software as a Service (SaaS):** One of the most common applications of cloud computing is Software as a Service (SaaS), where software applications are delivered over the internet. SaaS platforms are widely used for workflow automation, providing tools for project management, customer relationship management (CRM), document management, and more. These platforms can be accessed from anywhere, making it easy for teams to collaborate and automate workflows.
- **Infrastructure as a Service (IaaS):** IaaS provides virtualized computing resources over the internet, including servers, storage, and networking. Organizations can use IaaS to host and run their automation platforms, ensuring that they have the computing power and storage capacity needed to support large-scale automation initiatives.
- **Platform as a Service (PaaS):** PaaS provides a platform for developing, testing, and deploying applications. It includes tools and services that developers can use to build custom automation solutions. For example, a law firm might use a PaaS to develop a custom case management system that automates the tracking of legal cases and deadlines.
- **Cloud-Based Automation Tools:** Many modern automation tools are cloud-based, allowing organizations to automate workflows without the need for on-premises infrastructure. These tools offer flexibility and scalability, enabling organizations to deploy automation solutions quickly and scale them as needed. For example, a cloud-based document management system can automatically organize, store, and retrieve documents, making it easier for legal teams to manage case files and collaborate on legal work.

Benefits of Cloud Computing

- **Scalability:** Cloud computing allows organizations to scale their automation efforts up or down as needed, without the need for significant upfront investment in infrastructure.
- **Cost-Effectiveness:** Cloud services are typically offered on a pay-as-you-go basis, allowing organizations to pay only for the resources they use. This can reduce costs compared to maintaining on-premises infrastructure.

- **Accessibility:** Cloud-based automation tools can be accessed from anywhere with an internet connection, making it easier for teams to collaborate and work remotely.
- **Reliability:** Cloud providers typically offer high levels of uptime and reliability, ensuring that automation systems remain operational even in the event of hardware failures.

Challenges of Cloud Computing

- **Data Security:** Storing sensitive data in the cloud can raise security concerns, particularly in industries such as finance and healthcare, where data privacy is critical. Organizations must ensure that their cloud providers offer robust security measures and comply with relevant regulations.
- **Integration:** Integrating cloud-based automation tools with existing on-premises systems can be challenging, particularly for organizations with legacy infrastructure.
- **Dependence on Internet Connectivity:** Cloud-based systems require reliable internet connectivity. Any disruption in connectivity can impact access to automation tools and data.

Integrating Technologies for Enhanced Automation

The true power of workflow automation lies in the integration of AI, machine learning, RPA, and cloud computing. By combining these technologies, organizations can create sophisticated automation solutions that are both powerful and flexible.

- **AI-Driven RPA:** Integrating AI with RPA allows for the automation of more complex tasks that require decision-making or data analysis. For example, an AI-powered RPA bot can process invoices, identify discrepancies, and automatically resolve issues based on predefined rules and historical data.
- **Cloud-Based AI Platforms:** Cloud computing enables organizations to deploy AI and machine learning models at scale, providing the computational power needed to process large datasets and make real-time predictions. Cloud-based AI platforms also offer tools for developing, training, and deploying machine learning models, making it easier for organizations to integrate AI into their automation workflows.
- **API Integration for Seamless Connectivity:** Application Programming Interfaces (APIs) play a crucial role in connecting

disparate systems and platforms, enabling seamless communication between different tools in an automated workflow. APIs allow organizations to integrate various software applications, facilitating the exchange of data between cloud platforms, AI tools, and RPA systems. This connectivity enhances automation by enabling real-time data access and interoperability across systems, which is essential for creating efficient, scalable automation solutions.
- **End-to-End Automation:** By integrating RPA, AI, and cloud computing, organizations can create end-to-end automated workflows that handle everything from data entry to decision-making. For example, in the legal sector, an end-to-end automation solution might involve using RPA to collect and organize case data, AI to analyze legal precedents, and cloud-based tools to manage and share documents with clients and colleagues.

The Future of Workflow Automation

The technologies behind workflow automation—AI, machine learning, RPA, and cloud computing—are revolutionizing the way organizations operate. By leveraging these technologies, organizations can automate complex workflows, improve efficiency, and deliver better services to their clients.

As the legal profession continues to evolve, the integration of these technologies will play a crucial role in transforming how legal services are delivered. By understanding and embracing these technologies, law firms can create more efficient, scalable, and client-focused operations, positioning themselves for success in an increasingly competitive market.

Transforming Legal Workflows with Automation

The integration of workflow automation technologies—such as artificial intelligence (AI), machine learning, robotic process automation (RPA), and cloud computing—into legal workflows presents a transformative opportunity. By adopting these technologies, law firms and legal departments can address many of the inefficiencies that have long plagued the industry, enhance service delivery, and stay competitive in an increasingly dynamic market.

Workflow Adoption in Legal Services

Legal workflows traditionally involve a significant amount of manual labor, ranging from document drafting and review to legal research and case management. These processes often require meticulous attention to detail and are typically carried out by highly skilled professionals. However, despite the expertise involved, the reliance on manual processes has resulted in several persistent challenges:

- **Time-Consuming Tasks:** Many legal tasks, such as document review and due diligence, are time-intensive, requiring hours of manual work. This not only slows down the pace of legal work but also increases costs for clients.
- **Inconsistency and Human Error:** Manual processes are prone to variability in execution, leading to inconsistencies in quality and outcomes. Human error, even in minor tasks, can have significant legal and financial repercussions.
- **High Costs:** The reliance on manual labor, particularly in firms that bill by the hour, can lead to high costs for clients. This cost structure can also disincentivize efficiency, as time spent on a task directly correlates with revenue.
- **Limited Scalability:** Traditional legal workflows are difficult to scale, particularly for smaller firms or those with limited resources. As the volume of work increases, so does the need for additional manpower, which can be both costly and logistically challenging.
- **Client Expectations:** Clients are increasingly demanding greater transparency, efficiency, and predictability in legal services. The traditional billable hour model and manual processes often fail to meet these expectations, leading to client dissatisfaction and pressure to adopt alternative billing arrangements.

Given these challenges, the legal sector is ripe for transformation through workflow automation. By applying the same technologies that have revolutionized other industries, law firms can streamline their operations, reduce costs, and deliver higher-quality services.

Automating Routine Tasks

One of the most immediate and impactful applications of workflow automation in the legal sector is the automation of routine, repetitive tasks. These tasks, while essential, do not typically require the nuanced judgment or strategic thinking that lawyers are trained to provide.

Automating these processes can free up valuable time for legal professionals to focus on higher-value work.

Document Review and Analysis

Document review is a fundamental aspect of many legal workflows, particularly in litigation, due diligence, and contract management. Traditionally, this process involves lawyers or paralegals manually reviewing large volumes of documents to identify relevant information, assess risks, or ensure compliance with legal standards. This can be a tedious and time-consuming task, especially in cases involving thousands of documents.

AI-powered tools, such as those used in e-discovery platforms, can automate much of the document review process. These tools use machine learning algorithms to analyze documents, identify key terms and concepts, and flag potential issues for further review. By automating document review, law firms can significantly reduce the time and cost associated with this process while improving accuracy and consistency.

Contract Drafting and Management

Contract drafting is another area where workflow automation can have a substantial impact. Legal contracts often follow standard templates, with specific terms and conditions tailored to the needs of each client or transaction. Despite the repetitive nature of this work, contract drafting remains a labor-intensive process in many firms.

Automated contract management systems can streamline the drafting process by automatically populating standard templates with relevant information, such as client details, transaction terms, and legal clauses. These systems can also enforce consistency by ensuring that contracts adhere to predefined standards and legal requirements. Additionally, AI tools can assist in reviewing contracts for potential risks, such as ambiguous language or unfavorable terms, further enhancing the efficiency and effectiveness of the process.

Legal Research

Legal research is a critical component of legal practice, involving the identification and analysis of relevant statutes, regulations, case law, and legal precedents. Traditionally, this process has been carried out manually, with lawyers spending hours sifting through legal databases and resources to find pertinent information.

AI-driven legal research tools are transforming this process by automating the search and analysis of legal materials. These tools can quickly scan vast databases of legal texts, identify relevant cases and statutes, and provide lawyers with summaries and insights. Natural language processing (NLP) capabilities allow these tools to understand and interpret complex legal language, making them more effective at identifying relevant information than traditional keyword-based searches.

By automating legal research, law firms can reduce the time and effort required to find and analyze legal information, allowing lawyers to focus on applying this knowledge to their cases. This not only improves efficiency but also enhances the quality of legal analysis, as lawyers can spend more time on strategic thinking and less on information retrieval.

Billing and Invoicing

Billing and invoicing are essential administrative tasks in any law firm, but they can be time-consuming and prone to errors. Automated billing systems can streamline this process by tracking billable hours, generating invoices, and managing payments automatically. These systems can also provide clients with more transparent and detailed billing information, improving client satisfaction and reducing disputes over fees.

For example, a cloud-based billing system might integrate with the firm's time-tracking software, automatically generating invoices based on the hours logged by each lawyer. The system can then send these invoices to clients electronically, track payments, and issue reminders for overdue payments. This reduces the administrative burden on legal staff and ensures that billing is accurate and timely.

Enhancing Workflows With AI and Machine Learning

Beyond automating routine tasks, AI and machine learning offer the potential to enhance more complex aspects of legal work, such as decision-making, case strategy, and client advising. These technologies can provide lawyers with new insights, improve the accuracy of predictions, and help firms deliver more tailored and strategic legal services.

Predictive Analytics for Case Outcomes

One of the most promising applications of AI in the legal sector is predictive analytics, which involves using historical data to forecast the likely outcomes of legal cases.[29] By analyzing data from past cases, AI models can identify patterns and correlations that may not be immediately apparent to human observers. This information can help lawyers assess the strengths and weaknesses of their cases, develop more effective strategies, and provide clients with more accurate predictions of potential outcomes.

For instance, an AI-driven predictive analytics tool might analyze a database of past litigation cases, identifying factors that have influenced the outcomes of similar cases. The tool could then provide lawyers with an estimate of the likelihood of success based on these factors, allowing them to make more informed decisions about whether to pursue a case, negotiate a settlement, or take other actions.

Automated Due Diligence

Due diligence is a critical process in transactions such as mergers and acquisitions, where thorough investigation and analysis of the involved parties' legal, financial, and operational status are required. Traditionally, due diligence has been a labor-intensive process, involving the review of vast amounts of documentation and data.

AI and machine learning can significantly enhance the due diligence process by automating the analysis of documents and identifying potential risks. For example, an AI tool might analyze financial statements, contracts, and other relevant documents to identify red flags, such as undisclosed liabilities or unfavorable contract terms. This allows legal teams to conduct due diligence more quickly and accurately, reducing the risk of overlooking critical issues.

Client Communication and Relationship Management

Effective communication is key to maintaining strong client relationships, but managing client interactions can be challenging, especially for large firms with extensive client bases. AI-powered tools can assist in managing client communications by automating routine

---

[29] Katz, Daniel Martin, Bommarito, Michael J., and Blackman, Josh. "A General Approach for Predicting the Behavior of the Supreme Court of the United States." PLoS ONE, 2017

interactions, such as sending updates, scheduling meetings, and responding to common inquiries.

For example, a law firm might use an AI-driven chatbot to handle initial client inquiries, providing information about the firm's services, answering frequently asked questions, and directing clients to the appropriate legal professionals. This not only improves client service but also frees up lawyers to focus on more substantive client interactions.

Additionally, AI tools can be used to analyze client interactions and provide insights into client satisfaction, preferences, and needs. By understanding these factors, firms can tailor their services to better meet client expectations, improving client retention and satisfaction.

Leveraging Cloud Computing for Scalability and Collaboration

Cloud computing plays a critical role in enabling law firms to scale their operations and enhance collaboration, both internally and with clients. By leveraging cloud-based tools and platforms, law firms can access the computing power and resources needed to support large-scale automation initiatives while ensuring that their systems are accessible and secure.

Scalable Automation Solutions

One of the key benefits of cloud computing is its scalability. Cloud-based automation tools can be scaled up or down as needed, allowing law firms to handle fluctuating workloads without the need for significant investments in on-premises infrastructure. This is particularly valuable for firms that experience seasonal variations in workload or that are looking to expand their services.

For example, a law firm might use a cloud-based case management system that automatically adjusts its capacity based on the number of active cases. As the firm takes on more clients or larger cases, the system can scale up to accommodate the increased demand, ensuring that all cases are managed efficiently and effectively.

Enhanced Collaboration and Remote Work

Cloud computing also facilitates collaboration by providing lawyers with access to shared tools and resources from any location. This is particularly important in today's increasingly remote and globalized legal environment, where lawyers and clients may be spread across different locations and time zones.

Cloud-based platforms enable real-time collaboration on legal documents, case files, and other materials, allowing legal teams to work together more seamlessly. For example, multiple lawyers can collaborate on drafting a contract, with each team member making edits and comments that are instantly visible to others. This not only improves efficiency but also ensures that all team members are working with the most up-to-date information.

For clients, cloud-based tools provide greater transparency and convenience. Clients can access case updates, review documents, and communicate with their legal team through secure online portals, improving their overall experience and engagement with the firm.

Security and Compliance

Given the sensitive nature of legal work, security and compliance are paramount concerns for law firms. Cloud providers typically offer robust security measures, including encryption, multi-factor authentication, and regular security updates, to protect sensitive data from unauthorized access.

Additionally, many cloud providers offer tools and services that help law firms comply with legal and regulatory requirements, such as data privacy laws and industry-specific regulations. By leveraging these tools, law firms can ensure that their automated workflows meet the highest standards of security and compliance.

Overcoming Challenges and Embracing the Future

While the potential of workflow automation in the legal sector is immense, there are also challenges that firms must navigate to successfully implement these technologies. Cultural resistance, concerns about job displacement, and the complexity of integrating new technologies into existing workflows are all factors that must be carefully managed.

Cultural Resistance and Change Management

As with any significant change, there is likely to be resistance from within the organization, particularly from those who are accustomed to traditional ways of working. Lawyers may be skeptical about the benefits of automation or concerned that it could compromise the quality of legal work.

To overcome this resistance, it is essential to involve legal professionals in the implementation process, providing them with training and support to help them understand how automation can enhance their work rather than replace it. Change management strategies, such as clear communication, stakeholder engagement, and phased implementation, can also help to ease the transition and build buy-in across the organization.

Integration with Existing Systems

Integrating new automation tools with existing systems and processes can be complex, particularly for firms with legacy infrastructure. A thorough assessment of the firm's current technology stack, workflows, and needs is essential to identify the most effective automation solutions and ensure seamless integration.

In some cases, it may be necessary to upgrade or replace existing systems to fully leverage the benefits of automation. This can require significant investment, but the long-term benefits in terms of efficiency, scalability, and client satisfaction often outweigh the initial costs.

Ethical Considerations

As with the implementation of any new technology, ethical considerations must be carefully addressed. For example, the use of AI in legal decision-making raises questions about transparency, accountability, and bias. It is important to ensure that automated systems are designed and used in a way that upholds the ethical standards of the legal profession and protects the rights and interests of clients.

Law firms must also consider the potential impact of automation on employment, particularly for support staff whose roles may be most affected by the adoption of automated systems. By approaching automation as a tool to augment human work rather than replace it, firms can create opportunities for upskilling and career development, ensuring that their workforce is equipped to thrive in an increasingly automated environment.

Setting the Stage for Deeper Exploration

The potential for workflow automation in the legal sector is vast, offering opportunities to enhance efficiency, reduce costs, and improve service delivery. By automating routine tasks, leveraging AI and machine learning for complex legal work, and embracing cloud computing for scalability and collaboration, law firms can transform their operations and better meet the needs of their clients.

In the chapters that follow, we will delve deeper into specific applications of these technologies within the legal sector, exploring how law firms can implement automation strategies tailored to their unique needs and challenges. We will also examine case studies of successful automation initiatives, providing practical insights and lessons learned from firms that have already begun their automation journeys.

Chapter 3: The Problem with the Billable Hour

Like it or not, the billable hour model, long the cornerstone of legal billing practices, is fundamentally flawed in its approach to valuing legal services. While it provides a clear and straightforward method for tracking and charging for time spent on client matters, this model introduces several inherent inefficiencies that can negatively impact both the quality of legal services and the overall operation of law firms. These inefficiencies are not just theoretical—they manifest in everyday practice, often leading to suboptimal outcomes for both clients and lawyers.

Time Leakage and the Inefficient Use of Resources

One of the most significant inefficiencies associated with the billable hour is the phenomenon of time leakage. Time leakage refers to the unbilled hours that lawyers spend on tasks that are not directly billable to clients but are nonetheless necessary for the completion of legal work. This can include everything from internal meetings and administrative tasks to the time spent thinking through complex legal problems or preparing for client meetings.

In a billable hour system, there is little to no compensation for these essential activities unless they can be directly attributed to a client's matter and subsequently billed. As a result, lawyers often find themselves under pressure to minimize the time spent on these unbilled tasks, potentially compromising the quality of their work. For example, a lawyer might rush through legal research or the drafting of a document to maximize billable hours, even though taking more time might lead to a better outcome for the client.

The focus on billing hours can lead to inefficiencies in how legal work is allocated and performed within a firm. Senior lawyers, who command higher billing rates, might spend time on tasks that could be delegated to junior associates or paralegals at a lower cost to the client. However, because the firm's revenue model is tied to the total number of hours billed, there is little incentive to optimize the allocation of work in a way that maximizes efficiency rather than billable hours.

Misaligned Incentives

Another critical inefficiency of the billable hour model is the misalignment of incentives between lawyers and their clients. In an ideal world, both the lawyer and the client would be aligned in their desire to resolve legal matters as efficiently and effectively as possible. However, the billable hour model inherently creates a conflict of interest.

Since lawyers are compensated based on the number of hours they work, there is a built-in incentive to spend more time on tasks rather than less. This may lead to "padding" of hours, where lawyers may unconsciously (or in some cases, consciously[30]) extend the time they spend on a task to increase their billable hours. While ethical guidelines[31] and firm policies may discourage overt padding, the pressure to meet billable hour targets can subtly influence how lawyers allocate their time.

For clients, this misalignment can be particularly frustrating, as it creates unpredictability in legal costs. Clients may agree to an hourly rate without a clear understanding of how many hours a task will ultimately require, leading to significant cost overruns. Clients may also feel that their lawyer's incentive to bill more hours conflicts with their own desire for a quick and cost-effective resolution. This tension can strain the lawyer-client relationship and erode trust.

The Productivity Paradox

The billable hour model also creates a paradox where increased productivity does not necessarily lead to increased profitability. In most

---

[30] Cassens Weiss, Debra. "Lawyer Censured for Padding Internal Billing Records to Look Busy." ABA Journal, January 11, 2018
[31] American Bar Association. "Formal Ethics Opinion 93-379: Billing for Professional Fees, Disbursements, and Other Expenses." ABA Book Publishing, December 1, 1993

capitalistic industries, greater efficiency and productivity are rewarded because they allow a company to do more with less—producing more goods or services at a lower cost. However, in the legal profession, where revenue is tied directly to the number of hours billed, increased efficiency can actually reduce a lawyer's income.

For example, if a lawyer invests in technology that allows them to complete a task in half the time, their billable hours for that task are effectively cut in half, resulting in lower revenue unless they find a way to bill for the full value of the service provided. This creates a disincentive for lawyers to adopt new technologies or methods that could improve efficiency, as doing so could directly impact their bottom line.

The productivity paradox is particularly problematic in an era where clients are increasingly demanding more efficient and cost-effective legal services. Law firms that cling to the billable hour model may find themselves at odds with these client demands, struggling to reconcile the need for efficiency with the need to maintain profitability.

The Overhead Burden

As a final observation, the billable hour model contributes to high overhead costs for law firms. The focus on billing hours requires firms to invest in time-tracking systems, billing software, and administrative staff to manage the invoicing process. Because revenue is tied to the number of hours billed, firms may feel pressured to maintain a large staff of lawyers and support personnel, even if they are not fully utilized at all times. This can lead to inflated overhead costs, which are ultimately passed on to clients in the form of higher hourly rates.

In contrast, alternative billing models—such as flat fees or value-based billing—can streamline operations by reducing the need for extensive time tracking and billing management. These models allow firms to focus on delivering high-quality legal services without the constant pressure to log hours, potentially reducing overhead and creating a more sustainable business model.

The inherent inefficiencies of the billable hour model are significant and multifaceted – whether firms acknowledge them publicly or not. Time leakage, misaligned incentives, the productivity paradox, and the burden of overhead all contribute to a system that often prioritizes the quantity of time spent over the quality of legal work. As clients continue to demand more value for their legal expenditures and as technology offers new ways to deliver legal services, the limitations of the billable hour model are becoming increasingly apparent. In the next sections of this chapter, we will explore how these inefficiencies impact client satisfaction and why the billable hour model continues to persist despite its flaws.

Hourly Billing's Impact on Client Satisfaction

The billable hour model not only creates inefficiencies within law firms but also significantly impacts client satisfaction. Clients today are increasingly demanding more transparency, predictability, and value from their legal service providers. The traditional billable hour model, however, often falls short of meeting these expectations, leading to frustration, mistrust, and a strained lawyer-client relationship.

Unpredictable and Escalating Costs

One of the primary sources of client dissatisfaction with the billable hour model is the unpredictability of legal costs. Unlike fixed-fee arrangements, where the client knows upfront what the service will cost, the billable hour model provides no clear estimate of the total cost until the work is completed. This lack of cost predictability can be particularly concerning in complex or prolonged legal matters, where the number of billable hours can quickly escalate.

Clients may receive an initial estimate or budget for a legal matter, only to find that the final bill far exceeds expectations. This often leads to "sticker shock" when the invoice arrives, as clients are forced to reconcile the hours billed with the value they feel they received. The result can be a perception that the lawyer is more focused on billing hours than on providing efficient and effective legal solutions.

Studies and surveys consistently show that clients value cost certainty and transparency when it comes to legal services. For example, the 2024 Legal Trends Report[32] by Clio revealed that 63% of consumers want to know the final cost of legal services upfront, but only 25% of lawyers believe that providing such an estimate is important. This disconnect highlights the growing tension between client expectations and the traditional billing practices of law firms.

---

[32] 2024 Legal Trends Report. Clio, 2024

Perceived Inefficiency and Lack of Value

Clients often perceive the billable hour model as incentivizing inefficiency. Because lawyers are paid based on the number of hours they work, there is a natural concern that they might be inclined to spend more time on tasks than is necessary. Even when lawyers are working diligently and efficiently, the model itself can create the impression that time is being padded or that lawyers are more interested in maximizing their billable hours than in resolving the client's issues swiftly.

This perception is particularly problematic in cases where clients lack the expertise to evaluate the complexity or necessity of the work being done. For example, a client might question why a seemingly straightforward task, such as drafting a contract or reviewing a document, required so many hours of work. Without a clear understanding of the legal process, clients may struggle to see the value in the hours billed, leading to dissatisfaction and a potential loss of trust.

Clio's Legal Trends Report also found that clients who were satisfied with their lawyer's work cited "responsive communication" and "a clear understanding of expectations" as key factors in their satisfaction. The billable hour model, by focusing on time rather than outcomes, can obscure these factors and make it harder for lawyers to demonstrate the value of their services.

Strain on Lawyer-Client Relationships

The financial tension created by the billable hour model can strain the lawyer-client relationship. Clients who feel that their legal bills are excessive or unjustified may become less cooperative, more demanding, or even hostile. This can make it difficult for lawyers to do their jobs effectively, as they may be dealing with clients who are constantly questioning their decisions or pushing back against the time spent on various tasks.

In addition, the need to track and justify every billable hour can lead to an environment of micromanagement and mistrust. Lawyers may feel pressured to constantly explain or defend their time entries, which can be both time-consuming and detrimental to the overall relationship. Clients, on the other hand, may feel that they are being nickel-and-dimed, leading to a loss of confidence in their lawyer's ability to prioritize their best interests.

The focus on billable hours also limits the lawyer's ability to provide value-added services that are not directly billable but are important for client satisfaction, such as proactive legal advice, regular check-ins, and relationship-building activities. These activities, while not immediately profitable under the billable hour model, are essential for long-term client retention and the development of trust and loyalty.

Impact on Client Trust

Trust is the cornerstone of any successful lawyer-client relationship. Clients need to trust that their lawyer is working in their best interest and that the fees they are paying are fair and justified. The billable hour model, however, can erode this trust by creating a situation where clients may feel that their lawyer's financial incentives are not aligned with their own.

For example, a client might worry that their lawyer is dragging out a case to increase billable hours or that unnecessary tasks are being performed to pad the bill. Even if this is not the case, the mere possibility of such behavior can undermine trust and make clients more hesitant to engage fully with their lawyer.

Contrary to their original purpose, the lack of transparency in how billable hours are calculated and billed can further damage trust. Clients, particularly those who are less sophisticated or experienced with legal service providers, may not understand how time is tracked or why certain tasks took as long as they did, leading to suspicion and doubt. This lack of understanding can be exacerbated by vague or insufficient billing descriptions, which fail to convey the full scope and complexity of the work performed.

The impact of the billable hour model on client satisfaction is significant and multifaceted. From unpredictable and escalating costs to perceptions of inefficiency and strain on relationships, the model often falls short of meeting the needs and expectations of modern clients. As the legal market becomes more competitive and client demands continue to evolve, law firms that rely heavily on the billable hour model may find themselves at a disadvantage, struggling to maintain client satisfaction and trust.

In the next section, we will explore how the billable hour model discourages innovation within the legal profession, further compounding the challenges it presents and highlighting the need for a shift toward more modern, client-centric approaches to billing and service delivery.

Innovation and the Billable Hour

The legal profession is increasingly recognizing the need for innovation to stay competitive in a rapidly changing landscape. However, the billable hour model, which has long been the standard for pricing legal services, inherently discourages the adoption of innovative practices. This resistance to innovation stems from several factors rooted in the structure and incentives of the billable hour model, which ultimately prioritize time spent over the value delivered.

Resistance to Alternative Billing Models

Another way the billable hour model discourages innovation is by reinforcing a conservative approach to pricing and service delivery. The model is deeply ingrained in the culture of many law firms, where it has been the standard for decades. As a result, there is often significant resistance to exploring alternative billing models, such as flat fees, contingency fees, or value-based billing, which could encourage more innovative approaches to legal work.

Alternative billing models, particularly those that focus on value rather than time, can create a financial incentive for firms to innovate. For instance, under a value-based billing model, a firm might charge a fixed fee for a service based on the value it delivers to the client, rather than the time spent providing it. This shift in focus from hours worked to outcomes achieved can drive firms to seek out new methods and technologies that enhance their ability to deliver high-quality services more efficiently.

However, transitioning to such models requires a fundamental change in how firms operate and think about their work. It often involves rethinking how services are delivered, how success is measured, and how resources are allocated. The billable hour model, with its emphasis on tracking and billing time, creates a structural barrier to making this shift, as it locks firms into a cycle where time, rather than innovation, is the primary driver of revenue.

The Productivity Paradox: Innovation vs. Billable Hours

The billable hour model also creates a productivity paradox that further inhibits innovation. In most businesses, increased productivity—achieving more with less effort—leads to greater profitability. However, in the legal profession, where revenue is tied to the number of hours billed, increased productivity can actually reduce profitability unless the firm adapts its billing practices accordingly.

For example, if a lawyer finds a way to complete a task in half the time through the use of technology or process improvements, their billable hours—and therefore the firm's revenue—may decrease. This paradox creates a disincentive for individual lawyers and firms to adopt more productive methods, as doing so could directly impact their income.

The focus on billable hours often leads to a culture of "face time," where lawyers feel pressured to spend long hours in the office to meet their billable targets, even if those hours are not spent productively. This culture can discourage experimentation and the pursuit of innovative practices that might reduce the number of hours needed to complete a task. In such an environment, the emphasis is placed on maintaining or increasing billable hours, rather than on finding new ways to work smarter and deliver better value to clients.

Lack of Incentive for Process Improvement

Process improvement is a key component of innovation, involving the continuous analysis and refinement of workflows to enhance efficiency, quality, and client satisfaction. In industries where output and quality are prioritized, process improvement is often rewarded because it leads to better outcomes with fewer resources.

However, in the legal profession, where time spent is the metric by which work is valued, there is little incentive to streamline processes. In fact, process improvement can be seen as counterproductive under the billable hour model, as it may reduce the time required to complete tasks, thereby decreasing billable hours and revenue.

For example, a law firm might identify that certain administrative tasks, such as document management or client communication, could be automated or outsourced to reduce costs and improve efficiency. However, if these tasks are currently billable, automating or outsourcing them could reduce the firm's billable hours and, consequently, its revenue. As a result, there is little motivation to pursue process improvements that could ultimately benefit the client but potentially harm the firm's bottom line.

This lack of incentive for process improvement not only stifles innovation but also leads to a status quo where outdated and inefficient practices are maintained simply because they generate billable hours.

Over time, this can result in a firm that is less agile, less competitive, and less capable of meeting the evolving needs of clients.

The Impact on Lawyer Development and Specialization

The billable hour model also has implications for the professional development of lawyers, particularly in terms of specialization and the pursuit of innovative legal strategies. Under the billable hour system, junior lawyers are often encouraged to focus on generating billable hours, rather than on developing specialized expertise or exploring innovative approaches to legal problems.

This emphasis on billable hours can limit opportunities for lawyers to engage in non-billable activities that are critical for long-term professional growth, such as pro bono work, legal research, continuing education, and participation in professional organizations. These activities, while not immediately profitable, are essential for developing the skills, knowledge, and networks that drive innovation within the profession.

The pressure to meet billable hour targets can discourage lawyers from pursuing new areas of law or innovative legal strategies that might require significant upfront investment in learning and development. For example, a lawyer interested in specializing in a cutting-edge area of law, such as blockchain or artificial intelligence, may struggle to find the time to develop this expertise if they are constantly focused on generating billable hours in more traditional practice areas.

As a result, the billable hour model can lead to a profession that is less dynamic, less innovative, and less capable of adapting to new challenges and opportunities. This not only limits the potential for individual lawyers to grow and succeed but also restricts the ability of the profession as a whole to evolve in response to changing client needs and societal demands.

In the next section, we will delve into the psychological and economic factors that have kept the billable hour model entrenched in the legal profession, exploring why this model persists despite its many shortcomings and what it might take to move beyond it.

Psychological and Economic Factors

The billable hour model is more than just a billing practice; it is deeply ingrained in the culture and economics of the legal profession. Despite its inefficiencies and the growing demand for alternative approaches, the billable hour persists, supported by a combination of psychological comfort, economic incentives, and structural dynamics that make it difficult to displace. To understand why this model remains so entrenched, it is essential to explore the psychological and economic factors that reinforce its dominance.

Psychological Comfort and Familiarity

One of the primary reasons the billable hour model persists is the psychological comfort it provides to both lawyers and clients. For many lawyers, the billable hour is familiar and straightforward—it offers a clear, quantifiable measure of productivity and effort. Lawyers can easily track their time, and clients can see exactly how their money is being spent. This transparency, albeit often superficial, gives both parties a sense of control and predictability.

The Illusion of Objectivity

The billable hour creates an illusion of objectivity by quantifying legal work in precise units of time. Lawyers and clients alike can point to the number of hours billed as a tangible reflection of the work performed. This tangibility is comforting in a profession where the value of services can be difficult to measure, particularly in complex legal matters where outcomes are uncertain. By focusing on time, lawyers can avoid the more subjective task of valuing their work based on outcomes or client satisfaction, which can be harder to quantify and justify.

This comfort with the billable hour is reinforced by the fact that it has been the standard for so long. Many lawyers have spent their entire careers working within this model, and it is the only system they know. The prospect of moving to a different billing structure, such as flat fees or value-based billing, can be daunting because it requires a fundamental shift in how they think about and value their work. This fear of the unknown can create resistance to change, even when the current system is flawed.

Behavioral Inertia

Behavioral inertia—the tendency to stick with the status quo—is another psychological factor that helps to explain the persistence of the billable hour. People are naturally resistant to change, especially when it involves altering long-established practices and routines. This inertia is particularly strong in the legal profession, which is known for its conservative nature and adherence to tradition.

Lawyers, by training, are risk-averse and cautious. They are taught to prioritize consistency, precedent, and thoroughness, which can make them more reluctant to embrace new approaches or experiment with innovative billing models. The billable hour, with its clear and established structure, feels safe and reliable, whereas alternative models might seem risky or untested. This aversion to risk can make lawyers hesitant to move away from the familiar, even when there are compelling reasons to do so.

Economic Structures and Incentives

Beyond psychological comfort, the billable hour model is also reinforced by powerful economic structures and incentives that align the interests of law firms, individual lawyers, and even clients in ways that perpetuate its use. These economic factors create a complex web of incentives that make it challenging to transition to alternative billing models.

The Principal-Agent Problem

The Principal-Agent Problem, a well-known concept in economics,[33] provides a useful framework for understanding the dynamics at play in the billable hour model. In this context, the "principal" is the client, who seeks to have legal work performed efficiently and effectively, while the "agent" is the lawyer, who is tasked with carrying out the work. Ideally, the interests of the principal and agent would be perfectly aligned, with both parties focused on achieving the best possible outcome for the client.

However, the billable hour model creates a potential misalignment of incentives between the lawyer and the client. Because lawyers are compensated based on the number of hours they bill, they may be incentivized to spend more time on tasks than is strictly necessary. This misalignment can lead to inefficiencies, as the lawyer's financial interests may not fully align with the client's desire for cost-effective and timely legal services.

---

[33] Jensen, Michael C., and Meckling, William H.. "Theory of the Firm: Managerial Behavior, Agency Costs and Ownership Structure." Journal of Financial Economics, vol. 3, no. 4, 1976

Further, law firms, which act as principals to their lawyers (the agents), often set billable hour targets that lawyers must meet to achieve bonuses, promotions, and other forms of recognition. These targets further reinforce the focus on hours billed, rather than on outcomes achieved, and can exacerbate the potential for inefficiencies. The result is a system where both individual lawyers and law firms have strong economic incentives to maintain the billable hour model, even when it may not be in the best interest of clients.

Revenue Predictability

For law firms, the billable hour model provides a predictable and stable source of revenue. By tracking and billing hours, firms can easily project their income based on the number of hours worked by their lawyers. This predictability is particularly important for large firms with significant overhead costs, such as salaries, office space, and technology infrastructure. The billable hour model allows firms to manage their finances with a high degree of certainty, which can be more challenging under alternative billing models where revenue is tied to outcomes or value rather than time.

This economic stability is a powerful incentive for firms to stick with the billable hour model. Even when clients push for alternative billing arrangements, firms may be reluctant to move away from the predictability of hourly billing. This reluctance is often compounded by the fact that many law firms operate on a partnership model, where profits are distributed among partners based on the firm's overall revenue. The billable hour model, with its clear link between hours worked and revenue generated, fits neatly into this structure, reinforcing its continued use.

The Billable Hour as a Metric of Success

The billable hour also serves as a key metric of success within law firms, particularly in terms of evaluating individual lawyer performance. Lawyers are often judged based on the number of hours they bill, with those who consistently meet or exceed their targets being rewarded with bonuses, promotions, and partnership opportunities. This creates a powerful incentive for lawyers to focus on maximizing their billable hours, even if it means spending more time on tasks or avoiding efficiency improvements that could reduce the time required.

This focus on billable hours as a measure of success can create a culture of competition within firms, where lawyers feel pressured to work long hours and prioritize quantity over quality. It can also lead to a reluctance to delegate tasks to junior associates or support staff, as doing so could reduce the senior lawyer's billable hours. Over time, this emphasis on billable hours can become deeply ingrained in the firm's culture, making it difficult to shift to alternative models that prioritize value or outcomes over time spent.

The Impact on Lawyer Well-Being

The pressures associated with the billable hour model have significant implications for the well-being of lawyers, contributing to a culture of stress, burnout, and even substance abuse. The relentless focus on meeting billable hour targets can create a high-stress environment where lawyers feel constantly under pressure to work longer and harder to meet the demands of their firm.

Stress and Burnout

The pressure to meet billable hour targets can lead to chronic stress and burnout among lawyers. The need to log a certain number of hours each day, week, or year can result in long workdays, sacrificed weekends, and the blurring of boundaries between work and personal life. This relentless pace can take a toll on mental and physical health, leading to exhaustion, anxiety, and depression.

Research has consistently shown that lawyers are at a higher risk of burnout compared to other professions. A study[34] conducted by the American Bar Association (ABA) found that lawyers experience higher rates of depression, anxiety, and substance abuse than the general population. The billable hour model, with its emphasis on time spent rather than outcomes achieved, is a significant contributing factor to these mental health challenges.

Substance Abuse

The stress associated with the billable hour model can also lead to substance abuse as a coping mechanism. Lawyers may turn to alcohol,

---

[34] Krill, Patrick R., et al. "The Prevalence of Substance Use and Other Mental Health Concerns Among American Attorneys." Journal of Addiction Medicine, vol. 10, no. 1, 2016 > This landmark study, conducted by the ABA Commission on Lawyer Assistance Programs and the Hazelden Betty Ford Foundation, found that 28% of lawyers experience depression, 19% suffer from anxiety, and 21% engage in problematic drinking, significantly higher rates than in the general population.

drugs, or other substances to manage the pressure of meeting billable hour targets,[35] dealing with difficult clients, or coping with the demands of their work. The ABA's study on substance abuse in the legal profession found that a significant percentage of lawyers struggle with alcohol and drug dependency, with many citing work-related stress as a primary factor.

The culture of the legal profession, which often glorifies long hours and intense work schedules, can exacerbate these issues. Lawyers may feel that they have to keep up with their peers or meet the expectations of their firm, even at the expense of their health. This pressure can create a vicious cycle, where substance abuse leads to further stress and burnout, which in turn perpetuates the need for coping mechanisms.

Teaching the Billable Hour Model to Law Students

The billable hour model is often introduced to lawyers early in their careers, beginning with law school. Many law schools emphasize the importance of billing time, teaching students how to track their hours and instilling the idea that success in the legal profession is closely tied to the number of hours worked. While this training is intended to prepare students for the realities of legal practice, it also sets the stage for the stress-related pressures that many lawyers will face throughout their careers.

Law students who are taught to prioritize billable hours may internalize the idea that their worth as a lawyer is measured by the time they spend on their work. This mindset can lead to unhealthy work habits, such as overworking, neglecting self-care, and sacrificing personal relationships for the sake of meeting billable hour targets. It can also make it difficult for new lawyers to adjust to alternative billing models or to value their work based on outcomes rather than time spent.

The focus on billable hours in legal education can also contribute to a culture of competition among students, where those who log the most hours in internships or clerkships are seen as the most successful. This can create an environment where students feel pressured to overextend themselves, even before they enter the workforce, setting

---

[35] Sheldon, Kennon M., et al. "What Makes Lawyers Happy? A Data-Driven Prescription to Redefine Professional Success." George Washington Law Review, vol. 83, no. 2, 2015

the stage for the stress and burnout that many will experience as practicing lawyers.

The persistence of the billable hour model in the legal profession can be attributed to a combination of psychological comfort, economic incentives, and structural dynamics that reinforce its continued use. While the model provides predictability and a clear metric of success, it also creates significant barriers to innovation, efficiency, and lawyer well-being. The focus on time spent rather than value delivered can lead to a culture of stress, burnout, and even substance abuse, particularly for those who are introduced to the model early in their careers.

As the legal profession continues to evolve, it is essential to critically examine the impact of the billable hour model and explore alternative approaches that prioritize client satisfaction, innovation, and lawyer well-being. By moving away from the billable hour and embracing business models that align client results with firm profits, the legal profession can create a healthier and more sustainable environment for both lawyers and clients.

Chapter 4: The Rise of Productized Services

Imagine you're a client: Instead of booking hours with a lawyer and waiting weeks for a custom-tailored legal solution, you walk into a law office and pick a service off the shelf—like grabbing a neatly packaged product. No delays, no surprise costs, no endless back-and-forth. Just a streamlined, pre-designed solution to your legal problem, ready to go. This isn't some futuristic fantasy—it's an example of the rise of productized services in the legal industry. Just as companies like Netflix revolutionized how we consume entertainment by offering simple, subscription-based access to vast content, productized legal services offer clients clarity, speed, and affordability in an industry often seen as complex and opaque.

Productized Services

Productized services transform customized, labor-intensive tasks into streamlined, standardized solutions that can be offered to clients at a fixed price. Unlike the traditional model where law firms bill by the hour, productized services package expertise into clearly defined *deliverables*—eliminating the unpredictability of hourly rates and allowing clients to know exactly what they are getting and at what cost.

Key features of productized services include:

- **Predictability:** Clients know upfront what they will pay and the scope of the service, providing peace of mind and eliminating billing anxiety.
- **Standardization:** Processes are designed to be repeatable, allowing firms to deliver the same service to multiple clients efficiently.

- **Scalability:** With fixed workflows and pricing, firms can serve more clients without increasing overhead, leading to growth and profitability.

Transformation in Other Industries

The legal profession is not alone in its struggle with traditional business models that may hinder innovation and efficiency. Other industries, such as consulting and information technology (IT), have also grappled with similar challenges but have successfully transitioned to more innovative approaches, particularly through the adoption of productized services. By examining these industries, we can gain valuable insights into how the legal sector might similarly evolve to meet the demands of modern clients.

Consulting: From Billable Hours to Productized Services

The consulting industry, much like the legal profession, traditionally relied on a billable hour model. Consultants would work closely with clients, offering customized advice and solutions, and billing for their time. However, as client demands shifted towards more predictable pricing and measurable outcomes, the consulting industry began to explore new business models, leading to the rise of productized services.[36]

Consulting's Shift to Productization

Productized services in consulting refer to standardized, repeatable offerings that are designed to solve specific problems or achieve particular outcomes for clients. Unlike traditional consulting, where the work is highly customized and billed by the hour, productized services are typically offered at a fixed price and delivered through a standardized process. This approach allows consulting firms to scale their operations, reduce costs, and provide clients with greater predictability in terms of both pricing and outcomes.

For example, a consulting firm that specializes in digital transformation might develop a productized service that helps businesses migrate to

---

[36] Desabato, Nick. "Productized Services: 30+ Examples of Scalable Consulting." Coveted Consultant, August 3, 2015

the cloud. This service would be packaged with a clear scope, defined deliverables, and a fixed price, making it easier for clients to understand what they are getting and what it will cost. The consulting firm can then deliver this service to multiple clients using the same standardized process, increasing efficiency and profitability.

Benefits of Productized Services in Consulting

The transition to productized services has brought several benefits to the consulting industry:

- **Scalability:** By standardizing services, consulting firms can scale their operations more easily. They can deliver the same service to multiple clients without needing to reinvent the wheel each time, which increases efficiency and reduces the time required to deliver value.
- **Predictability:** Productized services provide clients with greater predictability in terms of both pricing and outcomes. Clients know exactly what they are paying for and what they can expect to receive, which reduces the risk of cost overruns and enhances client satisfaction.
- **Efficiency:** Standardized processes allow consulting firms to deliver services more efficiently, reducing the time and resources required to achieve the desired outcomes. This efficiency can lead to higher profitability and a more sustainable business model.
- **Focus on Outcomes:** Productized services shift the focus from time spent to results achieved. This aligns the interests of the consulting firm and the client, as both parties are working towards a clearly defined goal.

Case Study: McKinsey Solutions

McKinsey & Company, one of the world's leading consulting firms, has embraced productized services through its McKinsey Solutions division. McKinsey Solutions offers a range of productized services, such as advanced analytics tools and industry-specific solutions, that help clients address common challenges in a standardized way. These offerings are often delivered through digital platforms, allowing McKinsey to serve a broader range of clients more efficiently.

For example, McKinsey's Periscope[37] platform is a productized service that provides clients with advanced analytics tools to optimize pricing, marketing, and sales. Clients can access these tools on a subscription basis, with McKinsey providing ongoing support and updates. This productized approach allows McKinsey to deliver value at scale, while also providing clients with a predictable and transparent pricing model.

Information Technology: The Rise of SaaS and Managed Services

The IT industry has undergone a profound transformation over the past two decades, moving away from traditional service models to embrace productization through Software as a Service (SaaS) and managed services. This shift has revolutionized the way IT services are delivered and consumed, providing valuable lessons for the legal profession.

From Custom Development to SaaS

In the past, IT services were often delivered through custom software development projects, where clients would hire developers to build bespoke solutions tailored to their specific needs. These projects were typically billed by the hour, with costs and timelines often unpredictable due to the complexity and uncertainty involved.

However, as technology evolved, the IT industry began to shift towards SaaS, a productized model where software is developed, maintained, and delivered as a standardized service over the internet. SaaS providers offer their software on a subscription basis, allowing clients to access powerful tools and applications without the need for custom development or extensive on-premises infrastructure.

For example, Salesforce, one of the pioneers of the SaaS model, offers a standardized customer relationship management (CRM) platform that can be used by businesses of all sizes to manage their sales, marketing, and customer service operations. Clients pay a subscription fee based on the number of users and the features they need, and Salesforce takes care of all the development, maintenance, and updates. This model provides clients with predictable costs, quick

---

[37] McKinsey & Company. "Periscope by McKinsey | Growth, Marketing & Sales." McKinsey & Company, 2024

deployment, and ongoing access to the latest features and innovations.

Managed Services

In addition to SaaS, the IT industry has also seen the rise of managed services, another form of productized service. Managed service providers (MSPs) offer standardized IT services, such as network management, cybersecurity, and cloud hosting, on a subscription basis. Clients outsource these functions to the MSP, which takes responsibility for managing and maintaining the IT infrastructure, ensuring that it runs smoothly and securely.

Managed services differ from traditional IT consulting in that they are delivered as ongoing, standardized services rather than one-off projects. This model provides clients with continuous support and peace of mind, while also allowing MSPs to scale their operations and achieve greater efficiency.

Benefits of SaaS and Managed Services

The transition to SaaS and managed services has brought significant benefits to the IT industry:

- **Scalability:** SaaS and managed services are inherently scalable, allowing providers to serve a large number of clients with the same standardized offerings. This scalability leads to lower costs and higher margins for providers.
- **Predictable Revenue:** Subscription-based models provide IT service providers with predictable, recurring revenue streams. This financial stability allows providers to invest in innovation and continuous improvement, further enhancing their offerings.
- **Client Satisfaction:** Clients benefit from predictable costs, easy access to the latest technology, and ongoing support. This enhances client satisfaction and loyalty, as clients know they can rely on their providers to meet their needs.
- **Focus on Core Business:** By outsourcing IT functions to SaaS providers and MSPs, clients can focus on their core business activities, rather than being bogged down by the complexities of managing IT infrastructure.

Case Study: Microsoft Office 365

Microsoft's transition from selling perpetual software licenses to offering Office 365 as a SaaS product is a prime example of productization in the IT industry. Office 365 provides clients with access to Microsoft's suite of productivity tools, including Word, Excel, and Outlook, on a subscription basis. Clients receive regular updates, cloud storage, and collaboration features, all managed by Microsoft.

This productized approach has allowed Microsoft to generate recurring revenue, improve customer retention, and reach a broader market. It has also provided clients with a more flexible and cost-effective way to access essential software tools, without the need for expensive upfront investments or complex installation processes.

Lessons for the Legal Sector

The successful transformation of the consulting and IT industries offers valuable lessons for the legal sector, which faces many of the same challenges that these industries once did. By transitioning to productized services, law firms can achieve greater efficiency, scalability, and client satisfaction, while also reducing their reliance on the billable hour model.

Standardization and Efficiency

One of the key benefits of productized services is the ability to standardize processes and deliver services more efficiently. In the legal sector, this could involve developing standardized legal products, such as contract templates, compliance checklists, or automated legal research tools, that can be delivered to clients at a fixed price. By focusing on standardization, law firms can reduce the time and resources required to deliver these services, allowing them to serve more clients with greater consistency and quality.

Predictable Pricing and Client Trust

Productized services offer clients greater predictability in pricing, which is a significant advantage in an industry where legal costs are often seen as unpredictable and opaque. By offering fixed-price legal products, law firms can build trust with clients, who will appreciate the transparency and certainty that comes with knowing exactly what they are paying for. This approach can also help law firms differentiate themselves in a competitive market, where clients are increasingly looking for value and clarity.

Scalability and Growth

Productized legal services can also help law firms scale their operations more effectively. By creating standardized offerings that can be delivered to multiple clients, firms can expand their reach without a corresponding increase in costs. This scalability is particularly important in an era where technology is enabling law firms to serve clients remotely and across borders. By leveraging technology to deliver productized services, law firms can tap into new markets and client segments, driving growth and profitability.

Focus on Outcomes and Innovation

The transition to productized services can shift the focus from time spent to outcomes achieved, encouraging innovation and continuous improvement. By aligning their interests with those of their clients, law firms can create a culture of innovation, where the emphasis is on delivering value and solving problems, rather than simply billing hours. This shift in focus can drive the adoption of new technologies, process improvements, and innovative approaches to legal work, positioning law firms for success in a rapidly evolving market.

The successful transformation of industries like consulting and IT through the adoption of productized services provides a compelling blueprint for the legal sector. By moving away from the traditional billable hour model and embracing standardized, value-driven offerings, law firms can achieve greater efficiency, scalability, and client satisfaction. The lessons learned from these industries highlight the potential for legal productization to drive innovation, enhance client relationships, and create a more sustainable and competitive business model for the future.

Key Characteristics of Productized Services

Productized services represent a significant shift from traditional, custom-tailored professional services to standardized offerings designed to be scalable, repeatable, and easily delivered. In the context of the legal industry, this shift is particularly transformative, offering new ways for law firms to deliver value to clients while improving efficiency and predictability. To fully understand the potential of productized services in legal services, it is important to explore the key characteristics that define these offerings.

Fixed Pricing

One of the most defining features of productized services is fixed pricing. Unlike the billable hour model, where costs can fluctuate based on the time spent on a matter, productized services are typically offered at a set price. This pricing model provides clients with transparency and predictability, allowing them to know upfront what they will pay for a particular service

Transparency and Client Trust

Fixed pricing fosters greater transparency between law firms and their clients. Clients appreciate knowing exactly what they will be charged for a service, without the uncertainty and anxiety that often accompanies hourly billing. This transparency helps build trust, as clients are assured that there will be no unexpected charges or surprises when the bill arrives. For law firms, this trust can lead to stronger client relationships, increased client retention, and a reputation for fairness and reliability.

Incentivizing Efficiency

Fixed pricing also incentivizes law firms to be more efficient in their service delivery. Since the revenue from a productized service is not tied to the number of hours worked, firms are motivated to streamline processes, adopt technology, and reduce unnecessary steps to deliver the service as efficiently as possible. This focus on efficiency can lead to lower costs and higher profitability, as firms can deliver the same service to multiple clients with less time and effort.

Value-Based Pricing

In some cases, fixed pricing for productized services may be aligned with value-based pricing, where the price is set based on the value the service delivers to the client rather than the cost to the law firm. For example, a law firm might offer a standardized service for drafting employment contracts, priced according to the size of the client's workforce or the complexity of their legal needs. This approach ensures that the price reflects the client's perceived value of the service, leading to greater client satisfaction and a stronger alignment between the firm's interests and those of the client.

Standardization

Standardization is another key characteristic of productized services. In contrast to traditional legal services, which are often highly customized and tailored to the specific needs of each client, productized services are designed to be repeatable and consistent. This standardization allows law firms to deliver the same service to multiple clients with minimal variation, improving both efficiency and quality.

Consistency and Quality Control

Standardization ensures that clients receive the same level of service every time they engage with a productized offering. By creating standardized processes, templates, and workflows, law firms can maintain a high level of consistency in service delivery. This consistency not only enhances the client experience but also allows firms to implement robust quality control measures, ensuring that each service meets the firm's standards and client expectations.

For example, a law firm might develop a standardized process for conducting compliance audits for clients in a particular industry. This process would include predefined checklists, templates, and procedures that are followed for each audit, ensuring that all relevant legal issues are addressed in a consistent manner. By standardizing the service, the firm can deliver audits more efficiently while maintaining a high level of quality and accuracy.

Scalability and Efficiency

Standardization also makes productized services highly scalable. Because the service is based on a repeatable process, it can be easily scaled to serve a larger number of clients without a corresponding increase in costs or resources. This scalability is particularly valuable for law firms looking to expand their reach or serve new markets, as it allows them to grow their business without being constrained by the limitations of traditional, customized service delivery.

For example, a law firm might develop a standardized package for handling routine corporate filings, such as forming new entities or registering trademarks. This service could be offered to clients across multiple jurisdictions, with the same standardized process applied in each case. By leveraging technology and standardized workflows, the firm can handle a high volume of filings efficiently, allowing it to serve more clients and generate more revenue.

Process Optimization

Standardization also facilitates continuous process optimization. By creating standardized workflows, law firms can regularly review and refine their processes to improve efficiency, reduce costs, and enhance client satisfaction. This focus on process optimization is a key advantage of productized services, as it allows firms to continuously improve their offerings and stay competitive in a rapidly changing market.

Leveraging Technology

Technology plays a crucial role in enabling the scalability of productized services. By leveraging tools such as automation, cloud computing, and artificial intelligence, law firms can deliver standardized services to a large number of clients with minimal manual intervention. For example, a law firm might use a cloud-based document automation platform to generate legal documents for multiple clients, with each document customized based on client-specific data but generated through the same standardized process. This approach allows the firm to handle a high volume of work efficiently, without the need to hire additional staff or increase overhead costs.

Expanding Market Reach

Scalability also allows law firms to expand their market reach by offering productized services to a broader range of clients, including those in different geographical regions or industries. Because the service is standardized, it can be easily adapted to meet the needs of clients in different locations or sectors, without the need for extensive customization. This flexibility enables law firms to tap into new markets and grow their client base, driving revenue growth and increasing the firm's overall market presence.

For example, a law firm might develop a productized service for international business compliance, offering a standardized package that includes regulatory guidance, document preparation, and filing services for companies operating in multiple countries. By leveraging standardized processes and technology, the firm can offer this service to clients around the world, expanding its reach and generating new business opportunities.

Cost-Effective Growth

One of the key advantages of scalability is the ability to grow the business without a proportional increase in costs. Because productized services are based on standardized processes, they can be delivered at scale with minimal additional resources. This cost-effective growth allows law firms to increase their profitability while maintaining or even reducing their cost structure. For example, by automating routine legal tasks and standardizing service delivery, a law firm can increase its capacity to serve clients without needing to hire more lawyers or support staff. This scalability leads to higher margins and a more sustainable business model, as the firm can generate more revenue from the same or lower costs.

Flexibility and Adaptability

Scalability also provides law firms with the flexibility to adapt to changing market conditions or client demands. Because productized services are based on standardized processes, they can be easily modified or expanded to meet new challenges or opportunities. For example, a law firm might initially offer a productized service for trademark registration, but later expand the service to include trademark monitoring and enforcement as client needs evolve. This adaptability allows the firm to stay competitive and responsive to client demands, ensuring long-term success in a dynamic legal market.

Focus on Outcomes

One of the most significant shifts that comes with productized services is the focus on outcomes rather than time spent. In traditional legal services, particularly under the billable hour model, the emphasis is on the number of hours worked rather than the results achieved. Productized services, however, prioritize delivering specific outcomes or solutions for clients, aligning the interests of the law firm with those of the client.

Client-Centered Service

By focusing on outcomes, productized services place the client's needs at the center of the service delivery model. Clients engage with the service not because of the time or effort involved, but because of the value and results it delivers. This client-centered approach is particularly appealing in today's market, where clients increasingly demand measurable value and tangible results from their legal service providers.

For example, a law firm offering a productized service for dispute resolution might guarantee a specific outcome, such as a settlement or resolution within a certain timeframe. The client pays for the outcome, rather than the hours spent working on the case, ensuring that the service aligns with their goals and expectations. This outcome-based approach enhances client satisfaction and fosters long-term relationships, as clients feel confident that they are receiving real value for their investment.

Performance Metrics and Accountability

The focus on outcomes also encourages law firms to establish clear performance metrics and accountability for their productized services. By defining specific goals and outcomes for each service, firms can measure their success and continuously improve their offerings. This accountability is critical for building trust with clients and ensuring that the service consistently delivers the promised results.

For example, a law firm offering a productized service for compliance audits might establish key performance indicators (KPIs) such as the number of regulatory issues identified, the time taken to complete the audit, and client satisfaction ratings. These metrics allow the firm to assess the effectiveness of the service, identify areas for improvement, and demonstrate the value of the service to clients.

Aligning Incentives with Clients

Productized services align the incentives of the law firm with those of the client, as both parties are focused on achieving the desired outcome. This alignment creates a partnership dynamic, where the success of the service is measured by the value it delivers to the client, rather than the time spent on the service. This shift in focus can lead to stronger client relationships, greater trust, and increased client loyalty, as clients see the law firm as a true partner in achieving their goals.

Productized services offer a transformative approach to delivering legal services, characterized by fixed pricing, standardization, scalability, and a focus on outcomes. These key characteristics provide law firms with the tools they need to enhance efficiency, improve client satisfaction, and scale their operations in a cost-effective manner. By embracing productized services, law firms can move beyond the limitations of traditional billing models and create a more sustainable, client-centered approach to legal practice.

Adapting for Legal Work

Adapting the characteristics of productized services—such as fixed pricing, standardization, scalability, and a focus on outcomes—to legal work offers significant potential for transforming how legal services are delivered. By reimagining traditional legal tasks through the lens of productization, law firms can enhance efficiency, improve client satisfaction, and create more predictable revenue streams. This section explores how these characteristics can be effectively adapted to legal services, with practical examples like flat-fee billing for routine tasks.

Fixed Pricing in Legal Services

Fixed pricing is one of the most powerful ways to adapt productized services to the legal industry. By offering legal services at a set price, law firms can provide clients with greater cost certainty and transparency, which are increasingly important in a market where clients are demanding more value for their money.

Flat-Fee Billing for Routine Tasks

One of the most straightforward applications of fixed pricing in legal services is flat-fee billing for routine tasks. These tasks often involve repetitive, well-defined processes that can be standardized and delivered efficiently, making them ideal candidates for a fixed-fee structure.

Examples of Routine Tasks Suitable for Flat Fees:

- **Contract Drafting:** Law firms can offer a flat fee for drafting standard contracts, such as employment agreements, non-disclosure agreements (NDAs), or lease agreements. By using templates and automated document generation tools, firms can efficiently produce high-quality contracts at a predictable cost, providing clients with clear pricing upfront.
- **Trademark Registration:** Trademark registration is a process with well-defined steps and predictable outcomes, making it suitable for a flat-fee service. Law firms can package the entire process—from the initial trademark search to the filing and monitoring of the application—into a fixed-price service, offering clients transparency and peace of mind.
- **Business Formation:** Setting up a new business entity, such as a corporation or LLC, involves a series of routine legal steps, including filing articles of incorporation, drafting bylaws, and

obtaining necessary licenses. Law firms can offer a flat-fee package that covers all these steps, providing startups and small businesses with an affordable and predictable legal service.

Benefits of Fixed Pricing:

- **Client Trust:** Fixed pricing builds client trust by eliminating the uncertainty and anxiety associated with hourly billing. Clients know exactly what they will pay for a service, which helps to prevent disputes over billing and fosters stronger client relationships.
- **Efficiency Incentives:** Fixed pricing encourages law firms to be more efficient in delivering services. Since the revenue from a flat-fee service is not tied to the number of hours worked, firms are motivated to streamline processes and reduce the time required to complete tasks, ultimately improving profitability.
- **Competitive Advantage:** Offering flat-fee services can provide a competitive advantage in a market where clients are increasingly seeking cost-effective legal solutions. Law firms that can offer predictable pricing are more likely to attract price-sensitive clients, such as startups, small businesses, and individuals with limited budgets.

Standardization of Legal Processes

Standardization is another key characteristic of productized services that can be effectively adapted to legal work. By creating standardized processes and workflows, law firms can deliver consistent, high-quality services more efficiently, reducing the time and effort required to complete legal tasks.

Creating Standardized Legal Products

Standardization involves developing legal products that can be consistently delivered to multiple clients with minimal customization. These products are typically based on common legal needs and are designed to address specific client challenges through a repeatable process.

Examples of Standardized Legal Products:

- **Compliance Audits:** Law firms can develop standardized compliance audit packages for clients in regulated industries, such as healthcare, finance, or manufacturing. These packages

would include predefined checklists, templates, and reporting tools that ensure all relevant legal requirements are reviewed and documented consistently.
- **Legal Risk Assessments:** Firms can offer standardized legal risk assessment services for businesses, helping them identify potential legal risks in areas such as contracts, employment practices, or data protection. By using standardized assessment tools and processes, firms can efficiently deliver these services to multiple clients, providing valuable insights at a predictable cost.
- **Document Review Services:** For tasks like due diligence or discovery, law firms can create standardized document review services that leverage technology, such as AI-powered document analysis tools, to quickly and accurately review large volumes of documents. These services can be offered at a fixed price, based on the volume of documents or the complexity of the review.

Benefits of Standardization:

- **Consistency and Quality:** Standardization ensures that legal services are delivered consistently, with the same level of quality and attention to detail for each client. This consistency helps build client confidence and trust in the firm's ability to meet their legal needs.
- **Scalability:** By standardizing processes, law firms can scale their operations more easily, serving more clients with the same resources. This scalability is particularly important for firms looking to expand their client base or enter new markets.
- **Process Optimization:** Standardization facilitates continuous process improvement, allowing firms to refine and optimize their workflows over time. This focus on process optimization can lead to greater efficiency, lower costs, and enhanced client satisfaction.

Scalability in Legal Services

Scalability is a critical characteristic of productized services that allows law firms to grow their business without a proportional increase in costs. By leveraging technology and standardized processes, firms can deliver services to a larger number of clients efficiently and cost-effectively.

Leveraging Technology for Scalable Legal Services

Technology plays a central role in enabling the scalability of legal services. By automating routine tasks and using digital platforms to deliver services, law firms can expand their reach and serve more clients with minimal additional resources.

Examples of Scalable Legal Services:

- **Automated Document Generation:** Law firms can use document automation software to generate legal documents, such as contracts, wills, or corporate filings, based on standardized templates. This technology allows firms to produce documents quickly and accurately, serving more clients without increasing staff levels.
- **Online Legal Platforms:** Firms can develop online platforms that offer legal services directly to clients, such as contract drafting, trademark registration, or legal advice. These platforms can be accessed by clients from anywhere, allowing firms to reach a global audience and scale their operations without the limitations of traditional, in-person service delivery.
- **Subscription-Based Legal Services:** Some law firms are adopting subscription models, where clients pay a fixed monthly fee for access to a suite of legal services. This model allows firms to provide ongoing legal support to a large number of clients, with scalable processes and technology enabling efficient service delivery.

Benefits of Scalability:

- **Cost-Effective Growth:** Scalability allows law firms to grow their business and serve more clients without a corresponding increase in costs. This cost-effective growth is essential for firms looking to expand their market presence and increase profitability.
- **Increased Revenue Streams:** Scalable services, such as online platforms or subscription models, can generate recurring revenue streams, providing financial stability and predictability for the firm.
- **Flexibility and Adaptability:** Scalable legal services can be easily adapted to meet changing client demands or market conditions. This flexibility allows firms to stay competitive and responsive to client needs, ensuring long-term success.

Focus on Outcomes in Legal Services

Shifting the focus from time spent to outcomes achieved is a fundamental aspect of productized services that can be adapted to the legal profession. By prioritizing results rather than hours worked, law firms can align their interests with those of their clients, creating a more client-centered approach to legal services.

Outcome-based legal services are designed to deliver specific results or solutions for clients, rather than simply billing for the time spent on a matter. This approach aligns the firm's incentives with the client's goals, fostering a collaborative partnership focused on achieving the desired outcome.

Examples of Outcome-Based Legal Services:

- **Settlement Services:** Law firms can offer outcome-based services for dispute resolution, where the fee is tied to the successful settlement of a case. For example, a firm might charge a fixed fee or a success fee based on the amount recovered in a settlement or the resolution of a dispute within a specified timeframe.
- **Regulatory Compliance:** Firms can offer outcome-based services for regulatory compliance, where the goal is to achieve and maintain compliance with specific legal requirements. The fee might be structured based on the successful implementation of compliance measures or the client's continued compliance over a set period.
- **Transaction Closings:** In transactional work, such as mergers and acquisitions, firms can offer outcome-based services tied to the successful closing of a deal. The fee could be based on the value of the transaction, the complexity of the deal, or the successful resolution of key legal issues.

Benefits of Focusing on Outcomes:

- **Client Satisfaction:** Outcome-based services align the law firm's success with the client's goals, leading to greater client satisfaction and stronger relationships. Clients appreciate knowing that their lawyer is focused on achieving the best possible outcome, rather than simply billing for time spent.
- **Innovation and Efficiency:** Focusing on outcomes encourages law firms to innovate and find the most efficient ways to deliver results. This focus on efficiency can lead to the adoption of new

- technologies, streamlined processes, and a more agile approach to legal work.
- **Differentiation in the Market:** Offering outcome-based services differentiates law firms in a competitive market, where clients are increasingly looking for value-driven solutions. Firms that can deliver results, rather than just time, are more likely to attract and retain clients.

Adapting the characteristics of productized services to legal work—through fixed pricing, standardization, scalability, and a focus on outcomes—offers a powerful way to transform how legal services are delivered. By embracing these principles, law firms can enhance efficiency, improve client satisfaction, and create more sustainable business models that align with the evolving demands of the legal market.

In the chapters that follow, we will delve deeper into practical strategies for implementing productized legal services, including case studies, pricing models, and tips for overcoming common challenges. By exploring these approaches, law firms can unlock new opportunities for growth and innovation, positioning themselves for success in a rapidly changing legal landscape.

Chapter 5: Designing Workflow Automation for Legal Services

Workflow automation is a transformative tool for law firms, offering the potential to streamline operations, reduce inefficiencies, and enhance the overall quality of legal services. However, to fully realize these benefits, it is essential to carefully design and implement automated workflows that are tailored to the unique needs and processes of a legal practice. This chapter provides a practical guide to creating workflows that can be automated within a law firm, covering the step-by-step process of mapping legal tasks, identifying automation opportunities, and selecting the right tools. It also includes case studies of successful implementations to illustrate how these concepts can be put into practice.

Mapping Legal Workflows

The first step in designing workflow automation for legal services is to map out the existing workflows within the firm. Mapping workflows involves documenting the sequence of tasks and processes that are carried out to complete a particular legal matter. This process helps to identify routine tasks 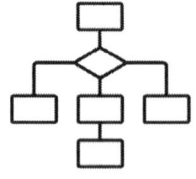 that are ripe for automation and provides a clear understanding of how work is currently being done, which is crucial for designing efficient automated workflows.

Step-by-Step Guide to Mapping Legal Workflows

- **Identify Key Processes:** Begin by identifying the key processes within the firm that are essential to delivering legal services. These processes might include tasks such as client intake, document drafting, legal research, contract review, litigation support, billing, and case management. Focus on processes

that are repetitive, time-consuming, and involve multiple steps, as these are often the best candidates for automation.
- **Break Down Each Process into Individual Tasks:** Once you have identified the key processes, break each one down into its component tasks. For example, the client intake process might include tasks such as scheduling initial consultations, collecting client information, conducting conflict checks, and setting up client files. Document each task in detail, noting who is responsible for completing it, what inputs are required, and what outputs are produced.
- **Create a Visual Workflow Diagram**: Use a visual tool, such as a flowchart or process map, to diagram the sequence of tasks within each process. This diagram should show the flow of work from start to finish, including decision points, handoffs between team members, and any parallel tasks that can be completed simultaneously. Visualizing the workflow helps to identify inefficiencies, redundancies, and bottlenecks that may not be immediately apparent when tasks are considered in isolation.
- **Identify Inputs and Outputs:** For each task within the workflow, identify the inputs (e.g., documents, data, or information) required to complete the task and the outputs (e.g., completed documents, reports, or communications) that result from it. This information is crucial for designing automation solutions, as it helps to determine what data and tools are needed at each stage of the process.
- **Analyze Current Pain Points:** Engage with the team members who are involved in each process to gather feedback on current pain points and challenges. Ask them to identify tasks that are particularly time-consuming, prone to errors, or require significant manual effort. Understanding these pain points will help you to prioritize tasks for automation and ensure that the automation solutions you implement address the most pressing needs of the firm.
- **Document Current Workflow Performance:** Before implementing any automation, it's important to document the current performance of each workflow. This includes tracking key metrics such as the time it takes to complete each task, the frequency of errors, and the overall efficiency of the process. Establishing a baseline allows you to measure the impact of automation and quantify the improvements achieved.

Example of Mapping a Legal Workflow: Client Intake Process

Let's consider the example of mapping the client intake process for a law firm:

Step 1: Identify the Process: The client intake process includes all tasks associated with bringing a new client into the firm, from the initial inquiry to the setup of the client file.

Step 2: Break Down the Process:

- Task 1: Receive and respond to the initial client inquiry (phone, email, or online form).
- Task 2: Schedule an initial consultation with the client.
- Task 3: Conduct a conflict check to ensure there are no conflicts of interest.
- Task 4: Collect detailed client information through an intake form.
- Task 5: Set up the client file in the firm's case management system.

Step 3: Create a Workflow Diagram: Use a flowchart to visualize the sequence of tasks, including decision points (e.g., if a conflict is found, escalate to a partner for review).

Step 4: Identify Inputs and Outputs:

Inputs: Client contact information, conflict check data, intake form responses.

Outputs: Scheduled consultation, completed conflict check, client file set up in the case management system.

Step 5: Analyze Pain Points: For example, team members identify that manually entering client information into the case management system is time-consuming and prone to errors.

Step 6: Document Current Performance: The firm may document that the current client intake process takes an average of 3 days to complete, with frequent delays due to manual data entry.

By mapping out the client intake process in this way, the firm can clearly see where automation could be implemented to streamline tasks, reduce errors, and improve the overall efficiency of the workflow.

Identifying Automation Opportunities

Once the workflows have been mapped out, the next step is to identify opportunities for automation. This involves analyzing the mapped workflows to spot inefficiencies, bottlenecks, and repetitive tasks that can be automated to save time and reduce the potential for errors.

How to Spot Automation Opportunities

Identify Repetitive Tasks: Look for tasks within the workflow that are repetitive and routine, as these are prime candidates for automation. Repetitive tasks often involve manual data entry, document generation, or routine communications, all of which can be automated using software tools.

Example: In the client intake process, manually entering client information into the case management system is a repetitive task that could be automated with data integration tools.

Analyze Decision Points: Decision points within a workflow are moments where a choice or judgment must be made, often based on predefined criteria. While some decision points require human judgment, others can be automated using decision-making algorithms or AI.

Example: The conflict check process often involves comparing client data against a database of existing clients and cases. This decision-making process can be automated using conflict-checking software that flags potential conflicts automatically.

Look for Bottlenecks: Bottlenecks are points in the workflow where tasks are delayed, causing a slowdown in the entire process. These bottlenecks often occur due to manual tasks that require significant time and effort, such as document review or approval processes. Automating these tasks can help to eliminate bottlenecks and speed up the workflow

Example: If the review and approval of legal documents are consistently delayed because they require multiple rounds of manual edits, implementing automated document review tools that flag potential issues for quick approval could significantly reduce these delays.

Consider High-Volume Tasks: Tasks that are performed frequently or involve large volumes of work are excellent candidates for automation.

Automating high-volume tasks can lead to significant time savings and allow lawyers to focus on higher-value activities.

Example: For law firms that handle a large number of similar contracts, automating the contract drafting process using template-based document generation can save substantial time and ensure consistency.

Evaluate Error-Prone Tasks: Tasks that are prone to errors due to manual data entry or complex processes should be prioritized for automation. Automating these tasks can reduce errors, improve accuracy, and enhance the overall quality of legal services.

Example: If manual entry of billing data frequently results in errors that need to be corrected, automating the billing process with integrated time-tracking and billing software can reduce these errors and streamline the invoicing process.

Prioritizing Automation Projects

Not all tasks can or should be automated immediately. It's important to prioritize automation projects based on factors such as the potential time savings, impact on efficiency, and ease of implementation. Consider starting with tasks that offer the greatest return on investment (ROI) and can be automated using readily available tools. As the firm gains experience with automation, more complex tasks can be addressed.

Selecting the Right Tools

Selecting the right tools is crucial for successful workflow automation. There are many software platforms and tools available that cater specifically to the needs of law firms, offering features such as case management, document automation, billing, and client communication. The key is to choose tools that integrate well with your existing systems and can be customized to fit the specific workflows of your firm.

Overview of Tools and Software for Legal Workflow Automation

In today's rapidly evolving legal landscape, workflow automation tools are becoming indispensable for law firms aiming to improve efficiency, reduce errors, and lower costs. While there are countless software options available, the following is a selection of prominent tools designed to streamline legal tasks. This list is not exhaustive but offers a glimpse into the diverse capabilities that modern legal technology can provide:

- **Clio:** Clio is a popular cloud-based practice management platform designed for law firms of all sizes. It offers a wide range of features, including case management, time tracking, billing, and client communication. Clio's automation capabilities include workflow automation for tasks such as client intake, document management, and billing, making it a versatile tool for automating various aspects of legal practice.
- **PracticePanther:** PracticePanther is another cloud-based legal practice management software that focuses on streamlining law firm operations. It offers features such as task management, document automation, billing, and time tracking. PracticePanther's workflow automation tools allow firms to automate repetitive tasks, such as sending reminders, generating invoices, and managing deadlines, helping to improve efficiency and reduce administrative burdens.
- **Lawyaw:** Lawyaw is a document automation tool specifically designed for law firms. It allows lawyers to create and manage templates for legal documents, which can then be automatically populated with client data. This automation reduces the time spent on drafting and ensures consistency across all documents. Lawyaw integrates with other practice management tools, making it easy to incorporate into existing workflows.
- **Lawcus:** Lawcus is a practice management tool that offers visual workflows, allowing firms to map out and automate their legal processes. It integrates with various tools and systems, providing a centralized platform for managing tasks, documents, billing, and client communication. Lawcus's workflow automation features help streamline case management, reduce manual tasks, and improve overall efficiency.
- **Microsoft Power Automate:** Microsoft Power Automate is a versatile cloud-based tool that enables businesses, like law firms, to automate repetitive tasks and integrate different applications. With its drag-and-drop interface and pre-built templates, Power Automate simplifies the process of creating workflows without the need for coding. Legal professionals can use it to automate tasks like document generation, data entry, client intake, and deadline reminders. It integrates seamlessly

with Microsoft Office applications, SharePoint, and third-party software.

Choosing the Right Tool for Your Firm

When selecting tools for workflow automation, it's important to consider the specific needs of your firm, including the size of your team, the complexity of your workflows, and your existing technology infrastructure. Look for tools that offer the features you need, integrate with your current systems, and provide customization options to fit your unique processes. It's also worth considering the level of support and training offered by the software provider, as this can be crucial for ensuring a smooth implementation.

Case Studies of Successful Implementations

To illustrate the impact of workflow automation in legal services, it's helpful to look at case studies of law firms that have successfully implemented these technologies. These examples provide practical insights into the process of designing and deploying automated workflows and demonstrate the tangible benefits that can be achieved.

Case Study 1: Streamlining Document Management at Foot Anstey

Foot Anstey, a UK-based law firm, identified inefficiencies in its document management and information workflows. The firm adopted a workflow automation platform[38] that integrated databases with existing systems to standardize information and streamline document handling. The automated system was designed to manage repetitive tasks like document creation and approval, significantly reducing manual intervention.

Outcome:

The automation enabled Foot Anstey to complete tasks four times faster than before, resulting in quicker turnaround times for client work. The improved efficiency helped the firm secure new business

---

[38] Thomson Reuters. "How Automation Turns Thousands of Tasks into One." Thomson Reuters Legal Blog, May 23, 2023

opportunities and increased staff productivity by automating repetitive tasks.

Case Study 2: Reducing Legal Processing Time at NetApp

NetApp, a Fortune 500 technology company, implemented TAP Workflow Automation by Mitratech[39] to address inefficiencies in document handling, specifically with Manufacturer's Authorization Forms (MAFs). The legal department faced significant challenges in manually tracking and processing up to 750 MAFs every quarter, which generated more than 2,250 related emails. The automation system was deployed to handle approvals, track document status, and reduce email volumes.

Outcome:

The automation reduced email volume by over 60%, saving the company 1,276 hours of attorney time in just six months. The overall cost savings amounted to approximately USD$236,694 in the first six months of implementation. Additionally, NetApp's legal department reported savings of $70,000 per week through the use of electronic signatures, resulting in a total annual savings of $3.6 million.

Case Study 3: Automating Employee Onboarding at Gilead Sciences

Gilead Sciences, a global biotech company, needed to streamline its employee onboarding process, which involved manual form submissions, approvals, and communication with IT. Gilead implemented similarly TAP Workflow Automation to automate these tasks. The automation system allowed employees to fill out onboarding forms, submit them digitally, and automatically route them through approval channels.

Outcome:

The onboarding process was automated and put into production within just two days. The automation saved significant time for the legal and HR departments, reduced the need for manual data entry, and

---

[39] O'Donnell, Steven. "Proven in Practice: Legal Workflow Automation in the Real World." Artificial Lawyer, June 21, 2019

improved the overall efficiency of onboarding new employees.

Designing workflow automation for legal services requires a thoughtful approach that begins with mapping existing workflows, identifying opportunities for automation, and selecting the right tools. By leveraging automation, law firms can streamline their operations, reduce inefficiencies, and deliver higher-quality services to their clients. The case studies presented in this chapter illustrate the real-world benefits of automation, demonstrating how it can transform legal practice and create a more efficient, client-focused firm.

In the next sections, we will explore how to build a productized legal service from these automated workflows, discussing pricing strategies, communication with clients, and the steps necessary to scale these services across the firm. By combining workflow automation with productization, law firms can unlock new levels of efficiency, profitability, and client satisfaction in a competitive legal market.

Chapter 6: Building a Productized Legal Service

In today's rapidly evolving legal landscape, the demand for efficiency and predictability is higher than ever. Clients increasingly seek not just legal expertise, but also streamlined services that deliver consistent value. This chapter delves into the concept of productized legal services, a model that transforms automated workflows into marketable offerings. By examining tasks like contract review, compliance checks, and legal research, we will explore how these services can be standardized, priced, and communicated effectively to clients. Together, we'll uncover strategies for turning routine legal work into scalable, profitable products that meet the needs of a modern clientele.

From Workflow to Product

Examples of Productizable Legal Tasks

Productizing legal services involves creating standardized, repeatable offerings that address common legal needs. These services can be delivered efficiently at a fixed price, providing clients with transparency and predictability while allowing law firms to scale their operations. The following are examples of legal tasks are ideally suited for productization:

Contract Drafting

Contract drafting is a fundamental legal task that is highly repetitive and can be standardized for various types of agreements. Many contracts, such as non-disclosure agreements (NDAs), employment agreements, and service contracts, follow similar structures and include common clauses. This makes them ideal candidates for productization.

How It Can Be Productized:

- **Standardized Templates:** Develop a series of contract templates that cover the most common types of agreements. These templates can be customized with specific client information, but the core structure and content remain consistent.
- **Automated Document Generation:** Use document automation tools to generate contracts quickly by populating templates with client-specific data. This reduces the time spent on drafting and ensures consistency across all contracts.
- **Fixed Pricing:** Offer contract drafting as a fixed-price service, with different pricing tiers based on the complexity of the contract or the level of customization required.

Example Offering: A law firm might offer a "Contract Essentials" package that includes the drafting of up to five standard contracts (e.g., NDAs, employment contracts, service agreements) for a flat fee. Clients can choose from pre-defined templates, and the firm will customize the contracts to meet their specific needs.

Compliance Reviews

Compliance reviews involve assessing a company's operations, policies, and procedures to ensure they meet legal and regulatory requirements. This task is often repetitive, especially for companies in highly regulated industries, such as healthcare, finance, or manufacturing. Compliance reviews can be standardized and offered as a productized service.

How It Can Be Productized:

- **Checklists and Templates:** Develop standardized checklists and templates for different types of compliance reviews, such as data privacy audits, environmental compliance, or workplace safety checks.
- **Automated Reporting:** Use software tools to automate the collection and analysis of compliance data, generating reports that highlight areas of non-compliance and recommend corrective actions.
- **Subscription Model:** Offer compliance reviews on a subscription basis, where clients receive regular (e.g., quarterly or annual) reviews as part of an ongoing service package.

Example Offering: A law firm could offer a "Regulatory Compliance Package" that includes an initial comprehensive compliance review followed by quarterly check-ins to ensure ongoing adherence to regulations. This service could be priced as an annual subscription, providing clients with continuous support and peace of mind.

Legal Research

Legal research is a critical component of many legal tasks, from drafting briefs to advising clients on complex legal issues. While some aspects of legal research require in-depth analysis and interpretation, much of the work involves finding and reviewing statutes, regulations, case law, and legal precedents—tasks that can be standardized and automated.

How It Can Be Productized:

- **Research Modules:** Develop standardized research modules for common legal topics, such as intellectual property law, employment law, or contract law. These modules can include curated collections of statutes, case summaries, and key legal principles.
- **AI-Powered Tools:** Utilize AI-powered legal research tools that can quickly analyze large volumes of legal data and identify relevant information. These tools can be integrated into the firm's research process to provide faster and more accurate results.
- **Flat-Fee Research Services:** Offer flat-fee legal research services for specific issues, such as preparing a legal memorandum on a particular topic or conducting due diligence research for a transaction.

Example Offering: A law firm could offer a "Legal Research On-Demand" service, where clients can request a research report on a specific legal issue for a fixed fee. The report would include a summary of relevant statutes, case law, and legal analysis, delivered within a set timeframe.

Future-Proof Tool for AI Legal Research: Alexi

Alexi is a cutting-edge AI-powered legal research platform that assists law firms in streamlining their research processes. By submitting a legal question, firms receive a comprehensive research memo that synthesize relevant case law, statutes, and legal principles. The platform uses advanced AI technology, supported by legal research experts, to quickly process vast amounts of data and deliver precise, actionable insights. This approach significantly reduces the time lawyers spend on manual research, allowing them to focus on strategic legal work and client engagement.

Firms such as Gowling WLG[40] and Stewart McKelvey have successfully integrated Alexi into their legal operations, improving the efficiency and accuracy of their research outputs. Lawyers report that Alexi's ability to generate well-researched legal arguments and summaries enhances their capacity to deliver higher-quality services. By automating this critical yet time-consuming aspect of legal practice, Alexi empowers firms to handle complex legal issues more effectively while maintaining high standards of accuracy and reliability.

Trademark Registration

Trademark registration is a highly standardized process that involves conducting a trademark search, preparing the application, and filing it with the relevant authorities. The steps involved in trademark registration are consistent across different clients, making it an ideal task for productization.

How It Can Be Productized:

- **Pre-Packaged Services:** Create a standardized trademark registration package that includes all necessary steps, such as conducting a trademark search, preparing the application, and managing the filing process.
- **Automated Workflow:** Implement automated workflows to handle routine tasks, such as generating search reports, preparing application documents, and tracking the status of filings.
- **Tiered Pricing:** Offer tiered pricing based on the complexity of the trademark registration, such as a basic package for single-class registrations and a premium package for multi-class or international registrations.

Example Offering: A law firm might offer a "Trademark Protection Package" that includes a comprehensive trademark search, preparation and filing of the application, and monitoring of the

---

[40] Hill, Caroline. "Canadian-Founded 'AI for Litigators' Platform Alexi Raises a US $11m Series A." Legal IT Insider, 10 June 2024

trademark's status. This service could be offered at a fixed price, with add-ons available for additional services, such as international filings or trademark enforcement.

Business Formation

Business formation involves the legal steps necessary to establish a new business entity, such as a corporation, limited liability company (LLC), or partnership. The process typically includes preparing and filing formation documents, drafting operating agreements or bylaws, and obtaining necessary licenses or permits. These steps are relatively standardized and can be offered as a productized service.

How It Can Be Productized:

- **Entity Formation Packages:** Create pre-packaged business formation services tailored to different types of entities, such as LLCs, corporations, or non-profits. These packages can include all necessary legal documents and filings, along with guidance on compliance requirements.
- **Fixed-Fee Services:** Offer business formation services at a fixed fee, with pricing based on the type of entity being formed and the level of customization required.
- **Ongoing Support:** Include ongoing legal support as part of the package, such as annual compliance checks or assistance with filing necessary reports and documents.

Example Offering: A law firm could offer a "Start-Up Essentials Package" that includes entity formation, drafting of foundational documents (e.g., operating agreement, bylaws), and initial regulatory compliance advice. This package could be priced at a fixed fee, with options for additional services like intellectual property protection or employment agreements.

Formation To Go: Stripe Atlas

Stripe Atlas, from payment tech giant Stripe, is an example of a productized business formation service designed to streamline the process of starting a new company. Entrepreneurs can use Stripe Atlas to form a corporation or LLC with just a few clicks.[41] The platform

---

[41] "The Stripe Atlas Review: How We Started a US Company as Non-US Residents." HackerNoon, February 8, 2021

provides a comprehensive package that includes the preparation and filing of incorporation documents, the creation of a tax identification number, and access to essential agreements, such as founder agreements and banking solutions. By automating these steps, Stripe Atlas reduces the complexity and cost associated with forming a business, making it an attractive option for startups globally.

In addition to entity formation, Stripe Atlas offers ongoing legal and financial support, such as tax guidance, banking setup, and compliance resources. The fixed-fee service provides transparency in pricing, allowing entrepreneurs to know the costs upfront and avoid surprises. This productized approach allows businesses to focus on growth while ensuring that their legal and financial foundations are solid, without the need for significant custom legal work. The success of Stripe Atlas highlights the potential for law firms to offer similarly packaged business formation services tailored to specific client needs.

Estate Planning

Estate planning involves the preparation of legal documents that outline how a person's assets will be managed and distributed after their death. This process typically includes drafting wills, trusts, powers of attorney, and healthcare directives. Estate planning can be highly repetitive and is well-suited for productization.

How It Can Be Productized:

- **Standardized Estate Plans:** Develop standardized estate planning packages that include all necessary documents, such as wills, trusts, and powers of attorney. These packages can be tailored to different client needs, such as basic plans for individuals or more complex plans for families with significant assets.
- **Document Automation:** Use document automation software to quickly generate estate planning documents based on client inputs. This ensures consistency and reduces the time spent on drafting.
- **Fixed-Price Packages:** Offer estate planning services at a fixed price, with different packages available based on the complexity of the client's estate and their specific needs.

Example Offering: A law firm might offer an "Estate Planning Essentials Package" that includes a will, living trust, power of attorney, and healthcare directive. This package could be priced at a flat fee, with options for more comprehensive plans that include additional services like tax planning or charitable giving.

Employment Law Compliance

Employment law compliance involves ensuring that a business's policies and practices adhere to federal, state, and local employment laws. This task often includes reviewing and drafting employee handbooks, conducting audits of employment practices, and providing guidance on compliance with labor laws. Employment law compliance is an area where standardized processes can be developed and offered as a productized service.

How It Can Be Productized:

- **Compliance Packages:** Develop employment law compliance packages that include services such as handbook review, policy drafting, and compliance audits. These packages can be tailored to different types of businesses, such as small businesses, startups, or large corporations.
- **Automated Audits:** Implement software tools to automate the audit process, identifying potential areas of non-compliance and generating reports with recommendations for corrective action.
- **Subscription-Based Services:** Offer ongoing compliance support as a subscription service, where clients receive regular updates on changes in employment law and assistance with maintaining compliance.

Example Offering: A law firm could offer an "Employment Compliance Package" that includes a comprehensive review of the client's employment practices, updating of employee handbooks, and regular compliance audits. This service could be priced as a one-time fee or as an annual subscription, providing clients with continuous support.

Immigration Services

Immigration services involve assisting clients with the legal processes related to visas, green cards, citizenship, and other immigration matters. These services are often standardized, following specific legal procedures and documentation requirements, making them suitable for productization.

How It Can Be Productized:

- **Pre-Packaged Services:** Create standardized immigration service packages, such as visa applications, green card processing, or citizenship applications. These packages can include all necessary legal documents and guidance on navigating the immigration process.

- **Automated Document Preparation:** Use document automation tools to streamline the preparation of immigration forms and applications, ensuring accuracy and consistency.

- **Fixed Pricing:** Offer immigration services at a fixed price, with different packages available based on the type of immigration service required.

Example Offering: A law firm might offer a "Visa Application Package" that includes all necessary legal assistance for obtaining a specific type of visa (e.g., H-1B, L-1, or F-1). This package could be offered at a flat fee, with additional services available for more complex immigration cases, such as family-based immigration or deportation defense.

These examples illustrate how various legal tasks can be effectively productized, offering clients standardized, efficient, and predictable services while allowing law firms to scale their operations and enhance profitability. By identifying the legal tasks most suited for productization and developing clear, consistent processes for delivering these services, law firms can create a more client-centered and competitive practice.

In the next sections, we will explore the practical steps for building and pricing productized legal services, as well as strategies for marketing and selling these offerings to clients.

Pricing Strategies

Pricing is a critical component of productizing legal services. The right pricing model not only ensures profitability for the law firm but also aligns with client expectations, offering transparency and predictability. Different pricing models can be applied depending on the nature of the service, the client base, and the firm's strategic goals. This section explores various pricing strategies for productized legal services, including subscription-based pricing, tiered pricing, and flat fees.

Subscription-Based Pricing

Subscription-based pricing involves clients paying a recurring fee—typically monthly, quarterly, or annually—in exchange for ongoing access to a suite of legal services. This model is particularly effective for services that clients need regularly or continuously, such as compliance monitoring, legal advice, or contract management.

Subscription Pricing Benefits:

- **Predictable Revenue:** Subscription pricing provides a steady and predictable revenue stream for the law firm, which can help with financial planning and cash flow management.
- **Client Loyalty:** The subscription model fosters long-term relationships with clients, as they are more likely to remain with the firm if they are continuously receiving value.
- **Scalability:** Firms can scale their subscription offerings to accommodate a growing client base without a corresponding increase in costs, especially if many services are automated.

Implementation Ideas:

- **Basic Legal Services Package:** A law firm might offer a basic subscription package that includes access to routine legal services, such as contract review, basic legal advice, and compliance updates. Clients could pay a flat monthly fee for this package, with the option to add on more specialized services as needed.
- **Premium Subscription Tiers:** Create multiple subscription tiers, each offering different levels of service. For example, a higher-tier subscription might include more comprehensive services like quarterly compliance audits, priority access to legal counsel, or unlimited document drafting. Clients can choose the tier that best fits their needs and budget.

Example Offering: A law firm specializing in employment law could offer an "HR Legal Support Subscription" where businesses pay a monthly fee for ongoing support. This could include services like updating employee handbooks, conducting compliance checks, and providing on-demand legal advice for HR-related issues.

Tiered Pricing

Tiered pricing involves offering different levels of service at different price points. Each tier provides a set of features or services that increase in scope and complexity with each higher level. This model allows clients to choose the level of service that best fits their needs and budget, making it a flexible option for both the firm and the client.

Tiered Pricing Benefits:

- **Customization and Flexibility:** Tiered pricing allows clients to select a package that closely matches their specific needs, making legal services more accessible and tailored.
- **Upsell Opportunities:** The tiered structure creates opportunities to upsell clients to higher service levels as their needs evolve, increasing the firm's revenue potential.
- **Market Segmentation:** This model helps law firms effectively segment their market, offering premium services to high-value clients while still providing basic services to those with smaller budgets.

Implementation Ideas:

- **Basic, Standard, and Premium Tiers:** Offer three pricing tiers—Basic, Standard, and Premium—each with a different set of services. For example, in a contract drafting service, the Basic tier might include standard template-based contracts, the Standard tier might offer customized contracts with some legal advice, and the Premium tier could include fully bespoke contracts with extensive legal consultation.
- **Add-On Services:** Allow clients to add specific services to their chosen tier for an additional fee. This flexibility ensures that clients can get exactly what they need without paying for unnecessary extras.

Example Offering: A corporate law firm could offer tiered pricing for its business formation services:

- *Basic Tier:* Formation of a single-member LLC with standard documents.
- *Standard Tier:* Formation of a corporation with customized articles of incorporation and bylaws.
- *Premium Tier:* Formation of a complex entity with multiple shareholders, including shareholder

agreements, regulatory compliance checks, and ongoing legal support for the first year.

Flat Fees

Flat-fee pricing involves charging a single, fixed price for a specific legal service. This model is straightforward and easy for clients to understand, as they know exactly what they will pay upfront. Flat fees are particularly suitable for well-defined legal tasks that can be standardized and delivered efficiently.

Flat Fee Benefits:

- **Transparency and Predictability:** Clients appreciate the certainty that comes with flat fees, as they don't have to worry about unexpected charges or escalating costs.
- **Efficiency Incentives**: Flat-fee pricing encourages law firms to work efficiently, as the fee is fixed regardless of the time spent on the task.
- **Simplified Billing:** Flat fees simplify the billing process, reducing the administrative burden on the firm and making it easier for clients to approve and pay invoices.

Implementation Ideas:

- **Service Packages:** Create flat-fee service packages for specific legal tasks, such as drafting a will, registering a trademark, or conducting a compliance audit. Each package should clearly outline what is included in the service and what the client can expect to receive.
- **Project-Based Pricing:** For more complex legal matters, consider offering flat fees for discrete phases of the project. For example, in a litigation matter, the firm could charge a flat fee for each stage—initial consultation, discovery, pre-trial motions, and so on—providing clients with clear pricing at each step.

Example Offering: An estate planning law firm could offer a "Simple Will Package" for a flat fee, which includes a consultation, the drafting of a simple will, and the execution of the document. Clients know the cost upfront and can proceed with confidence that there will be no hidden fees.

Value-Based Pricing

Value-based pricing sets the price of legal services based on the value delivered to the client rather than the time spent or the cost of delivering the service. This model is particularly effective when the legal service has a significant impact on the client's business or personal life, such as securing a major contract, winning a lawsuit, or obtaining a patent.

Value Pricing Benefits:

- **Alignment with Client Interests: Value**-based pricing aligns the lawyer's incentives with the client's goals, as both parties are focused on achieving a successful outcome.
- **Potential for Higher Revenue:** When the value of the service to the client is high, value-based pricing allows the law firm to capture a greater share of that value, potentially leading to higher fees than time-based billing.
- **Enhanced Client Relationships:** Clients appreciate the focus on results rather than time, which can lead to stronger, more trusting relationships.

Implementation Ideas:

- **Outcome-Based Pricing:** Set prices based on the anticipated value of the outcome to the client. For example, if a law firm is helping a startup secure venture capital funding, the fee could be based on the amount of funding secured, reflecting the value of the service to the client's business.
- **Risk Sharing:** Consider structuring value-based fees to include a performance component, where the firm's compensation increases if specific goals or outcomes are achieved. This approach aligns the firm's incentives with the client's success and can build stronger partnerships.

Example Offering: A patent law firm could offer value-based pricing for securing a patent, where the fee is tied to the potential commercial value of the patent. For a high-value invention, the firm could charge a higher fee based on the expected market impact and revenue potential of the patented product.

Hybrid Pricing Models

Hybrid pricing models combine elements of different pricing strategies to create a more flexible and customized approach to legal services. For example, a firm might use a combination of flat fees for certain tasks, subscription-based pricing for ongoing services, and value-based pricing for high-impact outcomes. This approach allows the firm to tailor its pricing to the specific needs of the client and the nature of the legal work.

Benefits of Hybrid Models:

- **Flexibility:** Hybrid models offer the flexibility to adapt pricing to the specific circumstances of each client and project, providing a more personalized service.
- **Client-Centric Approach:** By combining different pricing strategies, firms can better meet the diverse needs and preferences of their clients, enhancing client satisfaction.
- **Balanced Revenue Streams:** Hybrid models allow firms to balance predictable revenue from subscriptions or flat fees with the potential for higher earnings from value-based services.

Implementation Ideas:

- **Case-by-Case Pricing:** Develop a pricing strategy that is tailored to each client's needs, combining different pricing elements as appropriate. For example, a firm might offer a flat fee for initial consultation and document preparation, followed by value-based pricing for litigation outcomes.
- **Client Choice:** Offer clients a choice of pricing models, allowing them to select the option that best fits their budget and preferences. For instance, clients could choose between a flat fee for a one-time service or a subscription for ongoing support.

Example Offering: A corporate law firm could offer a hybrid pricing model for mergers and acquisitions, where the initial due diligence is billed at a flat fee, ongoing legal support is provided through a subscription, and the final closing of the deal is priced based on the value of the transaction.

Selecting the right pricing strategy is crucial for the successful productization of legal services. Whether using subscription-based pricing, tiered pricing, flat fees, value-based pricing, or a hybrid approach, law firms can tailor their pricing to meet the needs of their clients while ensuring profitability and sustainability. By offering transparent, predictable, and client-focused pricing, law firms can differentiate themselves in a competitive market and build stronger, long-term relationships with their clients.

Communicating Value to Clients

Effectively communicating the value of productized legal services is essential for gaining client buy-in and establishing long-term relationships. Clients need to understand not only what they are paying for but also why the service is valuable to them. This involves clearly articulating the benefits of productized services, such as transparency, predictability, and efficiency. By focusing on these key elements, law firms can differentiate their offerings in a competitive market and build trust with their clients.

Emphasizing Transparency

Transparency is a critical component of productized legal services. Clients want to know exactly what they are getting for their money, and they appreciate clarity around pricing, deliverables, and timelines. By emphasizing transparency, law firms can reduce the uncertainty that often accompanies traditional legal services and create a more client-friendly experience.

Strategies for Emphasizing Transparency:

- **Detailed Service Descriptions:** Provide clear, detailed descriptions of what each productized service includes. Break down the specific tasks, deliverables, and timelines so that clients have a complete understanding of what to expect. For example, if you are offering a flat-fee contract drafting service, outline the number of drafts included, the revision process, and the estimated time for completion.
- **Upfront Pricing Information:** Clearly communicate pricing upfront, including any potential additional costs or optional services. Use simple, straightforward language to explain the pricing structure, whether it's a flat fee, subscription, or tiered model. Ensure that clients understand exactly what they will be billed for and when.

- **Open Communication Channels:** Establish open lines of communication where clients can ask questions and receive prompt, transparent answers. This might include dedicated client portals, regular check-ins, or easy access to legal professionals who can clarify any concerns about the service.

Example Approach: A law firm offering a "Business Formation Package" could provide a detailed brochure or online landing page that outlines every step of the service, from initial consultation to final filing. The brochure would include a clear, fixed price, along with an FAQ section that addresses common client questions about timelines, additional services, and potential costs.

Highlighting Predictability

One of the most significant advantages of productized services is predictability—clients know exactly what they are getting, when they will get it, and how much it will cost. This predictability is a strong selling point, especially in a legal market where clients often feel anxious about unexpected costs and delays.

Strategies for Highlighting Predictability:

- **Clear Timelines and Milestones**: Provide clients with clear timelines and milestones for each service. Let them know when they can expect to receive drafts, reports, or updates, and stick to these deadlines as closely as possible. This not only reassures clients but also demonstrates your firm's commitment to reliability and efficiency.
- **Consistent Service Delivery:** Ensure that the quality and scope of the service are consistent across all clients and cases. Standardized processes and templates can help maintain this consistency, reinforcing the idea that clients can rely on your firm to deliver exactly what was promised.
- **Case Studies and Testimonials:** Use case studies and testimonials to show how your productized services have provided predictable, positive outcomes for other clients. Highlight examples where clients experienced smooth, hassle-free service delivery with no surprises in costs or timelines.

Example Approach: A law firm that offers a "Compliance Audit Package" could create a timeline infographic that visually maps out the audit process, from initial review to final report. The timeline would include specific dates for key milestones, such as document submission deadlines, interim updates, and the final delivery of the audit report. This visual tool can be shared with clients during the onboarding process to set clear expectations.

Demonstrating Cost-Effectiveness

Productized services often provide cost savings to clients by streamlining processes, reducing manual labor, and leveraging technology. It's important to communicate these cost savings effectively, showing clients that they are getting excellent value for their investment.

Strategies for Demonstrating Cost-Effectiveness:

- **Comparison with Traditional Billing:** Compare the cost of the productized service with the traditional billable hour model to show how much clients can save. For example, highlight how a flat-fee service for contract drafting might cost significantly less than billing by the hour for the same work.
- **Value for Money:** Emphasize the value that clients receive for the fixed price, including the quality of the service, the expertise of the legal team, and the convenience of a streamlined process. Show how the productized service provides comprehensive coverage for a predictable price, eliminating the risk of cost overruns.
- **Bundled Services:** Offer bundled services that combine multiple tasks at a discounted rate, providing clients with additional value. For example, a "Start-Up Legal Bundle" could include business formation, trademark registration, and employment contract drafting at a lower price than purchasing each service individually.

Example Approach: A law firm offering flat-fee estate planning services might create a cost comparison chart that shows the typical billable hours for drafting a will under the traditional model versus the flat fee for their "Estate Planning Essentials Package." The chart would highlight potential savings, making it clear that the client is receiving high-quality legal services at a competitive, predictable price.

Communicating the Benefits of Efficiency

Efficiency is a key selling point of productized legal services. By standardizing processes and using technology to automate routine tasks, law firms can deliver services more quickly and accurately. Communicating the benefits of this efficiency helps clients appreciate the convenience and speed of productized services.

Strategies for Communicating Efficiency:

- **Faster Turnaround Times:** Promote the faster turnaround times that result from standardized and automated processes. Clients often appreciate knowing that their legal matters will be handled promptly, without unnecessary delays.
- **Reduced Risk of Errors:** Highlight how automation and standardized templates reduce the risk of errors in legal documents and processes. Explain how your firm's approach ensures consistency and accuracy, providing clients with peace of mind.
- **Focus on High-Value Work:** Explain how productized services allow your firm to focus on high-value legal work, rather than getting bogged down in routine tasks. By automating repetitive processes, your legal team can dedicate more time to strategy, negotiation, and other critical aspects of the client's case.

Example Approach: A law firm that offers automated document review services might emphasize the speed and accuracy of their AI-powered tools in marketing materials. They could use metrics, such as "99% reduction in document review time" or "elimination of manual errors," to show how their service outperforms traditional methods, providing clients with faster and more reliable outcomes.

Leveraging Technology and Innovation

Clients are increasingly aware of the role that technology plays in improving legal services. By leveraging technology, law firms can offer innovative solutions that enhance the client experience, such as automated document generation, online client portals, and AI-driven legal research. Communicating these technological advantages helps position your firm as a forward-thinking, modern provider of legal services.

Strategies for Leveraging Technology and Innovation:

- **Highlight Technological Tools:** Clearly explain the technological tools and platforms your firm uses to deliver

productized services. Clients may not be familiar with the specifics, so it's important to translate the technical benefits into tangible advantages, such as faster service delivery, better communication, and enhanced security.
- **Showcase Innovation**: Position your firm as a leader in legal innovation by showcasing how you use cutting-edge technology to improve service delivery. This could include demonstrations of your online client portal, automated legal research tools, or AI-driven contract analysis software.
- **Client Education:** Educate clients about how technology benefits them directly, such as through webinars, blog posts, or informational brochures. Provide examples of how these innovations have improved outcomes for other clients, helping to build trust and confidence in your firm's capabilities.

Example Approach: A law firm that uses an online client portal to manage communications and document sharing could create a video walkthrough of the portal's features, showing clients how easy it is to access their case files, track progress, and communicate with their legal team. This video could be featured on the firm's website and shared with prospective clients as part of the onboarding process.

Using Testimonials and Case Studies

Testimonials and case studies are powerful tools for communicating the value of productized services. They provide social proof and real-world examples of how your services have benefited other clients, making it easier for potential clients to see the value in your offerings.

Strategies for Using Testimonials and Case Studies:

- **Client Testimonials:** Collect and feature testimonials from satisfied clients who have benefited from your productized services. Highlight specific outcomes, such as cost savings, faster service delivery, or successful case resolutions.
- **Case Studies:** Develop detailed case studies that showcase how your productized services have helped clients achieve their legal goals. Include metrics, such as time saved, costs reduced, or successful outcomes, to provide concrete evidence of the service's value.
- **Visual Storytelling:** Use visual elements, such as infographics, charts, and videos, to tell the story of how your services have positively impacted clients. Visual storytelling

can make complex information more accessible and engaging for potential clients.

Example Approach: A law firm that offers a productized "Trademark Protection Package" could create a case study highlighting how a client successfully registered multiple trademarks across different jurisdictions within a short timeframe, thanks to the firm's streamlined and automated process. The case study would include a testimonial from the client, emphasizing the ease and efficiency of the service.

Offering Demonstrations and Free Trials

Offering demonstrations or free trials of your productized services allows potential clients to experience the value firsthand before making a commitment. This approach can be particularly effective for services that leverage technology or are offered as part of a subscription model.

Strategies for Offering Demonstrations and Free Trials:

- **Service Demos:** Provide live or recorded demonstrations of your productized services, showing how they work and the benefits they offer. Demos can be presented in webinars, one-on-one client meetings, or on your website.
- **Free Trials:** Offer a limited-time free trial of certain services, such as access to an automated document generation tool or an online legal advice platform. This allows clients to test the service and see the value for themselves before committing to a purchase.
- **Introductory Offers:** Consider offering introductory discounts or promotions for new clients who sign up for a subscription service or purchase a bundled package. This can reduce the perceived risk for clients and encourage them to try your services.

Example Approach: A law firm offering a subscription-based "HR Legal Support" service could provide a 30-day free trial, during which clients can access the service's features, such as compliance updates, contract templates, and on-demand legal advice. The firm could follow up with the client at the end of the trial period to discuss their experience and encourage them to subscribe.

Communicating the value of productized legal services effectively is essential for building client trust, differentiating your offerings, and driving business growth. By focusing on transparency, predictability, cost-effectiveness, efficiency, and the benefits of technology, law firms can clearly articulate the advantages of their services to clients. Additionally, leveraging testimonials, case studies, demonstrations, and free trials can help clients see the value for themselves, making them more likely to engage with your firm.

Chapter 7: Automation Tech Stack

Software Platforms

Software platforms form the foundation of workflow automation in legal practices. These platforms enable law firms to automate routine tasks, manage cases efficiently, and maintain comprehensive records of client interactions and legal documents. Selecting the right software is critical to ensuring that automation efforts align with the firm's goals and enhance overall productivity. Below are some of the primary categories of software platforms that support legal workflow automation:

Practice Management Software

Practice management software is a comprehensive solution that integrates various aspects of law firm operations into a single platform. These platforms typically include features for case management, time tracking, billing, document management, and client communication. By centralizing these functions, practice management software facilitates the automation of many routine administrative tasks, allowing legal professionals to focus on higher-value work.

Key Features:

- **Case Management:** Automatically organize and track cases, including key dates, tasks, and deadlines. This feature ensures that nothing falls through the cracks and that cases progress smoothly.
- **Time and Billing Automation:** Streamline time tracking and billing processes by automatically generating invoices based on logged hours and predetermined billing rates. Some platforms also allow for the automation of payment reminders and tracking of outstanding balances.

- **Document Management:** Centralize the storage and retrieval of legal documents, with features for document version control, secure sharing, and automated organization based on case or client.
- **Task Automation:** Automate repetitive tasks, such as scheduling meetings, sending reminders, or generating standardized documents, based on predefined workflows.
- **Client Portal:** Provide clients with secure access to their case information, documents, and billing through an online portal, enhancing transparency and communication.

Popular Platforms:

Clio: A cloud-based practice management software that offers a wide range of features for managing cases, billing, and client communication. Clio's extensive automation capabilities make it a popular choice for law firms of all sizes.

PracticePanther: Another cloud-based platform known for its intuitive interface and robust automation features. PracticePanther excels in automating time tracking, billing, and document management.

MyCase: MyCase provides a comprehensive practice management solution with strong document management and client communication features, along with built-in billing automation.

Document Automation Tools

Document automation tools are designed to streamline the creation and management of legal documents. These tools allow law firms to generate documents quickly and consistently by populating standardized templates with client-specific data. This automation reduces the time spent on drafting and ensures that all documents adhere to the firm's standards and legal requirements.

Key Features:

- **Template Creation:** Develop and store templates for common legal documents, such as contracts, wills, or court filings. Templates can be customized with specific client or case information.
- **Data Integration:** Automatically populate templates with data from the firm's practice management system or client databases, reducing the need for manual data entry.

- **Document Assembly:** Combine multiple templates or clauses into a single document, automatically adjusting formatting and numbering to create a polished final product.
- **Workflow Integration:** Integrate document automation with other workflows, such as document review or approval processes, ensuring that documents are generated, reviewed, and finalized efficiently.

Popular Platforms:

Lawyaw: A document automation platform specifically designed for law firms. Lawyaw allows firms to create custom templates and automate the generation of various legal documents, integrating seamlessly with existing practice management systems.

HotDocs: A powerful document automation tool that supports complex document assembly and integration with other legal software. HotDocs is widely used for creating standardized legal forms and contracts.

Documate: A no-code document automation platform that enables lawyers to build custom document generation workflows without the need for programming knowledge. Documate is ideal for firms looking to automate highly specific or complex documents.

E-Discovery and Litigation Support Software

E-discovery and litigation support software is essential for managing large volumes of documents and data in litigation. These platforms automate the process of collecting, processing, reviewing, and analyzing electronic data, helping law firms to efficiently manage discovery in complex cases.

Key Features:

- **Data Collection and Processing:** Automate the collection of electronic data from various sources, including emails, databases, and cloud storage, while ensuring data integrity and compliance with legal standards.
- **Document Review:** Use advanced search and filtering tools, as well as AI-driven document review capabilities, to quickly identify relevant documents and flag potentially privileged or sensitive information.

- Analytics and Reporting: Provide detailed reports and visualizations that help legal teams analyze data trends, identify key issues, and prepare for trial.
- **Collaboration Tools:** Enable secure collaboration among legal teams, clients, and external experts, with features for sharing documents, tracking changes, and managing review workflows.

Popular Platforms:

Relativity: A leading e-discovery platform that offers comprehensive tools for data collection, processing, review, and analysis. Relativity is known for its scalability and robust analytics capabilities.

Everlaw: A cloud-based e-discovery platform that combines powerful search and review tools with intuitive collaboration features, making it a popular choice for litigation teams.

ZyLAB ONE: An AI-driven e-discovery platform that automates much of the document review process, using machine learning to categorize documents and identify key information efficiently.

Client Relationship Management (CRM) Software

Client Relationship Management (CRM) software helps law firms manage interactions with current and potential clients. By automating client communication and tracking, CRM platforms enhance client engagement and support business development efforts.

Key Features:

- **Contact Management:** Maintain a centralized database of client contacts, including communication history, case details, and preferences.
- **Automated Communication:** Schedule and automate follow-up emails, appointment reminders, and newsletters, ensuring consistent communication with clients and prospects.
- **Lead Tracking:** Track and manage leads from initial contact through to client conversion, with tools for automating follow-up and managing sales pipelines.
- **Reporting and Analytics**: Generate reports on client interactions, conversion rates, and other key metrics to inform business development strategies.

Popular Platforms:

Lexicata: A CRM specifically designed for law firms, offering features for client intake, lead tracking, and automated follow-ups. Lexicata integrates with Clio, making it a seamless addition to a law firm's technology stack.

Law Ruler: Another CRM tailored for legal practices, Law Ruler includes features for client intake, marketing automation, and detailed reporting on client interactions.

HubSpot CRM: While not exclusively for law firms, HubSpot CRM is a versatile, user-friendly platform that offers robust tools for managing client relationships and automating communication.

Selecting the right software platforms is critical to building a successful technology stack for legal workflow automation. Practice management software, document automation tools, e-discovery platforms, and CRM systems each play a vital role in streamlining operations, improving efficiency, and enhancing client service. By carefully choosing and integrating these platforms, law firms can lay a strong foundation for effective workflow automation, positioning themselves to meet the demands of a rapidly evolving legal market.

In the next sections, we will explore AI tools and capabilities that can further enhance legal automation, the importance of cybersecurity and data protection, and strategies for integrating new technologies with existing systems. These topics will help law firms build a comprehensive and secure technology stack that supports their automation goals and protects client data.

AI Tools and Capabilities

Artificial intelligence (AI) is rapidly transforming the legal industry by enhancing automation and enabling more sophisticated analysis of legal data. AI tools can significantly improve the efficiency and accuracy of legal workflows, offering capabilities that go beyond simple automation to provide deeper insights and more effective decision-making. This section explores key AI tools and capabilities that can be integrated into legal practice, focusing on technologies such as natural language processing (NLP) for document review, predictive analytics for case outcomes, and more.

Natural Language Processing (NLP) for Document Review

Natural language processing (NLP) is a subset of AI that enables machines to understand, interpret, and generate human language. In the legal field, NLP is particularly valuable for automating and enhancing document review processes. This technology can analyze vast amounts of text data quickly and accurately, identifying relevant information, categorizing documents, and even flagging potential issues.

Applications in Legal Practice:

- **Contract Analysis:** NLP tools can automatically analyze contracts, identifying key clauses, obligations, and risks. These tools can flag unusual or non-standard language, suggest revisions, and even compare contract terms against a database of similar agreements to ensure consistency.
- **E-Discovery:** During the discovery phase of litigation, NLP tools can sift through large volumes of electronic documents to identify relevant information. By recognizing patterns in the text, these tools can categorize documents, flag privileged information, and prioritize documents for human review.
- **Legal Research:** NLP-powered search engines can improve legal research by understanding the context and intent behind search queries. These tools can deliver more relevant case law, statutes, and legal opinions, saving time and improving the quality of legal research.

Popular NLP Tools:

Kira Systems: Kira uses NLP to automatically extract and analyze key provisions in contracts. It is widely used by law firms and corporate legal departments for due diligence, contract management, and regulatory compliance.

Lex Machina: Part of LexisNexis, Lex Machina uses NLP to analyze litigation data, helping legal professionals predict outcomes, understand opposing parties' strategies, and develop case strategies.

Predictive Analytics for Case Outcomes

Predictive analytics involves using AI and machine learning algorithms to analyze historical data and predict future outcomes. In the legal field, predictive analytics can be used to forecast case outcomes, assess litigation risks, and inform strategic decisions. By analyzing past cases, court rulings, and other relevant data, these tools provide lawyers with valuable insights into the likely direction of a case.

Applications in Legal Practice:

- **Case Outcome Prediction:** Predictive analytics tools can analyze historical case data to forecast the likely outcome of a current case. This can help lawyers assess the strengths and weaknesses of their case, advise clients on the likelihood of success, and develop more informed strategies.
- **Settlement Analysis:** AI can predict the likely settlement amounts based on data from similar cases, helping lawyers and their clients make informed decisions about whether to settle or proceed to trial. This can be particularly useful in personal injury, employment, or commercial litigation.
- **Jury Selection:** Some predictive analytics tools are designed to assist in jury selection by analyzing data on potential jurors, including their backgrounds, past verdicts, and social media activity. These tools help lawyers identify biases and select jurors who are more likely to be sympathetic to their case.

Popular Predictive Analytics Tools:

Premonition: Premonition is an AI platform that analyzes court data to predict the outcomes of cases, providing insights into judge and attorney performance. It helps law firms make data-driven decisions about case strategy and litigation risks.

Blue J Legal: Blue J Legal offers predictive analytics tools that use AI to forecast legal outcomes in areas like tax law, employment law, and commercial law. By analyzing case law and regulatory decisions, Blue J Legal helps lawyers and businesses assess their legal positions more accurately.

Lex Machina: In addition to its NLP capabilities, Lex Machina also provides predictive analytics for intellectual property litigation, helping lawyers predict case outcomes and develop winning strategies based on past rulings and trends.

Automated Legal Research and Insights

AI-driven legal research tools go beyond traditional keyword-based search engines by using advanced algorithms to understand the context of legal queries and deliver more relevant results. These tools can analyze large volumes of legal texts, including case law, statutes, and regulations, to provide insights that are both comprehensive and precise.

Applications in Legal Practice:

- **Contextual Search:** AI-powered legal research tools can understand the context and nuances of legal queries, providing more accurate and relevant search results than traditional methods. This reduces the time spent sifting through irrelevant information and improves the quality of research.
- **Brief Analysis:** Some AI tools can analyze legal briefs, automatically identifying relevant case law, statutes, and other supporting materials. These tools can suggest additional sources or highlight potential weaknesses in the argument.
- **Continuous Learning:** AI-driven research tools learn from user interactions, continually improving their accuracy and relevance over time. This ensures that the tool adapts to the specific needs and preferences of the lawyer, providing increasingly valuable insights.

Popular AI Legal Research Tools:

Casetext's CARA A.I.: CARA A.I. is an AI-driven legal research tool that analyzes briefs and legal documents to identify relevant case law. It can suggest cases that are on point but might have been overlooked, making it a valuable tool for strengthening legal arguments.

Westlaw Edge: Westlaw Edge, from Thomson Reuters, integrates AI into its legal research platform to provide advanced search capabilities, predictive analytics, and litigation insights. It offers a comprehensive suite of tools for legal research, case strategy, and litigation support.

Contract Review and Due Diligence

AI-powered contract review tools automate the process of analyzing and reviewing legal contracts. These tools can quickly identify key clauses, flag risks, and ensure compliance with relevant laws and regulations. AI is particularly valuable in due diligence processes, where large volumes of contracts need to be reviewed accurately and efficiently.

Applications in Legal Practice:

- **Automated Risk Assessment:** AI tools can analyze contracts to identify potential risks, such as unfavorable terms or non-compliance with legal standards. These tools provide a detailed risk assessment, allowing lawyers to address issues proactively.
- **Clause Extraction and Comparison:** AI can automatically extract key clauses from contracts and compare them to standard or preferred language. This ensures that contracts are consistent with the firm's guidelines and highlights any deviations that need attention.
- **Bulk Contract Review:** In due diligence processes, AI tools can review large volumes of contracts in a fraction of the time it would take a human team. This speeds up the due diligence process and ensures that no critical details are overlooked.

Popular AI Contract Review Tools:

Kira Systems: As previously mentioned, Kira Systems uses AI to automate the extraction and analysis of key contract clauses. It is widely used for due diligence, contract management, and regulatory compliance.

Luminance: Luminance is an AI-powered contract review tool that uses machine learning to analyze contracts, identify risks, and ensure compliance. It is designed to assist with due diligence, contract negotiation, and ongoing contract management.

eBrevia: eBrevia uses AI to analyze contracts and extract key data points, such as obligations, deadlines, and renewal terms. It is commonly used in contract review, due diligence, and compliance monitoring.

AI-Driven Client Insights and Communication

AI tools can also enhance client communication and relationship management by providing insights into client behavior, preferences, and needs. These tools can analyze client interactions, predict future needs, and automate personalized communication, improving client satisfaction and retention.

Applications in Legal Practice:

- **Client Interaction Analysis:** AI tools can analyze client communication patterns, identifying trends and potential issues. This helps law firms understand client needs better and tailor their services accordingly.
- **Automated Client Communication:** AI-driven chatbots and virtual assistants can handle routine client inquiries, provide updates on case status, and schedule appointments, freeing up time for legal professionals to focus on more complex tasks.
- **Predictive Client Needs**: By analyzing past interactions and case data, AI tools can predict when a client might need additional services, such as contract renewals, compliance updates, or legal audits. This allows firms to proactively offer services, enhancing client relationships and generating additional revenue.

Popular AI Tools for Client Insights:

Client Sense: Client Sense is an AI-driven platform that analyzes communication data to provide insights into client relationships, helping firms identify at-risk clients, cross-selling opportunities, and potential conflicts of interest.

LitiGate: LitiGate uses AI to analyze litigation data, providing insights into case strategy, potential outcomes, and client communication. It helps lawyers make data-driven decisions that improve case management and client satisfaction.

Conversica: Conversica is an AI-powered virtual assistant that automates client communication, handling tasks such as lead follow-up, appointment scheduling, and client inquiries. It is designed to enhance client engagement and improve operational efficiency.

AI tools and capabilities offer transformative potential for legal workflow automation, enabling law firms to enhance efficiency, accuracy, and decision-making across various aspects of their practice. From natural language processing for document review to predictive analytics for case outcomes, AI is reshaping the way legal professionals approach their work. By integrating these AI tools into their technology stack, law firms can stay ahead of the curve, delivering more effective and innovative services to their clients.

In the following sections, we will explore the importance of cybersecurity and data protection in legal automation, as well as strategies for integrating new technologies with existing systems. These topics are crucial for ensuring that the benefits of automation are realized without compromising the security and integrity of client data.

Cybersecurity and Data Protection

As legal practices increasingly adopt automation and digital technologies, the importance of cybersecurity and data protection cannot be overstated. The legal industry handles highly sensitive and confidential information, making it a prime target for cyberattacks. Ensuring that client data is protected and that the firm complies with relevant data protection regulations is critical to maintaining trust and safeguarding the firm's reputation. This section emphasizes the key considerations and strategies for cybersecurity in legal automation, including compliance with major data protection regulations such as the General Data Protection Regulation (GDPR) and the California Consumer Privacy Act (CCPA).

The Importance of Cybersecurity in Legal Automation

Cybersecurity involves protecting digital systems, networks, and data from unauthorized access, attacks, and damage. For law firms, robust cybersecurity measures are essential to protect client information, prevent data breaches, and comply with legal and ethical obligations. With the integration of automation and digital tools into legal workflows, firms must prioritize cybersecurity at every stage of their operations.

Major Law Firm Cyber Risks:

- **Data Breaches:** Law firms are attractive targets for cybercriminals due to the wealth of sensitive information they store, including personal data, financial records, and intellectual property. A data breach can lead to significant legal, financial, and reputational damage.
- **Ransomware Attacks:** Ransomware is a type of malware that encrypts a firm's data, rendering it inaccessible until a ransom is paid. Such attacks can cripple a law firm's operations, leading to downtime, lost revenue, and potential legal liabilities.

- **Phishing and Social Engineering:** Cybercriminals often use phishing emails or social engineering tactics to trick employees into revealing passwords or other sensitive information. These attacks can lead to unauthorized access to the firm's systems and data.

Strategies for Enhancing Cybersecurity:

- **Regular Security Audits:** Conduct regular cybersecurity audits to identify vulnerabilities in the firm's systems, software, and practices. Address any weaknesses promptly to minimize the risk of a breach.
- **Encryption:** Ensure that all sensitive data is encrypted, both at rest (stored data) and in transit (data being transmitted over the internet). Encryption protects data by making it unreadable to unauthorized users.
- **Access Controls:** Implement strict access controls to limit who can access sensitive information. Use role-based access control (RBAC) to ensure that employees only have access to the data and systems necessary for their job functions.
- **Multi-Factor Authentication (MFA):** Require multi-factor authentication for accessing the firm's systems, particularly for remote access. MFA adds an extra layer of security by requiring users to provide two or more verification factors, such as a password and a temporary code sent to their mobile device.
- **Employee Training:** Regularly train employees on cybersecurity best practices, including how to recognize phishing attempts, the importance of strong passwords, and how to handle sensitive data securely. Human error is often the weakest link in cybersecurity, so ongoing education is crucial.

Compliance with Data Protection Regulations

Data protection regulations are designed to safeguard individuals' personal information and ensure that organizations handle data responsibly. Law firms must comply with these regulations to avoid legal penalties, protect client data, and maintain trust. Key regulations include the General Data Protection Regulation (GDPR) in the European Union and the California Consumer Privacy Act (CCPA) in the United States.

General Data Protection Regulation (GDPR):

GDPR applies to any organization that processes the personal data of individuals in the European Union (EU), regardless of where the organization is based.[42] This regulation has broad implications for law firms that handle the personal data of EU clients.

Key GDPR Requirements:

- **Data Minimization:** Law firms must only collect and process data that is necessary for the specific purpose for which it was collected.
- **Consent:** Clients must give clear, informed consent for their data to be processed. Law firms must be transparent about how data will be used and allow clients to withdraw consent at any time.
- **Right to Access and Erasure:** Clients have the right to access their personal data held by the firm and request its deletion. Law firms must have processes in place to comply with such requests.
- **Data Protection Impact Assessments (DPIAs):** For high-risk data processing activities, firms must conduct DPIAs to assess and mitigate potential risks to data subjects.
- **Breach Notification:** In the event of a data breach, law firms must notify the relevant supervisory authority within 72 hours and inform affected individuals without undue delay if the breach poses a high risk to their rights and freedoms.

California Consumer Privacy Act (CCPA):

CCPA applies to businesses that collect personal information from California residents and meet certain thresholds, such as generating annual gross revenues over $25 million or processing data of more than 50,000 California residents annually.[43]

---

[42] Regulation (EU) 2016/679 of the European Parliament and of the Council of 27 April 2016 on the Protection of Natural Persons with Regard to the Processing of Personal Data and on the Free Movement of Such Data (General Data Protection Regulation). Official Journal of the European Union, L 119, 4 May 2016

[43] California Consumer Privacy Act of 2018 (CCPA), Civil Code §§ 1798.100 - 1798.199.100

Key CCPA Requirements:

- **Right to Know:** California residents have the right to know what personal information is being collected about them, how it is used, and with whom it is shared.
- **Right to Delete:** Clients can request the deletion of their personal information, and law firms must comply with such requests unless an exemption applies (e.g., data needed to complete a legal transaction).
- **Right to Opt-Out:** Clients can opt-out of the sale of their personal information. While law firms typically do not sell data, they must still provide this option if applicable.
- **Non-Discrimination:** Law firms cannot discriminate against clients who exercise their rights under CCPA, such as by denying services or charging different prices.

CCPA Compliance Strategies:

- **Data Inventory and Mapping**: Conduct a thorough data inventory to understand what personal information the firm collects, where it is stored, and how it is processed. Mapping data flows helps identify potential compliance risks and areas for improvement.
- **Privacy Policies:** Ensure that the firm's privacy policies are up to date and compliant with relevant regulations. Privacy policies should clearly explain how the firm collects, uses, and protects client data.
- **Client Consent:** Implement processes for obtaining and documenting client consent for data processing. This includes ensuring that consent requests are clear and specific, and providing clients with easy ways to withdraw consent.
- **Data Subject Rights:** Establish procedures for responding to client requests under GDPR and CCPA, such as requests for data access, deletion, or correction. Ensure that these procedures are efficient and comply with regulatory timelines.
- **Third-Party Risk Management:** If the firm shares data with third-party vendors, ensure that these vendors are also compliant with data protection regulations. Use data processing agreements to outline the responsibilities of each party and protect client data.

Data Protection Measures in Automated Legal Processes

Automation in legal workflows introduces additional data protection challenges, particularly when handling large volumes of personal and sensitive information. Law firms must ensure that automated processes are secure, compliant, and capable of protecting client data at every stage.

Key Data Protection Measures:

- **Secure Data Storage:** Use secure, encrypted storage solutions for all client data, especially when using cloud-based platforms. Ensure that data is stored in compliance with relevant regulations and that it can be easily retrieved, modified, or deleted as needed.
- **Automated Data Anonymization:** In some cases, it may be necessary to anonymize personal data to protect client privacy, particularly in large-scale data analysis or document review processes. Automated tools can help anonymize data by removing or obscuring identifying information before it is processed.
- **Regular Updates and Patching:** Ensure that all software used in automated legal processes is regularly updated and patched to protect against known vulnerabilities. Unpatched software can be a significant security risk, potentially exposing the firm to cyberattacks.
- **Audit Trails and Monitoring**: Implement audit trails to track access to and changes in client data. Automated monitoring tools can detect unusual activity or potential breaches in real-time, allowing the firm to respond quickly to security incidents.
- **Data Retention Policies:** Establish clear data retention policies that comply with legal requirements and client agreements. Automated processes should be configured to retain data only for as long as necessary and to securely delete data when it is no longer needed.

Incident Response and Data Breach Management

Even with robust cybersecurity measures in place, data breaches can still occur. Law firms must be prepared with an incident response plan that outlines how to respond to a data breach, mitigate damage, and comply with regulatory requirements for breach notification.

Key Components of an Incident Response Plan:

- **Incident Identification and Reporting:** Establish clear procedures for identifying potential data breaches and reporting them internally. Ensure that employees know how to recognize signs of a breach and who to contact if they suspect one.
- **Containment and Mitigation**: Once a breach is identified, take immediate steps to contain the breach and mitigate its impact. This might include disconnecting affected systems, revoking access, and applying security patches.
- **Investigation and Documentation:** Conduct a thorough investigation to determine the cause of the breach, the extent of the damage, and the affected data. Document all findings and actions taken, as this information may be required for regulatory reporting.
- **Notification Requirements:** Comply with regulatory requirements for breach notification, including informing the relevant authorities and affected clients within the required timeframe. Provide clear and transparent communication to clients about the breach, its impact, and the steps the firm is taking to protect their data.
- **Post-Incident Review:** After the breach is contained, conduct a post-incident review to identify lessons learned and improve the firm's security measures. Update the incident response plan as needed to address any gaps or weaknesses.

Cybersecurity and data protection are critical components of legal automation, ensuring that client data is safeguarded against threats and that the firm complies with relevant regulations. By implementing robust security measures, maintaining compliance with data protection laws like GDPR and CCPA, and preparing for potential data breaches, law firms can protect their clients' sensitive information while reaping the benefits of automation.

In the next section, we will explore strategies for integrating new automation technologies with a firm's existing IT infrastructure. Effective integration is essential for maximizing the benefits of automation while minimizing disruptions to the firm's operations.

Integration with Existing Systems

Integrating new automation technologies with a law firm's existing IT infrastructure is a critical step in ensuring the successful adoption and utilization of these tools. Effective integration minimizes disruptions, enhances productivity, and allows the firm to fully leverage the benefits of automation. However, integration can also present challenges, particularly when dealing with legacy systems or ensuring compatibility across different platforms. This section provides guidance on best practices for integrating new automation technologies into a law firm's existing IT environment.

Assessing Current IT Infrastructure

Before introducing new automation technologies, it is essential to assess the firm's current IT infrastructure. This assessment helps identify potential compatibility issues, understand the capabilities of existing systems, and determine what upgrades or adjustments may be necessary to support the integration.

Key Steps in Assessing IT Infrastructure:

- **Inventory Existing Systems:** Create a detailed inventory of the firm's current software, hardware, and network infrastructure. Include information on the age, version, and compatibility of each system to identify any outdated or incompatible components that might hinder integration.
- **Evaluate System Capabilities:** Assess the capabilities of existing systems to determine whether they can support the new automation technologies. For example, does the firm's practice management software have the necessary APIs for integration? Is the current network infrastructure robust enough to handle increased data traffic from automated processes?
- **Identify Gaps and Needs:** Identify any gaps in the current IT infrastructure that may need to be addressed before integration. This might include upgrading hardware, updating software to the latest versions, or enhancing network security measures.
- **Consult Stakeholders:** Engage with key stakeholders, including IT staff, lawyers, and administrative personnel, to gather insights on current pain points and expectations for the new technology. Understanding the needs and concerns of those who will be using the new system is crucial for successful integration.

Example: A law firm planning to integrate AI-powered document review tools should first evaluate its existing document management system.

The firm would need to ensure that the system can support the integration, possibly requiring an upgrade or a switch to a cloud-based platform that is compatible with the AI tool.

Ensuring Compatibility and Interoperability

Compatibility and interoperability between new automation technologies and existing systems are vital for seamless integration. Ensuring that different platforms and tools can work together without conflicts or disruptions allows the firm to create a cohesive, efficient workflow.

Strategies for Ensuring Compatibility:

- **Use Open Standards and APIs:** Choose automation tools that support open standards and have robust APIs (Application Programming Interfaces). APIs allow different software platforms to communicate and share data, facilitating integration with existing systems like practice management software, document management systems, and billing platforms.
- **Test for Compatibility:** Conduct thorough testing of the new technology in a controlled environment before full deployment. Testing should include compatibility checks with existing systems, ensuring that data can be transferred smoothly and that automated processes function as expected.
- **Modular Integration:** Consider a modular approach to integration, where new technologies are integrated one module or feature at a time. This approach allows for easier troubleshooting and minimizes the risk of widespread disruption if an issue arises during integration.
- **Vendor Collaboration:** Work closely with technology vendors to ensure compatibility. Vendors often provide integration support, including documentation, training, and technical assistance, to help firms connect their products with existing systems.

Example: If a law firm is integrating a new CRM (Client Relationship Management) system with its existing practice management software, the firm should work with both vendors to ensure that the CRM's API can seamlessly exchange data with the practice management system, allowing for unified client records and automated workflows.

Data Migration and Integration

Data migration is a critical aspect of integrating new automation technologies. This process involves transferring data from existing systems to the new platform, ensuring that all relevant information is accessible and usable within the automated workflows.

Best Practices for Data Migration:

- **Data Mapping:** Start by mapping the data fields in the existing system to those in the new system. This ensures that all data is accurately transferred and that there is no loss of critical information during migration.
- **Data Cleansing:** Before migrating data, conduct a thorough data cleansing process to remove duplicates, correct errors, and update outdated information. Clean data is essential for the success of the new automated processes.
- **Incremental Migration:** Consider migrating data incrementally rather than all at once. This phased approach allows the firm to validate the accuracy of the data transfer at each stage, reducing the risk of errors and ensuring that the new system functions as intended.
- **Backup and Contingency Planning:** Always create a backup of all data before starting the migration process. In the event of a migration failure, the backup ensures that no data is lost, and the firm can revert to the previous system if necessary.

Example: A firm implementing a new document automation tool would need to migrate all relevant document templates, client records, and case files to the new system. This process would involve mapping existing data fields (e.g., client names, case numbers) to the corresponding fields in the new tool, cleansing the data to ensure accuracy, and then gradually migrating the data to the new platform while testing each step.

Training and Change Management

Successful integration of new automation technologies depends not only on technical factors but also on the firm's ability to manage change effectively. Providing comprehensive training and managing the transition for all users is crucial to ensuring that the new system is adopted and utilized to its full potential.

Training and Change Management Strategies:

- **Comprehensive Training Programs:** Develop and implement training programs tailored to the needs of different user groups within the firm. Training should cover both the technical aspects of the new technology and how it will be integrated into existing workflows.
- **Hands-On Training:** Offer hands-on training sessions where users can interact with the new system in a controlled environment. This practical experience helps users become comfortable with the new technology before it goes live.
- **Ongoing Support:** Provide ongoing support during and after the integration process, including access to help desks, user manuals, and online resources. Encourage users to ask questions and provide feedback, which can be used to refine the system and address any issues.
- **Change Champions:** Identify change champions within the firm—staff members who are enthusiastic about the new technology and can help promote its benefits to their colleagues. These champions can provide peer support and act as liaisons between the IT team and end users.
- **Communication and Transparency:** Communicate clearly and frequently about the integration process, including timelines, expectations, and any potential disruptions. Transparency helps manage expectations and reduces resistance to change.

Example: When a law firm introduces a new AI-driven legal research tool, it should provide extensive training to its attorneys on how to use the tool effectively. This training might include webinars, in-person workshops, and a dedicated support team to assist with any challenges during the initial adoption phase.

Continuous Monitoring and Optimization

Integration is not a one-time event but an ongoing process that requires continuous monitoring and optimization. After the initial integration, the firm should regularly assess the performance of the new technology, identify any issues, and make adjustments as needed to ensure that the system continues to meet the firm's needs.

Continuous Monitoring and Optimization Strategies:

- **Performance Metrics:** Establish key performance indicators (KPIs) to measure the success of the integration. These metrics might include user adoption rates, system uptime, process efficiency gains, and client satisfaction scores.
- **Regular Audits:** Conduct regular audits of the integrated systems to ensure they are functioning as expected. Audits should check for data integrity, system performance, and security compliance.
- **Feedback Loops:** Create feedback loops where users can report issues, suggest improvements, and share their experiences with the new system. Use this feedback to make continuous improvements and to address any emerging challenges.
- **Scalability Planning:** As the firm grows or as new automation technologies are introduced, ensure that the existing system can scale to accommodate increased demand. Plan for future integrations and upgrades to avoid disruptions as the firm's needs evolve.
- **Vendor Updates:** Stay informed about updates and new features from technology vendors. Regularly update the integrated systems to take advantage of new capabilities, improve security, and enhance performance.

Example: After integrating a new practice management system, a law firm might set up monthly review meetings to assess the system's performance against established KPIs. The firm could also create a feedback portal where attorneys and support staff can report any issues or suggest enhancements. Based on this feedback, the IT team can make ongoing adjustments to optimize the system.

Integrating new automation technologies with a law firm's existing IT infrastructure is a complex but essential process for maximizing the benefits of legal automation. By carefully assessing current systems, ensuring compatibility, managing data migration, providing comprehensive training, and continuously monitoring performance, law firms can achieve a seamless integration that enhances efficiency and supports the firm's long-term goals.

With the right strategies in place, firms can minimize disruptions, improve adoption rates, and fully leverage the capabilities of their new automation tools. As the legal industry continues to evolve, effective integration will remain a critical factor in maintaining a competitive edge and delivering high-quality legal services in an increasingly digital world.

Chapter 8: Implementing Workflow Automation in a Law Firm

Implementing workflow automation in a law firm is a transformative process that can significantly enhance efficiency, reduce costs, and improve client service. However, successful implementation requires careful planning, a clear understanding of the firm's needs, and a strategic approach to managing change. This step-by-step guide provides a detailed roadmap for law firms looking to introduce workflow automation, from initial planning to full deployment.

Step-by-Step Implementation Guide

Implementing workflow automation involves multiple stages, each critical to the success of the initiative. Below is a comprehensive guide to each phase, offering practical advice and actionable steps.

Initial Planning and Goal Setting

Define Objectives:

- **Identify Key Goals:** Begin by defining the objectives of the automation project. What specific outcomes does the firm hope to achieve? Common goals might include reducing time spent on repetitive tasks, improving accuracy in document processing, or enhancing client communication.
- **Align with Firm Strategy:** Ensure that these objectives align with the overall strategic goals of the firm. For example, if the firm is focused on scaling operations, automation should support this by enabling greater efficiency and consistency in service delivery.

Conduct a Needs Assessment:

- **Audit Current Workflows:** Conduct a thorough audit of existing workflows to identify processes that are time-consuming, error-prone, or ripe for automation. Look at tasks such as document generation, client intake, billing, and case management.
- **Identify Pain Points:** Engage with staff at all levels to identify pain points in current workflows. Where do delays, errors, or inefficiencies occur? This feedback will be crucial in determining which processes to automate first.

Establish a Budget and Timeline:

- **Budgeting:** Determine the budget for the automation project. Consider the costs of software, hardware, training, and potential downtime during implementation.
- **Timeline:** Develop a realistic timeline for each phase of the project. This should include time for planning, testing, deployment, and training. Factor in potential delays or obstacles that could impact the timeline.

Selecting the Right Technology

Evaluate Potential Solutions:

- **Research Options:** Investigate the available automation tools and platforms that could meet the firm's needs. Look for solutions that integrate well with the firm's existing systems and offer the functionality required to achieve the defined objectives.
- **Software Demonstrations:** Schedule demonstrations with vendors to see the software in action. Assess the user interface, ease of use, and the level of support offered by the vendor.

Pilot Testing:

- **Select a Pilot Process:** Choose a single workflow to pilot the automation. This should be a process that is important but not mission-critical, allowing the firm to test the new system without significant risk.
- **Run a Pilot Program:** Implement the selected automation tool on a small scale. Monitor its performance, gather feedback from users, and identify any issues that need to be addressed before a full rollout.

- **Evaluate Results:** After the pilot, evaluate the results. Did the tool improve efficiency? Were there any unforeseen challenges? Use this information to refine the implementation plan.

Final Selection and Procurement:

- **Decision Making:** Based on the pilot test and vendor evaluations, select the automation tools that best meet the firm's needs. Obtain approval from stakeholders and proceed with procurement.
- **Contract Negotiation**: Negotiate the terms of the contract with the vendor, including pricing, support, training, and any customization required. Ensure that the contract includes clear deliverables and timelines.

Preparing for Implementation

Infrastructure Readiness:

- **Upgrade Systems if Necessary:** Ensure that the firm's IT infrastructure can support the new automation tools. This might involve upgrading hardware, improving network security, or expanding data storage capabilities.
- **Data Migration:** Plan for the migration of data to the new system. This includes mapping data fields, cleansing data, and creating backups. Ensure that data migration is tested before full deployment.

Developing Workflow Maps:

- **Detailed Workflow Mapping:** For each process to be automated, develop a detailed workflow map. This should include every step of the process, the inputs and outputs, decision points, and any exceptions that need to be handled.
- **Identify Automation Points:** Pinpoint the specific steps in each workflow that can be automated. Determine what triggers the automation, what tasks are performed automatically, and how the process is monitored.

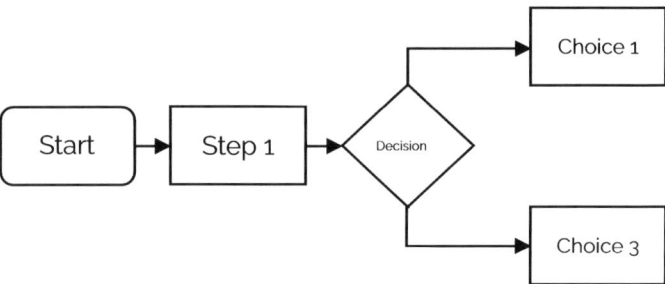

Customization and Configuration:

- **Tailor the Software:** Work with the vendor to customize the software to fit the firm's specific needs. This might include configuring templates, setting up automated alerts, and integrating the software with existing systems.
- **Testing and Validation:** Conduct thorough testing of the customized system to ensure that it functions as expected. Validate that all automated processes work correctly and that the system integrates smoothly with existing workflows.

Deployment and Rollout

Staged Rollout:

- **Phased Implementation:** Consider rolling out the automation in stages rather than all at once. Start with a single department or practice area to manage the transition more effectively.
- **Monitor Performance:** Closely monitor the performance of the new system during the initial rollout. Track key metrics such as time savings, error rates, and user satisfaction. Address any issues that arise promptly.

Full Deployment:

- **Firm-Wide Implementation:** Once the initial rollout has proven successful, expand the implementation to the rest of the firm. Continue to monitor performance and gather feedback from users.
- **Ongoing Support:** Provide ongoing technical support to address any challenges that users encounter. This support is crucial for ensuring that the system is adopted effectively across the firm.

Continuous Improvement:

- **Regular Reviews:** Schedule regular reviews of the automated workflows to ensure they continue to meet the firm's needs. Look for opportunities to further optimize processes and take advantage of new features or updates.
- **User Feedback:** Establish a feedback loop where users can report issues, suggest improvements, and share their experiences with the system. Use this feedback to make continuous improvements.

Post-Implementation Support and Optimization

Monitor and Measure Success:

- **Set Benchmarks:** Establish benchmarks for success, such as time saved, reduction in errors, or improved client satisfaction. Regularly compare these benchmarks to actual performance to measure the success of the automation.
- **Adjust as Needed:** Be prepared to make adjustments based on the metrics. This might involve reconfiguring the system, offering additional training, or tweaking workflows to better align with firm objectives.

Regular Updates and Maintenance:

- **System Maintenance:** Ensure that the software and systems are regularly updated and maintained. This includes installing updates, applying security patches, and optimizing performance.
- **Vendor Collaboration:** Maintain a close relationship with the software vendor to stay informed about new features, updates, and best practices. Regularly review the system with the vendor to ensure it continues to meet the firm's needs.

Training and Continuous Learning:

- **Ongoing Training:** Offer ongoing training sessions to keep staff updated on new features and best practices. This helps ensure that the firm continues to get the most out of the automation tools.
- **Encourage Innovation:** Foster a culture of continuous improvement by encouraging staff to suggest new ways to leverage automation in their work. Recognize and reward innovative ideas that lead to further efficiency gains.

Overcoming Resistance to Change

Resistance to change is a common challenge in implementing workflow automation, particularly in traditional law firms where established practices may be deeply ingrained. Overcoming this resistance requires a thoughtful approach that addresses concerns and engages stakeholders at all levels.

Engage Stakeholders Early:

- **Involve Key Decision-Makers:** Engage partners, department heads, and other key decision-makers early in the process. Ensure they understand the benefits of automation and how it aligns with the firm's strategic goals.
- **Communicate Benefits:** Clearly communicate the benefits of automation to all staff, including how it will reduce mundane tasks, improve work-life balance, and enhance client service. Tailor the message to different audiences to address their specific concerns.

Address Concerns Transparently:

- **Acknowledge Fears:** Recognize that some staff may fear that automation will lead to job losses or reduced responsibilities. Address these fears openly by explaining how automation will change their roles, focusing on how it can enhance their work rather than replace it.
- **Provide Reassurance:** Reassure staff that the firm is committed to supporting them through the transition, including offering retraining or new opportunities to adapt to the changes.

Foster a Culture of Innovation:

- **Promote a Growth Mindset:** Encourage a culture where innovation and continuous improvement are valued. Highlight how embracing automation positions the firm as a leader in the industry, attracting top talent and clients.
- **Celebrate Early Wins:** Publicly celebrate early successes in the automation initiative, showcasing how it has made work easier or more efficient. This positive reinforcement can help build momentum and reduce resistance.

Training and Adoption

Training is critical to the successful adoption of workflow automation. Effective training programs ensure that staff are comfortable using the new tools and understand how automation will benefit their work.

Develop a Comprehensive Training Plan:

- **Tailor Training to Roles:** Create training programs that are tailored to the specific roles within the firm. For example, lawyers might need training on automated document review tools, while administrative staff might focus on automated billing or client intake systems.
- **Use a Variety of Training Methods:** Combine different training methods, such as workshops, webinars, online tutorials, and hands-on practice sessions. This ensures that all learning styles are accommodated.

Provide Hands-On Practice:

- **Simulated Environments:** Offer practice sessions in a simulated environment where staff can interact with the new system without the pressure of real client work. This helps build confidence and proficiency.
- **Peer Learning:** Encourage peer learning by having early adopters or those who excel in the new system mentor their colleagues. This can create a supportive learning environment and promote knowledge sharing.

Offer Ongoing Support:

- **Help Desk:** Set up a help desk or dedicated support team that staff can contact with questions or issues as they arise. Quick access to support can alleviate frustration and encourage continued use of the new system.
- **Continuous Learning:** Keep the training ongoing by offering refresher courses, updates on new features, and advanced training for more complex tasks. Continuous learning ensures that staff remain engaged and proficient in using the automation tools.

Case Study: Dentons

Background:

Dentons is one of the world's largest law firms, with over 10,000 lawyers across more than 180 locations globally. The firm handles a wide array of legal services, from corporate law to intellectual property and dispute resolution. As part of its innovation strategy, Dentons recognized the need to improve efficiency and client service by automating repetitive workflows, especially in areas like contract generation, document review, and case management.

Implementation Process:

Dentons initiated the automation project through its in-house innovation team, NextLaw Labs. They first conducted a thorough audit of existing workflows, identifying that significant time was spent on drafting contracts, managing client intake, and other administrative tasks. The firm engaged with partners and staff to gather insights into pain points, and they aligned their objectives with the firm's strategy of scaling operations and improving service consistency.

After evaluating several technology solutions, Dentons selected an AI-driven platform designed for legal automation.[44] They began by piloting the automation in a non-mission-critical process: generating NDAs (non-disclosure agreements), a high-volume yet repetitive task. The firm worked closely with the vendor to customize the software, ensuring seamless integration with their existing practice management tools. Dentons mapped detailed workflows for the automated processes and ran extensive testing.

Challenges and Solutions:

The firm encountered several challenges during implementation, such as data migration complexities and initial resistance from some attorneys who were wary of changing long-standing practices. To address these issues, Dentons ensured thorough staff training and support. They set up a help desk to assist users with the new system and maintained open communication about the benefits of

---

[44] Downey, Sarah. "Bringing AI to a Law Firm Near You: Dentons' Nextlaw Venture Invests in IBM Watson App to Answer Lawyers' Questions." Legal Business, August 6, 2015

automation, focusing on how it would enhance—not replace—their roles.

Results and Outcomes:

After rolling out the automation firm-wide, Dentons saw significant improvements in efficiency. Tasks like contract generation, which used to take hours, could now be completed in minutes. The time savings allowed attorneys to focus on higher-value tasks, and client feedback indicated improved satisfaction with faster service delivery. Dentons also reduced error rates in document processing, leading to better compliance and reduced risk.

Lessons Learned:

Dentons learned that engaging staff early in the automation process and providing robust training and support are key to overcoming resistance. The firm also found that starting with a pilot project in a less critical area helped smooth the transition to full automation. For other firms considering automation, Dentons advises focusing on processes that are high-volume but low-complexity for the best initial results, and ensuring there is continuous feedback and improvement.

This case study demonstrates how a global law firm like Dentons successfully integrated workflow automation, improving both efficiency and client service while managing change effectively.

Implementing workflow automation in a law firm is a complex but rewarding process that can transform the way legal services are delivered. By following a structured approach, addressing resistance to change, providing thorough training, and learning from real-world examples, law firms can successfully adopt automation and reap the benefits of increased efficiency, accuracy, and client satisfaction.

Chapter 9: Overcoming Barriers to Innovation

Adopting new technologies and innovative practices in the legal industry is often met with resistance, stemming from deeply ingrained cultural, psychological, and institutional barriers. These barriers can slow down or even prevent the successful implementation of new technologies like workflow automation, which are essential for modernizing legal practices. Understanding and addressing these barriers is crucial for fostering a culture of innovation within a law firm. This chapter begins by exploring the cultural barriers that lawyers face when adopting new technologies.

Cultural Barriers

Cultural barriers are often the most challenging obstacles to overcome when introducing innovation in a law firm. These barriers are rooted in the traditional values, practices, and attitudes that have shaped the legal profession over many decades. Lawyers, by nature and training, tend to be risk-averse and cautious, particularly when it comes to changes that could disrupt established ways of working. Below, we explore the key cultural barriers to innovation and strategies for overcoming them.

Risk Aversion and Conservatism

The legal profession has long been characterized by a conservative approach to change, driven by the high stakes involved in legal work. Lawyers are trained to minimize risk and prioritize accuracy and precedent, which can lead to a reluctance to adopt new technologies or processes that are perceived as untested or risky.

Challenges:

Fear of Uncertainty

One of the most prevalent challenges when implementing new technologies in law firms is the fear of uncertainty. Lawyers often worry that automation and AI could introduce errors that wouldn't occur under traditional, human-led processes. This fear is not unfounded; even the best AI systems are prone to occasional inaccuracies, especially when handling complex or nuanced legal matters. The concern extends to the potential for these errors to expose the firm to legal liability. If AI misinterprets a legal clause or generates a document with an error, it could lead to significant consequences for both the client and the firm.

Moreover, many lawyers fear that automation could reduce the overall quality of their work. They may question whether AI can truly understand the complexity of legal language and nuances, particularly in areas requiring high levels of judgment and creativity. These fears are compounded by the fact that some AI systems, while improving efficiency, may lack transparency in how they reach conclusions, making it difficult for lawyers to trust their outputs.

Preference for Established Practices

Lawyers tend to adhere to traditional practices that have historically provided reliable results, which makes them reluctant to adopt new technologies. The legal profession is known for being risk-averse, with many professionals preferring methods that have been tested over time. For instance, manual document review and drafting are deeply ingrained practices that many believe deliver a level of scrutiny that automation cannot match. This preference for the familiar is often compounded by the time and effort required to learn new systems, which can disrupt daily operations.

Additionally, automation introduces a new way of thinking about workflows, which requires a shift in mindset. Lawyers often prioritize meticulousness over speed, and they may feel that relying on technology for tasks traditionally handled by human judgment undermines their core competencies. This resistance is particularly strong among senior attorneys who have spent decades working under manual processes and may view new technologies as unnecessary.

Concerns About Client Perception

A key challenge related to automation adoption is the potential perception clients might have of the technology. Lawyers fear that introducing automation, especially for critical tasks like document drafting or contract review, could signal to clients that the firm is cutting corners. Some worry that clients might believe the firm is reducing the personal attention that their case requires, or that the work is being delegated to machines rather than receiving the expertise of a seasoned attorney.

This concern is particularly acute in high-touch practice areas like family law, estate planning, or litigation, where clients often expect personalized service. Lawyers worry that clients may perceive automation as a reduction in quality, especially if they feel that human judgment is being replaced by impersonal software. Maintaining client trust and managing expectations is crucial, and introducing automation must be carefully communicated to clients to ensure that they understand the benefits, such as faster turnaround times and increased accuracy.

Strategies for Overcoming Risk Aversion:

- **Pilot Programs:** Introduce new technologies through pilot programs that allow the firm to test and evaluate them on a small scale before committing to a full rollout. This approach reduces perceived risk by providing evidence of the technology's effectiveness.
- **Emphasize Data-Driven Decisions:** Use data and case studies to demonstrate the benefits of new technologies, such as improved efficiency, accuracy, and client satisfaction. Showing concrete examples of successful implementations can help alleviate concerns.
- **Client Communication:** Proactively communicate with clients about how new technologies enhance service quality and reduce costs without compromising the attention to detail they expect. Transparency in how technology is used can build trust and acceptance.

Hierarchical Structures and Decision-Making

Many law firms operate within hierarchical structures where decision-making is concentrated at the top, often among senior partners who may be less familiar with or open to new technologies. This can create bottlenecks in the adoption of innovation, as younger, more tech-savvy lawyers may struggle to influence decisions.

Hierarchical Challenges:

- **Top-Down Decision-Making:** In hierarchical firms, decisions about technology adoption are often made by senior partners who may prioritize traditional approaches over innovation.
- **Resistance from Leadership:** Senior leaders who are less comfortable with technology may resist changes that they perceive as unnecessary or disruptive.
- **Lack of Empowerment:** Junior lawyers and staff who see the potential benefits of new technologies may feel disempowered to suggest or advocate for change.

Strategies for Addressing Hierarchical Barriers:

- **Create Innovation Committees:** Establish cross-functional innovation committees that include representatives from different levels of the firm, including junior lawyers and support staff. These committees can explore new technologies and present recommendations to senior leadership.
- **Champion Change from the Top:** Encourage senior leaders to champion innovation by highlighting the strategic benefits of adopting new technologies, such as staying competitive, attracting younger talent, and meeting client demands for efficiency.
- **Empower Staff to Innovate:** Foster a culture where all staff are encouraged to suggest new ideas and participate in discussions about technology adoption. Recognizing and rewarding contributions from across the firm can help flatten hierarchies and promote innovation.

The Billable Hour Mentality

The billable hour model, which ties revenue to the number of hours worked, is deeply embedded in the culture of many law firms. This model can create a disincentive to adopt technologies that increase efficiency because they could reduce the number of billable hours and, consequently, revenue.

Challenges:

- **Perceived Threat to Revenue:** Lawyers may view automation and other efficiency-enhancing technologies as a

threat to their billable hours, which directly impacts their income and the firm's profitability.
- **Ingrained Work Habits:** The focus on billable hours can lead to resistance against tools that automate tasks traditionally billed by the hour, as it requires a shift in how lawyers view and value their work.
- **Difficulty in Measuring Value:** Moving away from the billable hour model requires new ways of measuring and communicating the value provided to clients, which can be challenging for firms accustomed to time-based billing.

Strategies for Addressing the Billable Hour Mentality:
- **Value-Based Billing Models:** Introduce alternative billing models, such as fixed fees, subscription services, or value-based pricing, that align with the efficiencies gained through automation. These models can be more attractive to clients and can highlight the value of the firm's expertise rather than the time spent.
- **Internal Education:** Educate lawyers on the long-term benefits of automation, such as the ability to take on more clients, improve client satisfaction, and focus on higher-value work that cannot be easily automated.
- **Incentivize Efficiency:** Align incentives with efficiency by rewarding lawyers for delivering high-quality work efficiently rather than simply billing more hours. Performance metrics could include client satisfaction, successful case outcomes, or contributions to process improvements.

Tradition and Legacy Systems

Law firms, particularly those with long histories, may have deeply rooted traditions and legacy systems that have been in place for decades. These traditions can be a source of pride and identity for the firm, but they can also hinder the adoption of new technologies.

Challenges:
- **Attachment to Tradition:** Lawyers may be resistant to changes that disrupt the firm's traditional ways of working, especially if these traditions are seen as part of the firm's identity and success.
- **Dependence on Legacy Systems:** Many firms rely on legacy IT systems that were designed for different workflows

and may not easily integrate with modern automation tools. Replacing or upgrading these systems can be costly and disruptive.
- **Reluctance to Disrupt Established Processes:** Even when inefficiencies are recognized, there may be a reluctance to disrupt established processes, particularly if they have worked well in the past.

Strategies for Overcoming Tradition and Legacy Barriers:

- **Respect for Tradition:** Position new technologies as enhancements to, rather than replacements for, the firm's valued traditions. Emphasize how innovation can help the firm continue its legacy of excellence by adapting to the modern legal landscape.
- **Phased System Upgrades:** Plan a phased approach to upgrading legacy systems, starting with the most critical areas where automation can deliver immediate benefits. Gradual upgrades reduce disruption and allow the firm to adapt incrementally.
- **Pilot Programs with Legacy Integration:** Test new technologies on a small scale to demonstrate their compatibility with existing systems and processes. Success stories from these pilots can build confidence in the new tools and pave the way for broader adoption.

Cultural barriers are significant obstacles to innovation in law firms, but they are not insurmountable. By understanding the roots of these barriers and implementing targeted strategies to address them, law firms can create an environment where innovation is embraced rather than resisted. Overcoming cultural barriers requires a thoughtful, inclusive approach that respects the firm's traditions while encouraging the adoption of new technologies that can drive future success.

Psychological Barriers

Psychological barriers play a significant role in the resistance to adopting new technologies and innovative practices in law firms. These barriers are often rooted in deeper fears and anxieties, such as the fear of obsolescence, loss of professional identity, or uncertainty about the future of the legal profession. Understanding these psychological factors is crucial for effectively managing change and helping lawyers and staff overcome their apprehensions. This section explores the key psychological barriers to innovation in law firms and offers strategies for addressing them.

Fear of Obsolescence

One of the most pervasive psychological barriers in the legal profession is the fear of obsolescence. Lawyers and legal professionals may worry that the adoption of new technologies, particularly automation and artificial intelligence, will render their skills and expertise irrelevant. This fear can lead to resistance to learning new tools or adopting innovative practices, as individuals may feel that their hard-earned knowledge and experience are being devalued.

Challenges:

- **Perception of Replacement:** The fear that machines or software could replace human judgment and decision-making in legal work can cause significant anxiety among legal professionals. This is particularly true for tasks that are increasingly being automated, such as document review or legal research.
- **Resistance to Learning New Skills:** The prospect of having to learn and adapt to new technologies can be daunting, especially for those who have built their careers on traditional legal practices. This resistance can stem from a fear of being unable to keep up with younger, more tech-savvy colleagues.
- **Impact on Career Longevity:** Older lawyers, in particular, may fear that they will be pushed out of the profession earlier than planned if they are unable or unwilling to adapt to new technologies.

Strategies for Addressing the Fear of Obsolescence:

- **Emphasize the Complementary Role of Technology:** Position new technologies as tools that complement, rather than replace, human expertise. Highlight how automation can handle routine tasks, freeing up lawyers to focus on complex, strategic work that requires human judgment and creativity.
- **Skill Development and Lifelong Learning:** Encourage a culture of lifelong learning where continuous skill development is valued and supported. Provide training programs that help lawyers acquire new skills in a supportive environment, emphasizing that staying current with

technology is a way to enhance, not diminish, their professional value.
- **Showcase Success Stories:** Share examples of how other lawyers have successfully integrated new technologies into their practice, enhancing their efficiency and effectiveness without compromising their professional identity. Seeing peers thrive with new tools can reduce anxiety and build confidence.

Loss of Professional Identity

For many lawyers, their professional identity is closely tied to their expertise, experience, and the traditional ways of practicing law. The introduction of new technologies can challenge this identity, as it may require them to change how they work, interact with clients, and perceive their role in the legal process. The fear of losing this professional identity can create significant resistance to innovation.

Challenges:

- **Shift in Role Perception:** Automation and other innovations can change the nature of legal work, potentially shifting the lawyer's role from hands-on legal work to more strategic oversight. This shift can be unsettling for those who take pride in their direct involvement in legal tasks.
- **Erosion of Traditional Skills:** As more tasks become automated, there may be a concern that traditional legal skills, such as meticulous document drafting or in-depth legal research, will become less valued. Lawyers may worry that these changes will lead to a loss of respect or recognition within the profession.
- **Client Relationship Concerns:** Some lawyers fear that relying on technology could distance them from their clients, undermining the personal relationships that are a cornerstone of legal practice. The use of automation, particularly in client-facing tasks, might be seen as impersonal or detached.

Strategies for Addressing the Loss of Professional Identity:

- **Reframe the Role of the Lawyer:** Help lawyers see how their role is evolving rather than disappearing. Emphasize that their expertise is still crucial in guiding the use of technology, interpreting complex legal issues, and providing strategic advice to clients.

- **Integrate Technology with Human Insight:** Promote the idea that the most effective legal practice combines cutting-edge technology with human insight and experience. Lawyers can be positioned as the leaders in this new model, using technology to enhance their practice rather than diminish it.
- **Preserve Client Relationships:** Ensure that the introduction of new technologies does not erode the personal touch in client interactions. Use technology to enhance communication and service delivery while maintaining the lawyer's role as the primary point of contact and advisor for clients.

Fear of the Unknown and Uncertainty

Change is often accompanied by uncertainty, and the introduction of new technologies can create anxiety about the future. Lawyers may be uncertain about how new tools will impact their daily work, how their roles will evolve, or what the long-term implications will be for their careers and the legal profession as a whole. This fear of the unknown can lead to hesitation or outright resistance to innovation.

Challenges:

- **Uncertainty About Outcomes:** Lawyers may worry that new technologies will not deliver the promised benefits or that they will introduce unforeseen problems. This skepticism can be particularly strong if previous technology initiatives have failed or fallen short of expectations.
- **Impact on Job Security:** The uncertainty about how technology will impact job roles and security can create anxiety, especially among support staff whose tasks are more susceptible to automation. This fear can lead to resistance not only from those directly affected but also from others who sympathize with their colleagues' concerns.
- **Change Fatigue:** In firms where multiple changes have been implemented in a short period, lawyers and staff may experience change fatigue, leading to resistance to further innovation, regardless of its potential benefits.

Strategies for Addressing Fear of the Unknown:

- **Provide Clear Roadmaps:** Offer clear, detailed plans for how new technologies will be implemented, including timelines, expected outcomes, and how potential challenges will be

managed. Transparency reduces uncertainty and builds trust in the process.
- **Involve Stakeholders Early:** Engage lawyers and staff in the planning and decision-making process for new technologies. Involving them early on helps to demystify the changes and gives them a sense of control over the outcome.
- **Pilot Programs and Incremental Changes:** Introduce new technologies gradually, starting with pilot programs that allow the firm to test and refine the tools before full deployment. This approach reduces the perceived risk and allows for adjustments based on feedback.
- **Reassure on Job Security:** Clearly communicate how new technologies will impact job roles, emphasizing that the goal is to enhance rather than replace human work. Offer training and development opportunities to help staff adapt and grow within the new environment.

Psychological barriers such as the fear of obsolescence, loss of professional identity, and fear of the unknown can significantly hinder the adoption of new technologies in law firms. Addressing these barriers requires a deep understanding of the underlying fears and anxieties that drive resistance. By providing reassurance, emphasizing the complementary role of technology, and involving lawyers and staff in the change process, firms can help their people overcome these psychological hurdles and embrace innovation.

Institutional Barriers

Institutional barriers can be some of the most formidable obstacles to innovation within law firms. These barriers are rooted in the structural, regulatory, and organizational frameworks that govern legal practice. Unlike cultural or psychological barriers, which are often internal and personal, institutional barriers are external and systemic, often requiring changes in policy, governance, or regulation to overcome. This section explores the key institutional barriers to innovation in law firms and offers strategies for addressing them.

Regulatory Constraints

The legal profession is one of the most heavily regulated industries, with strict rules governing everything from client confidentiality to professional conduct and billing practices. These regulations, while essential for maintaining the integrity of the legal system, can also act as barriers to innovation, particularly when new technologies challenge traditional ways of delivering legal services.

Challenges:

- **Compliance with Ethical Rules:** Innovations such as AI-driven legal advice or automated document drafting must comply with ethical rules set by legal governing bodies. There is often uncertainty about how these rules apply to new technologies, leading to cautious adoption.
- **Client Confidentiality:** Maintaining client confidentiality is a cornerstone of legal practice. The use of cloud-based platforms, automated systems, or AI tools raises concerns about data security and the potential for breaches, which could violate regulatory requirements.
- **Restrictions on Legal Practice:** In some jurisdictions, regulations restrict who can provide legal services, which can limit the adoption of certain innovations. For example, the use of non-lawyer professionals in certain roles or the outsourcing of legal work to automated systems may be restricted by regulation.
- **Billing Regulations:** The shift from billable hours to alternative fee arrangements, which often accompany automation, can be hindered by regulations that are designed around traditional billing practices. These regulations may not easily accommodate new models that emphasize efficiency and outcomes over time spent.

Strategies for Navigating Regulatory Constraints:

- **Engage with Regulatory Bodies:** Law firms should actively engage with regulatory bodies to clarify how new technologies fit within existing regulations. By working closely with these organizations, firms can help shape the development of new rules that support innovation while maintaining ethical standards.
- **Implement Strong Data Protection Measures:** To address concerns about client confidentiality, firms must implement robust cybersecurity measures, including encryption, access controls, and regular security audits. Compliance with regulations such as GDPR or CCPA can also help mitigate risks associated with new technologies.

- **Pilot Programs with Regulatory Oversight:** Consider running pilot programs under the guidance of regulatory bodies. These programs can serve as test cases for how new technologies can be used within the bounds of existing regulations, providing a model for wider adoption.
- **Advocate for Regulatory Reform:** Where regulations are outdated or overly restrictive, law firms can advocate for reform. This might involve participating in industry groups, submitting proposals to regulatory bodies, or working with legal technology associations to push for changes that support innovation.

Firm Hierarchies

Many law firms operate within traditional hierarchical structures where decision-making power is concentrated at the top. These hierarchies can slow down or prevent the adoption of new technologies, especially if senior partners are resistant to change or if the decision-making process is cumbersome and bureaucratic.

Challenges:

- **Centralized Decision-Making:** In hierarchical firms, major decisions about technology adoption are typically made by a small group of senior partners. If these individuals are risk-averse or skeptical of new technologies, it can be difficult to push through innovation.
- **Resistance from Senior Leadership:** Senior leaders who have built their careers on traditional legal practices may be less open to adopting new technologies. They may also fear that these changes could undermine their authority or disrupt the firm's established culture.
- **Lack of Bottom-Up Innovation:** In firms with rigid hierarchies, junior lawyers and support staff may feel disempowered to suggest or drive innovation. This can stifle creativity and prevent the firm from benefiting from the insights and ideas of younger, more tech-savvy employees.

Strategies for Addressing Hierarchical Barriers:

- **Foster Inclusive Decision-Making:** Encourage a more inclusive approach to decision-making by involving representatives from different levels of the firm in discussions about technology adoption. Creating innovation committees

that include junior lawyers, IT staff, and support staff can provide a broader perspective and help build consensus.
- **Leadership Buy-In and Sponsorship:** For innovation to succeed, it is crucial to secure buy-in from senior leadership. This can be achieved by demonstrating how new technologies align with the firm's strategic goals, such as improving client service, increasing efficiency, or staying competitive in the market.
- **Empower Middle Management:** Middle managers, such as practice group leaders or department heads, can be key allies in driving innovation. Empower them to experiment with new technologies within their teams, creating a model for broader adoption across the firm.
- **Bottom-Up Innovation Initiatives:** Encourage bottom-up innovation by creating channels through which junior staff can propose ideas and participate in pilot projects. Recognizing and rewarding innovative ideas from all levels of the firm can help break down hierarchical barriers and promote a culture of continuous improvement.

Institutional Inertia

Institutional inertia refers to the tendency of organizations to resist change and continue operating as they always have, even when there are clear benefits to adopting new practices. In law firms, this inertia can be particularly strong due to the profession's reliance on precedent, long-standing traditions, and established workflows.

Challenges:

- **Comfort with the Status Quo:** Many law firms have established ways of working that have served them well for decades. There may be a strong preference for maintaining these familiar practices rather than taking risks with new technologies or workflows.
- **Perceived Complexity of Change:** The complexity of implementing new technologies—especially in large, multi-office firms—can be daunting. The potential disruption to daily operations, combined with the need for significant training and change management, can make firms reluctant to pursue innovation.
- **Lack of Urgency:** Without a clear and present threat to the firm's success, there may be little urgency to adopt new

technologies. This is especially true if the firm is currently profitable and clients appear satisfied with the status quo.

Strategies for Overcoming Institutional Inertia:

- **Highlight the Costs of Inaction:** Clearly articulate the risks of not adopting new technologies, such as falling behind competitors, losing clients who demand more efficient services, or missing out on growth opportunities. Case studies of other firms that have successfully innovated can provide compelling examples.
- **Start with Small Wins:** Begin with small, manageable projects that demonstrate the benefits of innovation. Successful small-scale initiatives can build momentum and make the case for larger, more comprehensive changes.
- **Create a Sense of Urgency:** Frame the adoption of new technologies as a necessity for staying competitive in an evolving legal market. This can be achieved by highlighting external pressures, such as changes in client expectations, industry trends, or economic conditions, that make innovation essential.
- **Leverage External Expertise:** Bringing in external consultants or partnering with legal technology vendors can help overcome inertia by providing the expertise and resources needed to implement change. External perspectives can also challenge internal assumptions and offer new approaches to overcoming resistance.

Institutional barriers, such as regulatory constraints, firm hierarchies, and institutional inertia, present significant challenges to innovation in law firms. These barriers are often deeply embedded in the structures and practices of the profession, making them difficult to overcome. However, with a strategic approach that includes engaging with regulators, fostering inclusive decision-making, and creating a sense of urgency, law firms can navigate these obstacles and successfully adopt new technologies that enhance their operations and client service.

Strategies for Overcoming Barriers

Overcoming the cultural, psychological, and institutional barriers to innovation in law firms requires a multifaceted approach. To successfully introduce new technologies and practices, law firms must foster a culture of innovation, align incentives with automation goals, and manage client expectations effectively. This section outlines actionable strategies that law firms can implement to overcome these barriers and drive meaningful change.

Fostering a Culture of Innovation

Creating a culture of innovation involves encouraging an environment where new ideas are welcomed, experimentation is encouraged, and continuous improvement is valued. In a law firm setting, this means shifting the mindset from one of risk aversion and adherence to tradition to one that embraces change and seeks out opportunities to improve efficiency, client service, and overall firm performance.

Strategies for Fostering Innovation:

Leadership Commitment:

- **Role of Leadership:** Senior partners and firm leaders must visibly commit to fostering innovation. This includes not only endorsing new technologies but also actively participating in the innovation process. When leadership demonstrates a willingness to embrace change, it sets the tone for the rest of the firm.
- **Innovation Champions:** Appoint innovation champions within the firm—individuals who are passionate about technology and process improvement. These champions can lead by example, advocate for new ideas, and mentor others in adopting innovative practices.

Encourage Experimentation:

- **Pilot Projects:** Allow teams to experiment with new technologies or processes through pilot projects. These small-scale initiatives provide a safe environment to test new ideas without the pressure of full-scale implementation. Successes from these pilots can be scaled up, while failures can be used as learning experiences.
- **Innovation Labs:** Consider establishing an innovation lab or task force dedicated to exploring new technologies and approaches. This group can research emerging trends, conduct trials, and report on potential benefits to the firm.

Create Open Communication Channels:

- **Idea Portals:** Implement idea portals or suggestion boxes where employees at all levels can submit ideas for improving workflows or adopting new technologies. Regularly review and respond to these suggestions to show that innovation is valued.
- **Regular Innovation Meetings:** Hold regular meetings or brainstorming sessions where staff can discuss new ideas and explore how the firm can innovate. These meetings should be inclusive, allowing contributions from all levels of the firm.

Recognize and Reward Innovation:

- **Incentive Programs:** Develop incentive programs that reward employees who contribute to successful innovation efforts. This could include bonuses, public recognition, or career advancement opportunities for those who drive meaningful change.
- **Celebrate Successes:** Publicly celebrate successful innovations within the firm, whether they are small process improvements or major technological implementations. Recognition encourages a positive attitude toward innovation and motivates others to contribute.

Aligning Incentives with Automation Goals

One of the key barriers to adopting new technologies, particularly automation, is the misalignment of incentives. Traditionally, law firms have rewarded lawyers based on the number of billable hours they generate. However, automation, which aims to improve efficiency and reduce time spent on routine tasks, can seem at odds with this model. To successfully implement automation, firms need to align their incentives with their automation goals, ensuring that lawyers and staff are rewarded for contributing to the firm's overall efficiency and success.

Strategies for Aligning Incentives:

Shift to Value-Based Billing:

- **Alternative Fee Arrangements (AFAs):** Encourage the adoption of alternative fee arrangements, such as fixed fees, value-based pricing, or subscription models. These models reward efficiency and results rather than time spent, aligning with the goals of automation.

- **Client-Centric Metrics:** Shift the focus from billable hours to metrics that reflect client satisfaction and outcomes. For example, measure success by the quality of the legal service provided, the speed of delivery, or the cost savings achieved for the client.

Redefine Performance Metrics:

- **Efficiency and Innovation:** Incorporate efficiency and innovation into performance evaluations. Reward lawyers who find ways to leverage technology to deliver high-quality work more quickly or who contribute to the development of new, automated workflows.
- **Team Collaboration:** Encourage collaboration between lawyers, IT staff, and support staff by including teamwork and knowledge-sharing in performance reviews. Recognize those who contribute to the firm's overall success, not just their individual billable hours.

Incentivize Adoption of New Technologies:

- **Technology Proficiency Bonuses:** Offer bonuses or other incentives to lawyers and staff who become proficient in new technologies. This could include completing training programs, successfully implementing new tools, or leading a technology adoption initiative.
- **Innovation Grants:** Provide internal grants or funding for teams that propose and successfully implement innovative projects that align with the firm's strategic goals. This financial support can help overcome initial resistance and encourage experimentation.

Managing Client Expectations

Clients are increasingly demanding more efficient, transparent, and cost-effective legal services. As law firms adopt new technologies, it is crucial to manage client expectations about how these changes will impact service delivery. Clear communication, transparency, and a focus on the benefits to the client are key to ensuring that clients understand and appreciate the value of innovation.

Strategies for Managing Client Expectations:

Transparent Communication:

- **Educate Clients:** Clearly explain to clients how new technologies and automation will benefit them. This could include faster turnaround times, more accurate document drafting, or lower costs due to increased efficiency.
- **Address Concerns:** Be proactive in addressing any concerns clients might have about the use of technology. For example, if a client is worried that automation will reduce the personal touch of their service, explain how the firm will continue to prioritize personalized attention while leveraging technology for routine tasks.

Demonstrate Value:

- **Case Studies and Testimonials:** Use case studies and client testimonials to demonstrate the positive impact of new technologies. Showing real-world examples of how innovation has improved outcomes for other clients can build trust and confidence.
- **Performance Metrics:** Provide clients with performance metrics that highlight the benefits of innovation. For example, share data on how automation has reduced errors, shortened delivery times, or provided more comprehensive risk assessments.

Involve Clients in the Process:

- **Client Feedback Loops:** Involve clients in the innovation process by soliciting their feedback on new tools or processes. This could be done through surveys, focus groups, or one-on-one meetings. Incorporating client input helps ensure that innovations are aligned with client needs and expectations.
- **Customized Solutions:** Offer customized solutions that integrate new technologies in ways that meet the specific needs of individual clients. This approach not only demonstrates flexibility but also reassures clients that their unique requirements are being considered.

Set Realistic Expectations:

- **Clear Timelines and Deliverables:** When introducing new technologies, set clear timelines and deliverables for clients.

This helps manage their expectations and reduces the risk of misunderstandings or dissatisfaction.
- **Transparency About Limitations:** Be upfront about the limitations of new technologies, especially during the initial implementation phase. While it's important to highlight the benefits, being honest about potential challenges or learning curves can build credibility and trust.

Overcoming the barriers to innovation in law firms requires a deliberate and strategic approach. By fostering a culture of innovation, aligning incentives with automation goals, and effectively managing client expectations, law firms can create an environment where new technologies are embraced and leveraged to their full potential. These strategies not only help overcome resistance but also position the firm for long-term success in an increasingly competitive and technology-driven legal landscape.

Chapter 10: The Economic Impact of Automation

Workflow automation and the adoption of productized services are not just about improving operational efficiency; they have profound economic implications for law firms. By reducing costs, increasing efficiency, and enabling new business models, automation can significantly alter the financial dynamics of legal practice. This chapter explores these economic impacts in detail, starting with the cost savings and efficiency gains that automation can bring to a law firm.

Cost Savings and Efficiency Gains

Automation has the potential to dramatically reduce the costs associated with running a law firm by streamlining processes, reducing the need for manual labor, and minimizing errors. These efficiency gains not only lower operational expenses but also allow firms to reallocate resources to more strategic activities, ultimately enhancing profitability and competitiveness.

Reducing Labor Costs:

- **Automating Routine Tasks:** Automation can significantly reduce the time and effort required for routine tasks such as document drafting, contract review, and legal research. By automating these processes, firms can reduce the reliance on paralegals, junior associates, and administrative staff, leading to lower labor costs.
- **Outsourcing and Offshoring:** Automation can also facilitate the outsourcing or offshoring of certain tasks that no longer require in-house expertise, further reducing costs. For example, routine document review can be outsourced to specialized service providers who use automated tools to

process large volumes of documents quickly and cost-effectively.

Global Efficiency: How Baker McKenzie's Offshore Operations and AI Drive Cost-Effective Legal Services

Baker McKenzie has developed extensive offshore operations to support its global legal services, particularly through its Global Services Centers (GSCs)[45] located in Manila, Philippines, and Buenos Aires, Argentina. These centers handle a wide array of routine legal and administrative tasks, such as document review, contract management, and compliance monitoring. By offshoring these services to regions with lower operational costs, Baker McKenzie can offer clients cost-efficient solutions without compromising quality. The firm's offshore teams work in close coordination with its onshore legal professionals, using automation tools and AI-driven platforms to process large volumes of legal documents quickly and accurately, particularly in areas like M&A and litigation. This offshoring strategy not only reduces costs but also allows for 24/7 operations due to the geographical spread of the service centers, enhancing efficiency and client satisfaction.

Minimizing Errors and Rework:

- **Error Reduction:** Automated systems can greatly reduce the risk of human error in tasks like data entry, billing, and document generation. Fewer errors mean less time spent on rework and corrections, which translates to cost savings.
- **Consistency and Standardization:** Automation ensures consistency and standardization across legal documents and processes. This reduces the variability that often leads to mistakes, improving overall quality and efficiency.

Improving Resource Allocation:

- **Freeing Up Lawyer Time:** By automating time-consuming tasks, lawyers can focus more on higher-value activities such as client consultations, strategic planning, and case analysis. This shift allows firms to maximize the utilization of their most

---

[45] Baker McKenzie Global Services Manila provides offshore support for the firm's legal and administrative operations. https://linkedin.com/company/bm-global-services-manila

valuable resource—attorney time—leading to better client outcomes and higher billing potential.
- **Optimizing Workflows:** Automation tools often come with analytics capabilities that allow firms to monitor and optimize their workflows continuously. This data-driven approach enables firms to identify bottlenecks, streamline processes, and allocate resources more effectively, leading to further efficiency gains.

Reducing Overhead Costs:

- **Decreased Paperwork:** Automation reduces the need for physical paperwork, leading to savings on printing, storage, and office space. Digital workflows also reduce the administrative burden associated with managing physical documents, further lowering overhead costs.
- **Technology Maintenance:** While implementing automation technologies involves upfront costs, these are often offset by the long-term savings in maintenance and support compared to traditional, manual processes. Automated systems can also reduce the need for IT support by minimizing the complexity of managing multiple disparate systems.

Enhancing Client Service and Retention:

- **Faster Turnaround Times:** Automation enables faster turnaround times for client deliverables, which can enhance client satisfaction and retention. Clients are more likely to stay with a firm that consistently meets deadlines and exceeds service expectations.
- **Cost Transparency:** Automation can also lead to more transparent and predictable pricing for clients, especially when combined with alternative billing models. This transparency builds trust and can attract cost-conscious clients who value clarity in pricing.

Case Study Example: Pinsent Masons – Enhancing Client Service Through Document Automation

Pinsent Masons, renowned for its innovative approach to legal services, implemented document automation to streamline routine tasks such as contract drafting, non-disclosure agreements, and other legal documents. Before automation, the firm's lawyers were spending significant time on repetitive document creation, which slowed service delivery and introduced risks of human error.[46]

After implementing document automation tools, Pinsent Masons achieved faster turnaround times, reducing the time required for document drafting by automating the use of pre-defined templates. This not only improved speed but also enhanced accuracy by minimizing errors associated with manual drafting. Clients experienced quicker service delivery and greater transparency in pricing, as automation enabled more predictable cost structures.

As a result, client satisfaction improved, with many clients appreciating the consistency and efficiency in the legal services they received. This boosted client retention and allowed the firm to focus its legal talent on higher-value, strategic tasks, contributing to its competitive edge in the legal market

New Revenue Streams

Automation not only leads to cost savings and efficiency gains but also opens up new revenue opportunities for law firms. By leveraging automated processes, firms can develop innovative service offerings that cater to a broader range of clients, provide more predictable revenue, and create scalable business models. This section explores how automation can enable law firms to generate new revenue streams, particularly through the introduction of subscription-based services, fixed-fee offerings, and scalable legal products.

Subscription-Based Legal Services:

- **Predictable Revenue:** Subscription models offer a steady and predictable revenue stream by charging clients a recurring fee for ongoing access to a suite of legal services. This model is particularly attractive for small and medium-sized businesses that need regular legal support but cannot afford the traditional hourly billing model.
- **Automated Service Delivery:** Automation allows firms to efficiently manage subscription services by automating routine tasks such as contract renewals, compliance updates, and document reviews. These tasks can be bundled into a

---

[46] Thomson Reuters. "Embracing Legal Document Automation: The Benefits Are Many." Thomson Reuters Legal Blog, November 8, 2019

subscription package, providing clients with ongoing legal support at a fixed monthly or annual rate.
- **Scalability:** With automation handling routine tasks, firms can easily scale their subscription offerings to accommodate a larger client base without a corresponding increase in labor costs. This scalability makes subscription services a highly profitable revenue stream.

Example Offering: A law firm specializing in employment law might offer a "Workplace Compliance Subscription" for small businesses. For a fixed monthly fee, clients receive regular updates on employment law changes, automated compliance audits, and access to a library of customizable HR documents. The firm uses automation to streamline the delivery of these services, ensuring efficiency and consistency.

Fixed-Fee Legal Products:

- **Standardized Services:** Automation enables the creation of standardized legal products that can be offered at a fixed fee. These products could include services such as trademark registration, basic contract drafting, or estate planning documents. By automating the majority of the work involved, firms can offer these services at a competitive price while maintaining profitability.
- **Lowered Barriers to Entry:** Fixed-fee services lower the financial barrier for clients, particularly individuals and small businesses who might be deterred by the unpredictability of hourly billing. This can attract a new client base that might otherwise forgo legal services.
- **Cross-Selling Opportunities:** Fixed-fee products can serve as an entry point for clients, leading to cross-selling opportunities for more complex, higher-value services. For example, a client who engages a firm for a fixed-fee contract review might later seek assistance with more complex business transactions.

Example Offering: A corporate law firm could offer a "Startup Legal Kit" that includes the formation of a limited liability company (LLC), basic operating agreements, and trademark registration for a fixed fee. The firm uses document automation tools to generate the necessary legal documents quickly and accurately, enabling them to offer the service at a competitive price.

Scalable Legal Products:

- **Automated Legal Tools:** Law firms can develop and sell automated legal tools, such as self-service platforms that allow clients to generate legal documents or perform legal research independently. These tools can be offered on a pay-per-use basis or as part of a subscription package.
- **White-Label Services:** Firms can also create white-label legal products that other professionals, such as accountants or financial advisors, can offer to their clients. By licensing these products, law firms can generate additional revenue streams without significantly increasing their workload.
- **Online Legal Portals:** An online legal portal offering automated services like will drafting, contract templates, or business formation can reach a wide audience and generate revenue with minimal human intervention. These portals are particularly appealing to tech-savvy clients who prefer to manage their legal needs independently.

Example Offering: A law firm could develop an automated online platform where clients can create customized contracts using a series of guided questions. The platform could be marketed to small businesses and entrepreneurs who need quick access to legal documents without the need for a full legal consultation. The firm could charge a one-time fee per document or offer a subscription for unlimited access.

Expanding Service Offerings:

- **Virtual Legal Services:** Automation enables the expansion of virtual legal services, where clients receive legal advice and document preparation remotely. This model is particularly relevant in a post-pandemic world, where remote work and virtual meetings have become the norm.
- **On-Demand Legal Support:** Firms can offer on-demand legal services through automated platforms that connect clients with lawyers for brief consultations, document reviews, or legal advice on specific issues. These services can be monetized through flat fees or time-based pricing models.
- **Customized Legal Solutions:** By leveraging data analytics and automation, firms can offer highly customized legal solutions tailored to specific industries or client needs. These

solutions can be packaged as premium services, commanding higher fees.

Example Offering: A family law firm could offer virtual mediation services, where clients participate in online mediation sessions facilitated by an automated scheduling and document preparation system. The firm could offer this service on an on-demand basis, allowing clients to resolve disputes quickly and efficiently without the need for in-person meetings.

Automation not only enhances the efficiency and cost-effectiveness of legal services but also opens up new revenue opportunities for law firms. By developing subscription-based services, fixed-fee products, scalable legal tools, and expanding service offerings, firms can tap into new markets, attract a broader client base, and create sustainable, long-term revenue streams. These innovations allow law firms to stay competitive in a rapidly changing legal landscape while meeting the evolving needs of their clients.

Broader Industry Implications

The adoption of workflow automation and productized legal services is not only transforming individual law firms but is also reshaping the broader legal industry. As these innovations become more widespread, they are driving significant shifts in how legal services are valued, billed, and delivered. This section explores the broader economic implications of automation for the legal industry, including changes in the traditional billing models, the evolving role of legal professionals, and the potential impact on access to justice.

Shifts in Billing Models

The traditional billable hour model has long been the dominant billing method in the legal industry. However, the efficiency gains brought about by automation are prompting a shift towards alternative billing models that prioritize value over time. This shift is fundamentally altering the economics of legal practice and client expectations.

Implications:

- **Decline of the Billable Hour:** As automation reduces the time required to complete routine legal tasks, the billable hour model becomes less viable. Clients are increasingly demanding greater transparency, predictability, and fairness in

billing, leading to the rise of alternative fee arrangements (AFAs).
- **Rise of Value-Based Billing:** Value-based billing models, such as fixed fees, contingency fees, and subscription services, are becoming more prevalent. These models align the cost of legal services with the value delivered to the client, rather than the time spent by the lawyer. This shift encourages efficiency and innovation, as firms are rewarded for delivering results rather than for the hours billed.
- **Client Empowerment:** Clients are gaining more control over legal costs and are better able to compare services across providers. This increased transparency is putting pressure on law firms to demonstrate the value they bring, driving competition and encouraging the adoption of technology to maintain profitability.

Example: A corporate client might prefer a fixed-fee arrangement for routine contract review, knowing exactly what the service will cost upfront. The law firm, using automated document review tools, can complete the task efficiently and profitably while providing the client with cost certainty.

Evolving Role of Legal Professionals

The integration of automation into legal workflows is changing the role of legal professionals, shifting their focus from routine, administrative tasks to higher-value, strategic activities. This evolution is impacting how lawyers, paralegals, and support staff work, how they are trained, and how they are valued within the legal ecosystem.

Implications:

- **Focus on Strategic Work:** Automation frees lawyers from time-consuming tasks such as document drafting, legal research, and data entry, allowing them to concentrate on more complex and strategic activities. This shift enhances job satisfaction and enables lawyers to provide more value to their clients.
- **Redefining Legal Roles:** The role of paralegals and support staff is also evolving. These professionals are increasingly taking on more sophisticated tasks, such as managing automated workflows, interpreting data analytics, and supporting client-facing activities. This requires new skill sets and continuous learning.

- **New Career Paths:** The rise of legal technology is creating new career paths within the industry, such as legal technologists, project managers, and data analysts. These roles are essential for implementing and managing automation tools, bridging the gap between legal expertise and technological innovation.
- **Changing Skill Requirements:** As technology becomes more integral to legal practice, the demand for tech-savvy lawyers is growing. Law schools and continuing education programs are increasingly incorporating technology training into their curricula to prepare future lawyers for a tech-driven industry.

Example: A litigation lawyer might use predictive analytics tools to assess the likely outcome of a case based on historical data, allowing them to focus on strategy and client counseling rather than time-consuming legal research. Meanwhile, a paralegal might oversee the automated document production process, ensuring accuracy and compliance.

Impact on Access to Justice

Automation has the potential to significantly impact access to justice by making legal services more affordable, efficient, and widely available. By lowering the cost of legal services and enabling self-service options, automation can help bridge the justice gap for individuals and small businesses who may otherwise be unable to afford legal representation.

Implications:

- **Lower Costs for Clients:** Automation reduces the cost of delivering legal services, allowing law firms to offer more affordable options to clients. This is particularly important for individuals and small businesses who may struggle to pay traditional legal fees.
- **Self-Service Legal Tools:** The development of automated legal tools, such as online document generators and guided legal advice platforms, empowers individuals to handle straightforward legal matters on their own. This democratization of legal services increases access to justice, particularly in underserved communities.
- **Pro Bono and Legal Aid:** Automation can also enhance the capacity of pro bono and legal aid organizations by

streamlining case management, document preparation, and client intake processes. This allows these organizations to serve more clients with limited resources, improving access to justice for vulnerable populations.

- **Challenges and Risks:** While automation offers many benefits, there are also challenges, such as ensuring that automated tools are accurate, unbiased, and accessible to all. Additionally, there is a risk that over-reliance on automation could lead to a reduction in personalized legal advice, particularly for complex cases that require human judgment.

Example: A legal aid organization might implement an automated intake system that helps clients quickly determine their eligibility for services and provides them with customized legal information. This system can handle a high volume of inquiries efficiently, allowing the organization to focus its limited resources on providing direct representation to those in need.

The broader economic implications of automation in the legal industry are profound, affecting everything from billing models and the role of legal professionals to access to justice. As automation continues to reshape the legal landscape, firms that embrace these changes will be better positioned to thrive in a competitive market. By adopting new billing models, redefining the roles of legal professionals, and expanding access to legal services, law firms can leverage automation to create a more efficient, equitable, and sustainable legal ecosystem.

Chapter 11: Case Studies of Successful Legal Automation

This section presents a series of case studies from different types of law firms and legal departments. Each case study details the firm's background, the specific automation technologies implemented, the process of adoption, and the results achieved. These examples cover a range of practice areas and firm sizes to demonstrate the versatility and impact of workflow automation and productized services.

Case Study 1: Clifford Chance – AI and Workflow Automation

Background

Clifford Chance, one of the largest international law firms, faced increasing pressure to improve efficiency and accuracy in high-volume transactions, particularly in mergers and acquisitions (M&A). With the growing complexity of legal documents and rising client expectations for faster and more transparent service, the firm recognized the need to integrate advanced technologies into their operations.[47]

Automation Implementation

Clifford Chance adopted Kira Systems, an AI-powered platform designed for document review and analysis. Kira's machine learning capabilities enabled the firm to automate contract review and due diligence processes. Additionally, the firm introduced workflow

---

[47] Clifford Chance drives innovation strategy with artificial intelligence. https://www.cliffordchance.com/news/news/2016/07/clifford-chance-drives-innovation-strategy-with--artificial-inte.html

automation tools to streamline internal collaboration and communication between its international offices.

Process

The firm started with a pilot program, using Kira Systems for document review in select M&A transactions. After the pilot's success, Clifford Chance expanded the use of Kira across other practice areas. To ensure smooth adoption, the firm provided extensive training and integrated the AI tool into their existing IT infrastructure to minimize workflow disruption. The firm also introduced project management software to enhance communication and collaboration across offices globally.

Results

Clifford Chance reported a 30% reduction in the time spent on document review. The implementation of AI improved both efficiency and accuracy, reducing the likelihood of human error and freeing up lawyers to focus on more complex legal tasks. The firm's workflow automation tools also improved communication between international offices, enhancing their ability to handle cross-border cases effectively. As a result, the firm experienced increased client satisfaction due to faster turnaround times and more transparent billing practices.

Case Study 2: Allen & Overy – Productization with Fuse

Background

Allen & Overy, a global law firm, established Fuse, an innovation hub[48] aimed at exploring how technology could revolutionize legal services. The firm saw an opportunity to productize routine legal work, creating standardized services that could be delivered efficiently and at scale while maintaining high-quality client service.

Automation Implementation

Through Fuse, the firm collaborated with legal tech companies to implement tools such as Legatics, a deal management platform that automates routine administrative tasks involved in legal transactions. This included managing document checklists, tracking approvals, and

---

[48] Fuse – Allen & Overy's legal tech innovation hub. https://fuse.allenovery.com

automating contract execution processes. The firm also integrated AI-driven tools for legal research, contract analysis, and compliance monitoring, allowing for faster and more consistent legal work.

Process

Allen & Overy piloted Legatics in their corporate M&A practice to automate deal management. Following successful results, they expanded the platform's use to other areas like capital markets and regulatory compliance. Fuse allowed the firm to productize these services, offering clients fixed-price packages that provided greater cost transparency. The firm also engaged in extensive training to ensure that staff could effectively use the new tools.

Results

The productization of legal services led to a 50% reduction in time spent on deal management tasks. The ability to offer standardized, scalable legal services at a fixed price resulted in increased client satisfaction and improved efficiency. Lawyers were able to focus on higher-value work, while clients benefitted from predictable pricing and faster service. The success of Fuse cemented Allen & Overy's position as a leader in legal innovation.

Case Study 3: Orrick, Herrington & Sutcliffe – Virtual Law Firm and AI Integration

Background

Orrick, Herrington & Sutcliffe, known for its focus on innovation and technology clients, was one of the early adopters of a virtual-first law firm model. The firm recognized that operating virtually, coupled with AI-driven tools, would offer flexibility, reduce overhead costs, and enhance service delivery, particularly for clients in technology and startups.[49]

---

[49] The Law Firm Disrupted: "Orrick, Reed Smith, and Dechert Make Time to Get Comfortable with AI." Law.com, March 7, 2024. https://www.law.com/2024/03/07/the-law-firm-disrupted-orrick-reed-smith-and-dechert-make-time-to-get-comfortable-with-ai/?slreturn=20240806143313.

Automation Implementation

Orrick implemented a range of AI-driven tools, including ROSS Intelligence[50], an AI-powered legal research tool, and Luminance, an AI system for document review and contract analysis. These tools enabled Orrick to provide efficient, high-quality legal services while allowing lawyers to work remotely. Additionally, the firm adopted cloud-based collaboration platforms to facilitate seamless communication between remote teams and clients.

Process

Orrick's shift to a virtual-first model required substantial investment in IT infrastructure, including enhanced cybersecurity and cloud-based collaboration tools. Training programs were implemented to ensure that all lawyers and staff were proficient in using AI tools like ROSS Intelligence and Luminance. The firm also restructured internal workflows to support remote work, ensuring that lawyers could collaborate effectively regardless of their location.

Results

Orrick's virtual law firm model allowed it to significantly reduce its physical office space, lowering overhead costs without compromising client service. AI tools like ROSS and Luminance led to a 40% reduction in the time spent on legal research and document review. The firm's ability to operate virtually and leverage AI tools positioned it as a leader in the legal industry, particularly during the global shift to remote work during the COVID-19 pandemic. Orrick's success demonstrated the viability of a virtual law firm model in providing high-quality, client-focused legal services.

---

[50] *ROSS Intelligence*, an AI-powered legal research platform, faced legal challenges in 2020 when Westlaw (Thomson Reuters) sued the company for allegedly misappropriating copyrighted materials to train its AI systems. Westlaw claimed that ROSS unlawfully accessed its proprietary content through a third-party provider. Although ROSS denied the allegations, the lawsuit placed financial pressure on the company, leading to its decision to largely cease operations in December 2020. This case highlights broader issues regarding the use of proprietary data to train AI models in legal tech.

Chapter 12: The Future of Legal Services

As the legal industry continues to evolve, automation and advanced technologies like artificial intelligence (AI) are poised to play an increasingly transformative role. AI, in particular, has the potential to redefine the practice of law, driving new efficiencies, enhancing decision-making, and even challenging the traditional roles of legal professionals. This section explores the future role of AI in the legal profession, speculating on how advances in AI could further disrupt the industry.

Future-Proof: Imagining The State of Legal Services in 2050

Introduction: Imagining the Future of Legal Services

As we look ahead to the year 2050, we envision a legal landscape transformed by the full integration of artificial intelligence (AI) and automation. Today's emerging technologies—tools that streamline tasks like document review, contract drafting, and predictive analytics—will have become essential pillars of legal practice. But this evolution does not signal the decline of the legal profession; instead, it represents a new chapter where lawyers, empowered by technology, deliver more strategic, creative, and client-focused services than ever before.

In this imagined future, AI does not replace human judgment but complements it, automating routine processes while enabling legal professionals to focus on the aspects of their work that demand human insight, empathy, and ethical decision-making. This section explores what legal services may look like in this transformed world: how virtual law firms will operate seamlessly, how lawyers will become proactive risk managers, and how AI will allow them to craft dynamic strategies with unprecedented precision. Welcome to a future where the practice of law is more agile, accessible, and human-centered than ever.

2050: AI-Driven Efficiency and Enhanced Decision-Making

Today, AI handles the majority of routine tasks that once occupied significant portions of a lawyer's time. Document review, legal research, and contract drafting are now automated processes, completed with a speed and accuracy that were unimaginable just a few decades ago. Lawyers no longer spend countless hours poring over documents or sifting through case law—instead, AI systems quickly generate results, allowing legal professionals to focus on high-level analysis and strategy.

Predictive analytics, powered by AI, have become indispensable tools for legal teams. These systems can analyze vast amounts of historical data and social trends to forecast case outcomes with impressive accuracy. Judges' tendencies, jury compositions, and even economic indicators are considered in these predictions, helping lawyers craft strategies that are data-driven and precise. This predictive capacity not only improves case outcomes but also allows clients to make better-informed decisions about pursuing litigation or exploring settlement options.

2050: Risk Management and Proactive Legal Strategy

Law firms in 2050 also play a proactive role in managing legal risks for their clients. AI systems continuously scan contracts, policies, and business practices to identify areas of potential exposure. By flagging issues before they escalate into disputes, lawyers are able to offer a preventative approach to legal counsel, shifting their focus from reactive problem-solving to proactive risk mitigation.

This shift in focus has redefined the role of the lawyer. Legal professionals now serve as strategic advisors, using real-time data to guide business decisions, negotiate favorable outcomes, and manage risks across multiple industries.

2050: The Rise of Virtual Law Firms

The traditional law firm, with its physical offices and large staff, has been largely replaced by the fully virtual law firm. Enabled by cloud-based systems and AI-driven processes, legal professionals now work from anywhere, meeting clients through secure digital platforms. Virtual client portals allow for seamless document sharing, real-time updates, and direct communication between clients and their legal teams. This shift has not only made legal services more accessible to clients but has also allowed firms to reduce overhead costs and increase flexibility.

2050: Ethical Considerations and Human Oversight

While AI handles many aspects of legal practice, the need for human oversight remains critical. Lawyers continue to play a key role in ensuring that AI-driven processes adhere to ethical standards, particularly in areas like client confidentiality and the mitigation of bias in legal decisions. Human judgment is still central to the legal profession, particularly in complex cases where emotional intelligence, empathy, and ethical considerations come into play.

2050: A Human-Centered Future

The integration of AI has not diminished the role of the lawyer—instead, it has enhanced it. By automating routine tasks, AI has allowed legal professionals to focus on what truly matters: developing legal strategies, advising clients, and delivering the personalized, thoughtful counsel that AI cannot replicate. In this new era, law firms are more agile, competitive, and client-focused, proving that the adoption of AI has led to a more efficient and human-centered legal practice.

In 2050, the legal profession is thriving, driven by technologies that support, rather than replace, the skills and expertise that only human lawyers can provide. The future of law is one where AI and human intelligence work hand-in-hand to deliver better outcomes, greater access to justice, and a more dynamic, responsive legal system.

Becoming Future-Proof Lawyers

The Role of AI

Artificial intelligence is already making significant inroads into the legal profession, with applications ranging from document review and legal research to contract analysis and predictive analytics. However, the future of AI in law promises even more profound changes, potentially reshaping how legal services are delivered, how legal decisions are made, and how lawyers interact with both clients and the law itself.

Advances in Predictive Analytics:

Predictive analytics uses AI to analyze historical data and predict future outcomes. In the legal field, this technology is increasingly used to forecast case outcomes, assess litigation risks, and inform legal strategy. As AI technology advances, predictive analytics is likely to become even more sophisticated, offering deeper insights and greater accuracy.

Future Potential:

- **Case Outcome Prediction:** AI could eventually predict case outcomes with a high degree of accuracy, factoring in a broader range of variables, such as judge behavior, jury demographics, and even real-time analysis of social and economic trends. This would allow lawyers to craft more effective strategies, advise clients with greater confidence, and potentially avoid costly litigation by steering clients toward settlement or alternative dispute resolution.
- **Risk Assessment and Mitigation:** Predictive analytics could be used to proactively identify and mitigate legal risks for clients. For example, AI could analyze a company's contracts, policies, and business practices to identify areas of potential legal exposure, recommending changes to minimize risks before they escalate into legal issues.
- **Dynamic Legal Strategy:** AI-driven predictive analytics could enable dynamic legal strategies, where lawyers adjust their approach in real-time based on ongoing analysis of new data. This could include monitoring developments in case law, regulatory changes, or even public sentiment, allowing for more agile and responsive legal representation.

Automated Legal Reasoning:

Legal reasoning—the process of applying legal rules to specific facts to reach a —has traditionally been the domain of human lawyers. However, advances in AI are beginning to enable machines to perform increasingly complex legal reasoning tasks. While AI is not yet capable of fully replicating human judgment, the future may see AI systems that can handle many aspects of legal reasoning, particularly in well-defined areas of law.

Future Potential:

- **AI-Driven Legal Research:** Future AI systems could conduct legal research that goes beyond simply finding relevant cases or statutes. These systems could analyze the nuances of legal language, context, and precedent to provide more sophisticated and contextually relevant insights. Lawyers might receive not just search results but also AI-generated arguments or strategies based on the research.
- **Automated Decision-Making:** In certain areas of law where rules are clear and consistent, AI could be used to automate legal decision-making. For example, in routine administrative law cases, such as immigration applications or social security claims, AI could process applications, apply the relevant law, and issue decisions. This could significantly reduce the backlog in such cases and make the legal system more efficient.
- **AI-Assisted Judgments:** While it is unlikely that AI will replace judges, it could assist in judicial decision-making by providing detailed analyses of case law, predicting the impact of different rulings, and even suggesting possible outcomes based on past decisions. This could help judges make more informed decisions and reduce the time required to deliver judgments.

Ethical and Practical Challenges:

The increasing role of AI in legal practice also raises important ethical and practical challenges. These challenges must be addressed to ensure that AI enhances, rather than undermines, the legal profession and the justice system as a whole.

Key Challenges:

- **Bias and Fairness:** AI systems are only as good as the data they are trained on. If the data reflects historical biases, the AI could perpetuate or even exacerbate these biases. Ensuring that AI systems are fair, transparent, and accountable will be critical as they take on more significant roles in legal decision-making.
- **Client Confidentiality:** As AI systems handle more sensitive legal data, ensuring the confidentiality and security of client

information will be paramount. Firms will need to implement robust cybersecurity measures and develop protocols for AI usage that protect client privacy.
- **Human Oversight:** While AI can enhance legal practice, it should not replace human judgment, particularly in complex or high-stakes cases. Lawyers will need to remain vigilant in overseeing AI-driven processes, ensuring that the final decisions are in the best interests of their clients and comply with legal and ethical standards.

The role of AI in the legal profession is poised to expand dramatically, offering new tools and capabilities that can transform how legal services are delivered. While the potential benefits are significant—ranging from greater efficiency and accuracy to new forms of legal practice—these advances must be carefully managed to address ethical concerns and ensure that AI serves as a tool for justice rather than a source of inequity. As the legal profession navigates this future, the integration of AI will likely become a defining feature of modern legal practice.

Rise of Virtual Law Firms

The legal profession, traditionally rooted in brick-and-mortar offices, is undergoing a significant transformation. The rise of virtual law firms is a key component of this change, driven by advances in technology, shifting client expectations, and the need for greater flexibility and efficiency. Automation plays a crucial role in enabling and accelerating the shift to virtual law firms, providing the tools necessary for remote collaboration, service delivery, and client interaction. This section explores the potential rise of virtual law firms and how automation could facilitate this shift.

Defining the Virtual Law Firm

A virtual law firm operates without a physical office, leveraging technology to provide legal services entirely online. Lawyers, paralegals, and support staff work remotely, often from different locations, while clients access legal services through digital platforms. This model contrasts with the traditional law firm, where in-person meetings and physical document exchanges are the norm.

Key Characteristics:

- **Remote Work Environment:** All firm activities, including client consultations, document preparation, and internal

meetings, are conducted online. Lawyers and staff have the flexibility to work from anywhere, using cloud-based tools and communication platforms.
- **Digital Client Interaction:** Clients interact with the firm through secure online portals, video conferencing, and digital communication channels. Documents are shared and signed electronically, and legal advice is provided through virtual consultations.
- **Automation-Driven Processes:** Many routine tasks, such as document generation, legal research, and case management, are automated. This reduces the need for administrative support and allows the firm to operate efficiently with a leaner team.

Automation as an Enabler of Virtual Law Firms

Automation is a key enabler of the virtual law firm model, providing the technological infrastructure needed to manage remote operations, streamline workflows, and maintain high standards of client service. The following sections explore how specific automation technologies facilitate the rise of virtual law firms.

Cloud-Based Practice Management:

- **Centralized Access:** Cloud-based practice management platforms allow virtual law firms to centralize all case-related information in a secure, easily accessible environment. Lawyers and staff can access case files, calendars, billing information, and client communications from any location, ensuring seamless collaboration.
- **Task Automation:** These platforms often include automation features such as task reminders, document templates, and automated billing processes. This reduces the administrative burden and ensures that tasks are completed on time, even in a remote work setting.
- **Scalability:** Cloud-based systems are highly scalable, allowing virtual law firms to expand their operations easily as their client base grows. Firms can add new users, practice areas, or services without the need for significant infrastructure investments.

Virtual Client Portals:

- **Client Engagement:** Automation enables the creation of secure client portals where clients can access their case files, communicate with their lawyer, upload documents, and track the progress of their case. These portals enhance client engagement and provide a more transparent, interactive experience.
- **Document Automation:** Virtual client portals often integrate with document automation tools, allowing clients to generate and review legal documents through guided workflows. This self-service approach not only improves efficiency but also empowers clients to take an active role in their legal matters.
- **24/7 Accessibility:** Clients can access the portal at any time, providing greater flexibility and convenience. This is particularly valuable for clients in different time zones or with busy schedules, making the virtual law firm an attractive option.

Remote Collaboration Tools:

- **Real-Time Communication:** Automation facilitates real-time communication and collaboration through tools such as video conferencing, instant messaging, and collaborative document editing. These tools enable lawyers and staff to work together effectively, regardless of their physical location.
- **Project Management:** Automation-driven project management tools help virtual law firms manage complex cases involving multiple team members. These tools provide visibility into task progress, deadlines, and resource allocation, ensuring that everyone stays on track.
- **Data Security:** Remote collaboration tools incorporate robust security features, such as encryption and access controls, to protect sensitive client information. This is critical for maintaining client trust and complying with data protection regulations.

Benefits and Challenges of Virtual Law Firms

While the virtual law firm model offers numerous benefits, it also presents unique challenges. Understanding these factors is essential for firms considering the transition to a virtual or hybrid model.

Benefits:

- **Cost Efficiency:** Operating without a physical office significantly reduces overhead costs, including rent, utilities, and office supplies. These savings can be passed on to clients, making legal services more affordable and competitive.
- **Flexibility and Work-Life Balance:** Virtual law firms offer lawyers and staff greater flexibility in their work arrangements, which can lead to improved work-life balance. This flexibility can also attract top talent who value the ability to work remotely.
- **Client Reach:** Virtual law firms can serve clients across a broader geographic area, unrestricted by the need for physical proximity. This expands the potential client base and allows firms to tap into new markets.
- **Sustainability:** The virtual model is more environmentally sustainable, reducing the firm's carbon footprint by minimizing commuting, paper usage, and energy consumption.

Challenges:

- **Maintaining Firm Culture:** Building and maintaining a strong firm culture can be challenging in a virtual environment. Firms need to be intentional about fostering team cohesion, communication, and a sense of belonging among remote workers.
- **Technology Dependence:** Virtual law firms are heavily dependent on technology, which means they must invest in reliable IT infrastructure and cybersecurity measures. Any disruption in technology can impact service delivery and client satisfaction.
- **Client Perception:** Some clients may still value face-to-face interactions and may be hesitant to engage with a law firm that operates entirely online. Virtual firms must work to build trust and demonstrate the effectiveness of their digital services.
- **Regulatory Compliance:** Virtual law firms must navigate the complex regulatory landscape, ensuring compliance with jurisdiction-specific rules regarding the practice of law, data protection, and client confidentiality.

The Future of Virtual Law Firms

As automation and technology continue to advance, the virtual law firm model is likely to become more prevalent. The COVID-19 pandemic accelerated the adoption of remote work and virtual services, and many of these changes are expected to persist. The future of virtual law firms will likely be shaped by ongoing technological innovations, evolving client expectations, and the broader shift toward digital transformation in the legal industry.

Trends to Watch:

- **Hybrid Models:** Many traditional law firms may adopt a hybrid model, combining physical office spaces with virtual services. This approach offers the best of both worlds, providing flexibility while maintaining a physical presence for clients who prefer in-person interactions.
- **AI-Driven Virtual Assistants:** AI-powered virtual assistants could become a standard feature of virtual law firms, handling routine client inquiries, scheduling, and document preparation, further enhancing efficiency and client service.
- **Global Reach:** Virtual law firms will continue to expand their reach globally, leveraging technology to provide cross-border legal services and collaborate with international clients and partners.
- **Customization and Personalization:** As AI and data analytics become more sophisticated, virtual law firms will be able to offer highly personalized legal services tailored to the specific needs and preferences of individual clients.

The rise of virtual law firms represents a significant shift in the legal profession, enabled by automation and other technological advancements. While the virtual model offers numerous benefits, including cost savings, flexibility, and broader client reach, it also presents challenges that firms must address to succeed in this new environment. As the legal industry continues to evolve, virtual law firms are likely to play an increasingly important role, reshaping how legal services are delivered and experienced.

Evolution of Productized Services

Productized legal services—standardized, scalable offerings that deliver specific legal solutions at a fixed price—are transforming how legal services are delivered and consumed. As technology continues to advance and client expectations evolve, the concept of productized services is likely to expand and diversify, giving rise to entirely new legal service models. This section explores how productized services might evolve in the coming years and the potential impact on the legal industry.

Expansion of Productized Service Offerings

As the demand for more accessible, transparent, and cost-effective legal services grows, law firms are likely to expand their productized offerings. This expansion will be driven by advancements in automation, AI, and data analytics, which will enable firms to productize increasingly complex and specialized legal services.

Potential Developments:

- **Industry-Specific Products:** Law firms may develop productized services tailored to specific industries, such as healthcare, technology, or real estate. These offerings could include compliance packages, regulatory updates, or industry-specific contract templates, all designed to address the unique legal needs of particular sectors.
- **Lifecycle Legal Services:** Firms might offer productized services that cover the entire lifecycle of a legal matter, from initial consultation to resolution. For example, a productized divorce service could include everything from the filing of initial documents to final settlement, bundled into a single package with a fixed fee.
- **Bundled Legal Solutions:** Firms could bundle multiple productized services into comprehensive legal solutions that address a range of client needs. For instance, a "Business Formation and Compliance" package might include entity formation, trademark registration, and ongoing compliance monitoring, all delivered as a single, cohesive service.

Example Offering: A law firm specializing in technology startups could offer a "Startup Legal Suite" that includes business formation, intellectual property protection, and employment contracts, all standardized and delivered at a fixed price. This would provide startups with a one-stop legal solution tailored to their specific needs.

Integration of AI and Data Analytics

The integration of AI and data analytics into productized services will drive the evolution of these offerings, enabling more personalized, efficient, and predictive legal solutions. As these technologies mature, they will allow firms to deliver more sophisticated services at scale, further enhancing the value proposition of productized legal services.

Potential Developments:

- **Predictive Legal Services:** AI-driven predictive analytics could be integrated into productized services to provide clients with insights into the likely outcomes of their legal matters. For example, a productized litigation service might include an AI-generated report that predicts the chances of success based on historical data, helping clients make informed decisions about whether to proceed with a case.
- **Personalized Legal Products:** By leveraging data analytics, firms could offer personalized legal products that adapt to the specific circumstances and preferences of each client. For example, a contract review service might automatically highlight clauses of particular concern based on the client's industry, risk tolerance, and previous legal history.
- **Dynamic Pricing Models:** AI and data analytics could enable dynamic pricing models for productized services, where fees are adjusted based on factors such as case complexity, client needs, or market conditions. This would allow firms to offer more competitive pricing while maintaining profitability.

Example Offering: A real estate law firm could develop a productized service that includes AI-driven contract review, which analyzes market trends, local regulations, and historical data to identify potential risks in property transactions. The service could also adjust pricing based on the complexity of the transaction and the level of customization required by the client.

Emergence of New Legal Service Models

The continued evolution of productized services may give rise to entirely new legal service models that break away from traditional legal practice. These models could redefine the client-lawyer relationship, introduce new forms of legal engagement, and expand access to legal services in innovative ways.

Potential Developments:

- **Subscription-Based Legal Services:** Building on the success of subscription models in other industries, law firms might offer subscription-based legal services that provide ongoing access to legal advice, document preparation, and compliance monitoring. Clients would pay a monthly or annual

fee for continuous legal support, rather than engaging with a lawyer on a case-by-case basis.
- **Self-Service Legal Platforms:** Firms could develop self-service legal platforms that allow clients to handle routine legal matters independently, with automated tools guiding them through the process. These platforms would offer standardized legal products, such as wills, contracts, or business agreements, that clients can customize to their needs.
- **Legal Marketplaces:** The future may see the rise of legal marketplaces where clients can purchase productized legal services from multiple providers. These marketplaces would allow clients to compare offerings, read reviews, and select the service that best meets their needs. Legal professionals would compete based on price, quality, and specialization, driving innovation and improving access to legal services.

Example Offering: A consumer rights law firm could offer a subscription-based service for small businesses, providing ongoing legal advice, contract review, and compliance updates. Clients would access these services through an online portal, where they could also purchase additional productized services as needed.

Impact on the Legal Profession

The evolution of productized services will have a profound impact on the legal profession, influencing how lawyers work, how legal services are priced, and how clients interact with the law. As productized services become more prevalent, the role of the lawyer may shift from that of a traditional advisor to that of a service provider, facilitator, or legal technologist.

Potential Impacts:
- **Shift in Lawyer Roles:** Lawyers may increasingly take on roles that involve designing, managing, and improving productized services, rather than providing bespoke legal advice. This shift will require new skills, such as proficiency in legal technology, project management, and data analysis.
- **Increased Competition:** The rise of productized services will likely increase competition in the legal market, as firms compete on price, quality, and innovation. This competition could drive down costs for clients while encouraging firms to continuously improve their offerings.

- **Access to Justice:** Productized services have the potential to greatly expand access to justice by making legal services more affordable and widely available. This could help bridge the gap for individuals and small businesses who might otherwise struggle to access traditional legal services.

Example Offering: A law firm specializing in elder law could develop a self-service platform that allows clients to create customized wills, powers of attorney, and healthcare directives. The platform would use AI to guide clients through the process, offering recommendations based on their personal circumstances and legal needs.

The evolution of productized services represents a significant shift in the legal profession, offering new opportunities for innovation, efficiency, and client engagement. As technology continues to advance, law firms will need to adapt by expanding their productized offerings, integrating AI and data analytics, and embracing new service models. These changes will not only reshape how legal services are delivered but also redefine the role of the lawyer in a rapidly evolving legal landscape.

Chapter 13: Ethical Considerations in Legal Automation

The Case of Risky Predictive Policing Algorithms

In recent years, predictive policing—an AI-driven system designed to predict where crimes are likely to occur—has garnered significant controversy due to its reliance on biased data. One high-profile case occurred in Chicago, where the city adopted a system intended to prevent violent crimes by focusing law enforcement on individuals and neighborhoods deemed at high risk.[51] However, the system relied heavily on historical crime data, which disproportionately targeted minority communities. As a result, it reinforced existing racial biases in law enforcement.[52]

For law firms adopting AI for tasks such as predictive litigation outcomes or automated legal research, this example serves as a cautionary tale. If the data used to train AI tools is biased or incomplete, the AI's output will be similarly flawed. In a legal context, this could lead to biased legal advice, discriminatory hiring practices within firms, or unjust case outcomes.

Ethically, law firms are bound to ensure that automation tools do not perpetuate inequality or discrimination. This means being vigilant

---

[51] Yale Law School Media Freedom and Information Access Clinic, Predictive Policing: AI and Racial Bias Concerns, available at https://law.yale.edu/sites/default/files/area/center/mfia/document/infopack.pdf
[52] American Civil Liberties Union (ACLU), Statement of Concern About Predictive Policing: ACLU and 16 Civil Rights, Privacy, and Racial Justice Organizations, available at https://www.aclu.org/documents/statement-concern-about-predictive-policing-aclu-and-16-civil-rights-privacy-racial-justice

about the sources of data fed into AI systems and regularly auditing algorithms to detect and mitigate bias.

Automation in the legal field brings with it a host of ethical considerations that must be carefully managed to ensure that technological advancements do not compromise the core values of the legal profession. Among these considerations, client confidentiality is paramount. As legal work becomes increasingly automated, safeguarding the privacy and security of client information becomes more complex and challenging. This section delves into the ethical implications of automating legal work with a focus on maintaining client confidentiality.

Client Confidentiality

Client confidentiality is a foundational principle of legal practice, ensuring that all communications between a lawyer and their client are kept private and secure. This principle is not only a professional obligation but also a legal requirement in most jurisdictions. As law firms adopt automation tools—ranging from AI-driven document review systems to cloud-based practice management platforms—the potential risks to client confidentiality increase. It is essential for law firms to navigate these risks carefully, implementing robust security measures and ethical guidelines to protect client data.

Risks to Client Confidentiality in Automation

Automation introduces several potential risks to client confidentiality, primarily related to data security, unauthorized access, and the use of third-party services. These risks must be thoroughly understood and mitigated to ensure that the trust clients place in their legal advisors is not compromised.

Key Risks:

- **Data Breaches:** Automated systems, particularly those hosted on cloud platforms, are susceptible to data breaches. Cyberattacks, hacking, or accidental exposure of sensitive information can lead to unauthorized access to client data, resulting in severe legal and reputational consequences for the firm.
- **Third-Party Involvement:** Many automation tools involve third-party vendors who provide software, cloud storage, or other services. When client data is handled by these vendors, there is a risk that it could be accessed or misused by

unauthorized parties. Ensuring that third-party providers adhere to strict confidentiality standards is critical.
- **Inadequate Security Measures:** Not all automation tools are created equal in terms of security. If a law firm uses a platform that lacks adequate encryption, access controls, or other security features, client data could be vulnerable to interception or unauthorized access.
- **Data Aggregation and AI Processing:** AI systems often require large datasets to function effectively, leading to the aggregation of client data across multiple cases or jurisdictions. This concentration of data can increase the risk of exposure, particularly if the AI system itself is not adequately protected or if the data is used beyond its intended scope.

Example: A law firm using a cloud-based document management system to automate contract reviews might inadvertently expose client information if the system is breached or if the data is accessed by unauthorized users. Even if the breach is accidental, the firm could face legal consequences, including penalties for failing to protect confidential information.

Ethical Obligations in Protecting Client Confidentiality

Lawyers have a duty to protect client confidentiality, and this duty extends to any technology they use in their practice. When automating legal work, firms must take proactive steps to ensure that client information is as secure in digital formats as it is in traditional, physical formats. This involves both selecting the right technologies and implementing stringent security protocols.

Key Ethical Obligations:

- **Due Diligence in Technology Selection:** Before adopting any automation tool, law firms must conduct thorough due diligence to assess its security features, data handling practices, and the reputation of the vendor. This includes ensuring that the tool complies with relevant data protection laws, such as the General Data Protection Regulation (GDPR) in Europe or the California Consumer Privacy Act (CCPA) in the United States.
- **Client Consent:** Firms should inform clients about the use of automation tools, particularly when these tools involve storing or processing data off-site (e.g., in the cloud). Clients should be

made aware of the potential risks and give informed consent before their data is entered into automated systems.
- **Encryption and Access Controls:** All client data stored or processed through automated systems should be encrypted both at rest and in transit. Additionally, firms must implement strict access controls, ensuring that only authorized personnel can access sensitive information. This includes using multi-factor authentication (MFA) and regularly reviewing access logs.
- **Ongoing Monitoring and Auditing:** To maintain client confidentiality, law firms should continuously monitor their automated systems for any signs of unauthorized access or data breaches. Regular security audits can help identify vulnerabilities and ensure that the firm's data protection practices remain robust.

Example: A law firm automating its billing process through a third-party vendor must ensure that the vendor's platform is secure and that client billing information is encrypted. The firm should also provide clients with transparency about how their billing data will be handled and stored, and secure their consent before processing payments through the platform.

Best Practices for Maintaining Confidentiality in Automated Legal Work

To effectively manage the risks associated with automation, law firms should adopt best practices that go beyond the minimum legal requirements. These practices are designed to enhance the security of client data and ensure that the firm's use of technology aligns with ethical standards.

Best Practices:

- **Vendor Contracts and Agreements:** Ensure that all contracts with third-party vendors include robust confidentiality clauses that specify how client data will be handled, stored, and protected. These agreements should also include provisions for auditing the vendor's security practices and obtaining assurance of compliance with industry standards.
- **Regular Training and Awareness:** Law firm staff, including attorneys, paralegals, and IT personnel, should receive regular training on the importance of client confidentiality and the

specific risks associated with automation. This training should cover best practices for data security, recognizing potential threats, and responding to data breaches.
- **Client Data Minimization:** Adopt a principle of data minimization, where only the necessary amount of client data is collected, stored, or processed. This reduces the risk of exposure in the event of a breach and ensures compliance with data protection regulations.
- **Incident Response Planning:** Develop a comprehensive incident response plan that outlines the steps to be taken in the event of a data breach involving client information. This plan should include immediate actions to contain the breach, notification procedures for affected clients, and measures to prevent future incidents.

Example: A law firm specializing in intellectual property might implement a data minimization strategy where only essential client information is uploaded to its automated patent filing system. The firm could also require that all staff undergo annual cybersecurity training to stay updated on the latest threats and best practices for protecting client data.

The ethical obligation to protect client confidentiality is a critical consideration in the adoption of legal automation tools. As law firms increasingly rely on automation to enhance efficiency and service delivery, they must also take proactive steps to ensure that these technologies do not compromise the privacy and security of client information. By conducting thorough due diligence, implementing strong security measures, and adhering to best practices, law firms can leverage automation responsibly while upholding the highest standards of client confidentiality.

Bias in AI

Artificial Intelligence (AI) is increasingly being integrated into legal practice, offering tools that can streamline processes such as document review, legal research, and even decision-making. However, one of the most significant ethical concerns surrounding AI in legal automation is the potential for bias. AI systems, which learn from historical data, can inadvertently perpetuate or even amplify existing biases. This section explores the risks of bias in AI tools used for legal automation, the potential consequences of such bias, and strategies for mitigating these risks to ensure that AI serves to enhance, rather than undermine, fairness and justice in the legal profession.

Understanding Bias in AI

AI systems are trained on large datasets, which they use to make predictions, classify information, or provide recommendations. If the data used to train these systems reflects historical biases—whether based on race, gender, socioeconomic status, or other factors—the AI can replicate and even exacerbate those biases in its outputs. In the legal context, this can have serious implications for the fairness and impartiality of legal processes.

Types of Bias:

- **Data Bias:** This occurs when the data used to train the AI is biased. For example, if historical legal data reflects racial disparities in sentencing, an AI system trained on this data might predict harsher sentences for certain racial groups.
- **Algorithmic Bias:** This occurs when the algorithms themselves are biased, either due to flawed design or the use of biased features. For instance, an AI tool might weigh certain factors more heavily than others, leading to skewed outcomes.
- **Human Bias in Development:** Bias can also be introduced by the humans who design, develop, and implement AI systems. If the developers have unconscious biases, these can be embedded in the system's logic and decision-making processes.

Example: An AI tool designed to predict the likelihood of a defendant reoffending might rely on data that includes previous biased policing practices or judicial decisions. As a result, the tool could unjustly predict higher recidivism rates for minority defendants, influencing bail decisions and sentencing outcomes.

Consequences of Bias in Legal AI Tools

The consequences of bias in AI tools used in the legal profession can be profound, affecting not only individual cases but also broader public trust in the legal system. Understanding these consequences is crucial for developing strategies to mitigate bias and ensure that AI tools are used ethically.

Key Consequences:

- **Unfair Outcomes:** The most direct consequence of biased AI is the potential for unfair legal outcomes. For example, biased AI tools could lead to discriminatory practices in bail decisions,

sentencing, or hiring within law firms, perpetuating inequality and injustice.
- **Erosion of Trust:** The use of biased AI in the legal system can erode public trust in the fairness and impartiality of the law. If people perceive that legal decisions are influenced by biased algorithms, they may lose faith in the justice system's ability to deliver fair outcomes.
- **Legal and Ethical Liability:** Law firms and legal professionals who rely on biased AI tools may face legal and ethical liabilities. They could be held accountable for decisions influenced by biased AI, leading to potential lawsuits, reputational damage, and disciplinary action.

Example: If a law firm uses an AI tool to screen job applicants and that tool disproportionately rejects candidates from certain demographic groups, the firm could face discrimination lawsuits. Beyond legal consequences, such practices could damage the firm's reputation and undermine its diversity and inclusion efforts.

Strategies for Mitigating Bias in Legal AI Tools

To ensure that AI tools are used responsibly in legal practice, law firms and developers must take proactive steps to mitigate bias. These strategies include improving the quality of training data, incorporating fairness checks into AI systems, and maintaining human oversight throughout the AI lifecycle.

Key Strategies:

Data Quality and Diversity:

- **Diverse Datasets:** Ensure that AI systems are trained on diverse datasets that accurately represent different demographic groups and avoid reinforcing historical biases. This might involve sourcing data from multiple jurisdictions, time periods, and case types.
- **Data Audits:** Regularly audit the training data for biases, omissions, or inaccuracies. This includes checking for disproportionate representation of certain groups and ensuring that the data reflects fair and just legal outcomes.

Algorithm Transparency and Fairness Checks:

- **Transparent Algorithms:** Develop AI systems with transparent algorithms that allow for scrutiny and

understanding of how decisions are made. This transparency is crucial for identifying and correcting biased outcomes.
- **Fairness Metrics:** Implement fairness metrics within AI systems to detect and measure bias. For example, firms can use statistical tools to assess whether the AI's predictions or decisions disproportionately affect certain groups.
- **Regular Testing and Validation:** Continuously test and validate AI systems to ensure that they produce fair and unbiased results. This includes running simulations with diverse inputs to see how the AI performs across different scenarios.

Human Oversight and Accountability:

- **Human-in-the-Loop:** Maintain human oversight over AI-driven decisions, particularly in high-stakes legal matters. Lawyers should review AI-generated outputs and ensure that final decisions are made with human judgment, considering the ethical implications.
- **Bias Training for Developers and Users:** Provide training for both AI developers and users on recognizing and mitigating bias. This includes educating them on the ethical risks of biased AI and how to implement safeguards effectively.
- **Accountability Frameworks:** Establish clear accountability frameworks that specify who is responsible for monitoring, addressing, and correcting bias in AI tools. This ensures that there is a process for handling biased outcomes and making necessary adjustments to the AI system.

Example: A law firm using AI for predictive analytics in litigation might implement a fairness check that analyzes whether the AI's predictions differ significantly based on race, gender, or other protected characteristics. If a bias is detected, the firm would adjust the algorithm or retrain the AI on a more balanced dataset to eliminate the bias.

Bias in AI poses a significant ethical challenge in the legal profession, with the potential to undermine fairness, justice, and public trust. However, by understanding the sources and consequences of bias, and by implementing proactive strategies to mitigate it, law firms can use AI tools responsibly and ethically. Ensuring that AI systems are transparent, fair, and subject to human oversight is crucial for integrating these powerful technologies into legal practice without compromising the core values of the legal profession.

Job Displacement

As automation and AI technologies become more integrated into legal practice, concerns about job displacement within the legal profession are increasingly prevalent. These concerns revolve around the potential for automation to reduce the need for certain roles, particularly those involving routine, repetitive tasks. While automation offers significant efficiency gains, it also raises important ethical and practical questions about the future of legal employment. This section addresses the concerns surrounding job displacement, explores the potential impact on different legal roles, and discusses strategies to mitigate the negative effects of automation on the workforce.

Case Study: Baker McKenzie's Response to AI-Driven Job Displacement

Background

Baker McKenzie, a global law firm known for its innovation, has been at the forefront of integrating AI and automation into its legal services. In response to the growing role of AI in handling routine tasks such as document review, e-discovery, and contract analysis, the firm faced the challenge of job displacement, particularly for paralegals and legal assistants whose work traditionally involved these tasks.

Challenge

The introduction of AI-driven tools at Baker McKenzie threatened to displace many legal professionals whose jobs were centered around repetitive, data-heavy tasks. This raised concerns not only about employment but also about how AI could be effectively integrated into the firm without compromising the quality of legal services.[53]

Solution

To address these concerns, Baker McKenzie employed a two-pronged strategy:

- **Reskilling Programs:** The firm invested in training programs that allowed paralegals and legal assistants to learn new skills

---

[53] Baker McKenzie. Responsible AI and the War for Talent. https://www.bakermckenzie.com/en/insight/publications/resources/responsible-ai

related to legal technology and AI management. This enabled many employees to shift into new roles where they could oversee and manage AI tools, ensuring that human judgment remained integral to the legal process.
- **Hybrid Roles:** Employees were transitioned into hybrid positions where they continued to contribute to the firm's operations but in more strategic and supervisory roles. Rather than merely performing repetitive tasks, these roles focused on managing AI systems, maintaining client relationships, and handling tasks requiring human intuition and judgment.

Outcomes

Baker McKenzie's strategy allowed the firm to:

- **Retain Key Talent:** By reskilling employees, Baker McKenzie avoided layoffs, maintaining workforce stability while embracing cutting-edge AI tools.
- **Enhance Efficiency:** The AI tools significantly improved the firm's efficiency in handling large-scale document reviews and contract analyses, allowing human employees to focus on higher-value tasks.
- **Lead Industry Innovation:** The firm's proactive approach earned it recognition, including the AI Innovation Award at the 2022 Legal Innovation Awards[54], highlighting its role as a leader in legal tech adoption.

Conclusion

Baker McKenzie's approach to job displacement due to AI offers a model for balancing technological advancement with workforce management. By investing in reskilling and creating hybrid roles, the firm has successfully integrated AI into its operations without sacrificing the human elements essential to effective legal services.

The Potential for Job Displacement

Automation has the potential to significantly reduce the demand for certain types of legal work, particularly those tasks that are repetitive, time-consuming, and can be easily standardized. Roles that involve

---

[54] Baker McKenzie wins AI Innovation Award at The Legal Innovation Awards 2022. https://www.bakermckenzie.com/en/newsroom/2022/05/ai-innovation-award-2022

document review, data entry, and basic legal research are particularly vulnerable to automation. However, the impact of automation is not uniform across all legal roles, and its effects are likely to vary depending on the nature of the work, the level of expertise required, and the firm's approach to integrating technology.

Key Areas of Impact:

- **Paralegals and Legal Assistants:** These roles are among the most likely to be affected by automation, as they often involve routine tasks such as drafting documents, managing case files, and conducting preliminary research. Automated systems can perform these tasks more quickly and accurately, potentially reducing the need for a large support staff dedicated to these tasks.
- **Junior Associates:** Junior associates in law firms traditionally spend a significant amount of time on tasks like document review, due diligence, and legal research—areas where automation is increasingly making inroads. While automation can free associates from these time-consuming tasks, it may also reduce the opportunities for them to gain experience and develop their skills.
- **Legal Research:** AI-driven legal research tools can process vast amounts of information quickly, potentially reducing the demand for human researchers. These tools can provide more comprehensive and relevant results in less time, but they may also displace roles that focus on traditional research methods.

Example: A large law firm implementing AI-powered document review tools for e-discovery may reduce the number of paralegals needed for large-scale litigation projects. While the firm gains efficiency, the paralegals whose tasks are automated may face job insecurity or the need to transition to new roles.

Ethical Considerations of Job Displacement

The potential for job displacement raises significant ethical concerns, particularly regarding the responsibility of law firms to their employees. As firms adopt automation technologies, they must balance the pursuit of efficiency with the need to support their workforce. Ethical considerations include the duty to provide fair treatment to employees, the impact on career development, and the broader implications for the legal profession.

Key Ethical Issues:

- **Fair Treatment of Employees:** Law firms have an ethical obligation to treat their employees fairly, even as they adopt technologies that may reduce the need for certain roles. This includes providing adequate notice of changes, offering retraining opportunities, and ensuring that displaced workers are supported in transitioning to new roles.
- **Impact on Career Development:** For junior lawyers and support staff, automation can limit opportunities to develop critical skills through hands-on experience. Law firms must consider how to provide alternative pathways for skill development and career advancement in an increasingly automated environment.
- **Social Responsibility:** The legal profession plays a vital role in society, and the widespread displacement of legal workers could have broader social implications. Firms should consider the long-term impact of their automation strategies on employment within the legal sector and explore ways to mitigate negative effects.

Example: A mid-sized law firm decides to automate its contract review process using AI, potentially displacing several paralegals who previously handled this work. The firm's ethical response could include offering these paralegals retraining in other areas, such as legal technology or project management, to help them transition to new roles within the firm.

Strategies for Mitigating Job Displacement

While automation will undoubtedly change the landscape of legal employment, law firms can take proactive steps to mitigate the negative impact on their workforce. These strategies include reskilling and upskilling employees, redefining roles to incorporate new technologies, and creating new opportunities within the firm that leverage human skills in ways that complement automation.

Key Strategies:

Reskilling and Upskilling:

- **Training Programs:** Law firms should invest in training programs that help employees develop new skills that are relevant in an automated environment. This could include training in legal technology, data analytics, or AI tool

management, enabling employees to take on more complex and valuable tasks.
- **Continuing Legal Education (CLE):** Firms can encourage lawyers and support staff to pursue continuing legal education focused on emerging technologies and their applications in legal practice. This ensures that the workforce remains adaptable and capable of working alongside new tools.

Redefining Roles:

- **Hybrid Roles:** As automation takes over routine tasks, firms can redefine roles to focus on tasks that require human judgment, creativity, and client interaction. For example, paralegals might transition to roles that involve managing client relationships, overseeing automated processes, or providing more strategic support to attorneys.
- **Technology Specialists:** Firms can create new roles specifically focused on the integration and management of automation tools. These roles could include positions like legal technologists, who bridge the gap between legal expertise and technological innovation.

Creating New Opportunities:

- **Innovation and R&D Teams:** Establishing teams dedicated to exploring and implementing new technologies can create opportunities for employees to engage in innovative work. These teams can lead the firm's efforts to stay ahead of technological trends and ensure that automation is leveraged to its fullest potential.
- **Client-Facing Roles:** As automation frees up time, firms can encourage lawyers and support staff to focus more on client-facing activities, such as business development, personalized client service, and advisory roles. These activities not only add value to the firm but also provide meaningful work for employees.

Example: A small law firm automates its billing and invoicing process, reducing the workload for its administrative staff. Instead of downsizing, the firm offers these employees training in client management and technology integration, enabling them to take on new roles that support the firm's growth and client engagement efforts.

The Future of Legal Work

The future of legal work will be shaped by the interplay between automation and human expertise. While some traditional roles may diminish, new opportunities will emerge for those who are adaptable and willing to embrace change. Law firms that successfully navigate this transition will be those that recognize the value of both technology and human talent, and that invest in the development of their workforce.

Key Considerations:

- **Balancing Technology and Human Skills:** The most successful law firms will be those that strike a balance between leveraging technology for efficiency and maintaining the human touch that clients value. Automation should be seen as a tool to enhance, not replace, the expertise and judgment that lawyers bring to their work.
- **Fostering a Culture of Innovation:** By fostering a culture of innovation and continuous learning, law firms can ensure that their workforce remains engaged and motivated, even as their roles evolve. Encouraging creativity, flexibility, and a willingness to experiment with new technologies will be key to thriving in the future legal landscape.
- **Emphasizing Ethical Leadership:** As the legal profession undergoes this transformation, ethical leadership will be crucial. Law firms must prioritize the well-being of their employees and the integrity of their practice, ensuring that technological advancements are pursued in a manner that benefits both clients and the legal workforce.

Example: A forward-thinking law firm might establish an innovation hub where lawyers and technologists collaborate on developing new legal products and services. This initiative not only drives the firm's growth but also creates new career paths for employees who are interested in working at the intersection of law and technology.

While automation presents challenges related to job displacement within the legal profession, it also offers opportunities for growth, innovation, and the development of new skills. Law firms have an ethical responsibility to manage the transition to automation in a way that supports their employees, ensuring that they are equipped to thrive in a changing environment. By investing in reskilling, redefining roles, and creating new opportunities, law firms can mitigate the negative impacts of automation and build a more dynamic, adaptable workforce that is prepared for the future of legal work.

Responsible Implementation

As legal automation becomes more prevalent, it is essential to ensure that these technologies are implemented in a manner that upholds the ethical standards of the legal profession. Responsible implementation involves not only leveraging the benefits of automation but also addressing the potential risks and challenges it presents. This section provides guidelines for law firms on how to adopt automation technologies responsibly, with a focus on maintaining ethical integrity, protecting clients, and supporting the legal workforce.

Ethical Guidelines for Automation Adoption

Law firms must establish clear ethical guidelines when adopting automation technologies to ensure that these tools are used in a manner consistent with professional responsibilities. These guidelines should address issues such as client confidentiality, the potential for bias, and the impact on the quality of legal services.

Key Ethical Considerations:

- **Client-Centered Approach:** Automation should be implemented with the client's best interests in mind. This means ensuring that automated tools enhance, rather than detract from, the quality of legal services provided. Lawyers should remain involved in the decision-making process, particularly in complex cases where human judgment is critical.
- **Transparency and Disclosure**: Clients have the right to know when their legal services are being automated. Firms should be transparent about the use of automation tools and ensure that clients understand how these tools will be used in their cases. This includes disclosing any limitations of the technology and ensuring clients are informed about how their data will be handled.
- **Accountability:** Even as tasks become automated, lawyers must remain accountable for the outcomes. This means maintaining oversight of automated processes, regularly reviewing the work produced by AI and other tools, and being prepared to intervene when necessary. The ethical duty to

provide competent representation cannot be delegated to a machine.

Example: A law firm implementing an AI-driven document review system should inform clients that AI will be used to analyze their documents, explain the benefits (such as faster turnaround times), and clarify that a human lawyer will review the AI's findings to ensure accuracy and relevance.

Ensuring Data Security and Privacy

Data security and privacy are critical concerns in the digital age, particularly when it comes to automating legal work. Legal documents often contain sensitive information, and any breach of this data could have serious consequences. Law firms must take proactive steps to protect client data when implementing automation technologies

Key Strategies for Data Protection:

- **Encryption:** All client data processed by automation tools should be encrypted both at rest and in transit. This ensures that even if data is intercepted or accessed without authorization, it cannot be read or used by malicious actors.
- **Access Controls:** Implement strict access controls to limit who can view or interact with client data within automated systems. This includes using multi-factor authentication, role-based access, and regular audits of access logs to detect any unauthorized activity.
- **Vendor Vetting:** When using third-party automation tools, thoroughly vet vendors to ensure they comply with the highest standards of data security and privacy. This includes reviewing their data handling practices, security certifications, and history of data breaches or incidents.
- **Regular Security Audits:** Conduct regular security audits of all automated systems to identify vulnerabilities and ensure compliance with data protection regulations. These audits should include penetration testing, vulnerability assessments, and reviews of incident response plans.

Example: A law firm using a cloud-based case management system should ensure that all client data stored in the cloud is encrypted and that only authorized personnel have access to it. The firm should also regularly audit the system for security vulnerabilities and have a clear protocol for responding to any data breaches.

Balancing Automation with Human Oversight

While automation can significantly enhance efficiency, it is crucial to balance the use of technology with human oversight. Lawyers must remain actively involved in automated processes to ensure that legal work is completed accurately and ethically. Human oversight is particularly important in areas where automation tools may lack the nuance and judgment required to make complex legal decisions.

Key Approaches to Human Oversight:

- **Human-in-the-Loop Systems:** Design automation systems with a "human-in-the-loop" approach, where human lawyers are required to review and approve the outputs generated by AI or other automated tools. This ensures that the final decisions are made by experienced professionals who can apply context and judgment.
- **Review and Quality Assurance:** Establish robust review and quality assurance processes to monitor the outputs of automated systems. Lawyers should regularly check the accuracy, relevance, and completeness of the work produced by these tools, making adjustments as needed.
- **Continuous Learning and Improvement:** Automation tools should be subject to continuous learning and improvement, informed by human feedback. Lawyers should be encouraged to provide input on how automation systems can be enhanced and to report any issues or inconsistencies they encounter.

Example: A law firm using an AI tool to draft legal documents might implement a process where each document generated by the AI is reviewed by a lawyer before being sent to the client. The lawyer would check for accuracy, ensure that the document meets the client's specific needs, and make any necessary revisions.

Supporting the Legal Workforce

As automation transforms the legal profession, law firms have a responsibility to support their workforce through this transition. This includes providing opportunities for reskilling, fostering a culture of continuous learning, and ensuring that employees can adapt to new technologies without fear of obsolescence.

Key Strategies for Workforce Support:

- **Reskilling and Training:** Offer reskilling programs that help employees develop new skills relevant to an automated environment. This might include training in legal technology, project management, data analysis, or other areas where human expertise complements automation.
- **Career Pathways:** Create clear career pathways for employees affected by automation. This could involve transitioning to roles that focus on managing automated systems, client relations, or higher-level legal work that requires human judgment and creativity.
- **Employee Involvement in Innovation:** Involve employees in the innovation process by encouraging them to contribute ideas for how automation can be used effectively within the firm. This helps build buy-in and ensures that the technology is implemented in a way that aligns with the firm's culture and values.

Example: A law firm automating its e-discovery process could offer its paralegals training in managing AI tools and data analysis. This not only helps them transition to new roles within the firm but also ensures that the firm retains their valuable expertise in handling complex legal matters.

Responsible implementation of legal automation requires a thoughtful approach that prioritizes ethical considerations, protects client data, balances technology with human oversight, and supports the legal workforce through change. By adhering to these principles, law firms can leverage the benefits of automation while maintaining the high standards of professionalism and integrity that define the legal profession. As automation continues to reshape the legal landscape, firms that commit to responsible implementation will be best positioned to navigate the challenges and opportunities that lie ahead.

Chapter 14: Marketing and Selling Productized Legal Services

As law firms increasingly adopt productized legal services, effective branding becomes essential to differentiate these offerings from traditional legal services and to capture the attention of potential clients. Branding productized services requires a strategic approach that leverages the principles of e-commerce, where clear messaging, strong brand identity, and an understanding of client needs are critical to success. This section explores key strategies for branding productized legal services, drawing insights from successful branding practices in the e-commerce industry.

Branding Strategies

Branding productized legal services involves creating a distinct identity that resonates with clients and clearly communicates the value of these services. Unlike traditional legal services, which often rely on the reputation of individual lawyers or the firm, productized services require a brand that stands out in a competitive market, is easily recognizable, and appeals to a broad audience. This section outlines strategies for developing a strong brand for productized legal services, using lessons learned from the e-commerce sector.

Define a Unique Value Proposition (UVP)

The foundation of any successful brand is a clear and compelling Unique Value Proposition (UVP). For productized legal services, the UVP should highlight what sets these services apart from both traditional legal offerings and competing productized services. This could include factors such as convenience, affordability, transparency, or specialization in a niche market.

Key Strategies:

- **Focus on Client Needs:** Identify the specific needs and pain points of your target clients and tailor your UVP to address these directly. For example, if your productized service is designed for small businesses, emphasize how it simplifies legal processes, saves time, and reduces costs compared to traditional legal services.
- **Emphasize Efficiency and Predictability:** Many clients value predictability in legal services, particularly when it comes to pricing and timelines. Your UVP should underscore how your productized services offer clear, upfront pricing and faster turnaround times, eliminating the uncertainty often associated with traditional legal billing.
- **Highlight Specialization:** If your productized services cater to a specific industry or legal area, make this specialization a central part of your brand. Specialization not only differentiates your services but also builds trust with clients who need expertise in a particular field.

Example: A law firm offering a productized service for startup legal needs might define its UVP as follows: "Legal solutions for startups, designed to get you up and running quickly with transparent, flat-fee pricing and specialized advice from experienced startup attorneys." This UVP directly addresses the key concerns of startup founders—speed, cost, and expertise.

Develop a Strong Brand Identity

A strong brand identity goes beyond a logo or a tagline; it encompasses the entire visual and verbal representation of your productized services. This identity should be consistent across all touchpoints, from your website and marketing materials to client communications and service delivery. A cohesive brand identity builds recognition and trust, making it easier for clients to connect with your services.

Key Strategies:

- **Visual Branding:** Invest in professional design for your logo, website, and marketing materials to create a cohesive visual identity. The design should reflect the values and professionalism of your productized services, whether that's modern and tech-savvy, or traditional and trustworthy.

- **Consistent Messaging:** Develop a brand voice that aligns with your UVP and resonates with your target audience. Whether your tone is authoritative, approachable, or innovative, it should be consistent across all platforms and communications.
- **Brand Storytelling:** Craft a brand story that explains why your productized services exist and how they benefit clients. This story should be authentic and relatable, helping clients understand the passion and expertise behind your services.

Example: A firm offering productized compliance services might develop a brand identity centered on simplicity and reliability. Their visual branding could include clean, straightforward design elements with a color palette that conveys trust and professionalism. Their messaging might emphasize "Compliance made simple—trust us to keep your business on track with our expert, hassle-free legal services."

Leverage E-Commerce Principles for Branding

The principles of e-commerce offer valuable insights for branding productized legal services. E-commerce brands succeed by making it easy for customers to understand, access, and trust their products. Applying these principles to legal services can help law firms create brands that are client-centric, transparent, and easy to engage with.

Key Strategies:

- **User-Centric Design:** Ensure that your website and digital platforms are designed with the user in mind. Navigation should be intuitive, information should be easy to find, and the purchasing process should be straightforward. Clients should be able to understand your services and make decisions with minimal friction.
- **Clear Product Descriptions:** Just as e-commerce sites provide detailed product descriptions, your productized legal services should be clearly explained. Break down what each service includes, the benefits it offers, and any additional features or options. Transparency in what clients are purchasing builds trust and reduces the potential for misunderstandings.
- **Client Reviews and Testimonials:** In e-commerce, customer reviews are a powerful tool for building credibility. Encourage satisfied clients to leave testimonials that you can feature on your website and marketing materials. Positive

feedback from real clients reinforces the value of your services and helps potential clients feel confident in their choice.

Example: A firm offering flat-fee estate planning services could apply e-commerce principles by creating a dedicated webpage for each service, complete with a clear description of what's included, client testimonials, and a simple "Buy Now" option for immediate purchase. The webpage might also feature a FAQ section to address common questions and provide additional reassurance.

Differentiate Through Personalization

In a competitive market, personalization can be a key differentiator for productized legal services. While the services themselves are standardized, the way they are presented and delivered can be tailored to meet the specific needs of individual clients. Personalization enhances the client experience and creates a stronger connection between the client and your brand.

Key Strategies:

- **Tailored Communication:** Use client data to personalize communications, such as emails and follow-up messages. For example, addressing clients by name and referencing their specific legal needs or previous interactions with your firm can make communications feel more relevant and personal.
- **Customizable Service Options:** Offer clients the ability to customize certain aspects of your productized services. This could include choosing the level of service, adding optional features, or selecting from different pricing tiers. Customization allows clients to feel in control of the process and ensures that the service meets their specific needs.
- **Client Onboarding:** Develop a personalized onboarding process for new clients, where you walk them through the service they've purchased and how it will be delivered. This not only sets clear expectations but also makes clients feel valued and supported from the start.

Example: A firm offering productized business formation services could differentiate itself by offering a personalized onboarding session for each new client, where they discuss the client's business goals and how the firm's services can be tailored to meet those goals. This personalized approach makes the client feel like they are receiving more than just a standardized service.

Branding productized legal services requires a strategic approach that emphasizes a strong unique value proposition, cohesive brand identity, and client-centric design principles. By applying these strategies, law firms can create a distinct and compelling brand that differentiates their services from traditional legal offerings and resonates with clients. Drawing on e-commerce principles, firms can build brands that are accessible, transparent, and trusted, helping them to stand out in a competitive market.

Client Communication

Clients may be unfamiliar with the concept of productized legal services, so it's essential to highlight the specific benefits these services offer compared to traditional legal models. Clear communication of these benefits can help clients see the value in choosing a productized approach.

Key Benefits to Communicate:

- **Predictable Pricing:** One of the most attractive aspects of productized services is their fixed or transparent pricing. Clients appreciate knowing upfront what their legal costs will be, without the uncertainty of billable hours. Emphasize how this pricing structure removes the risk of unexpected legal fees, making budgeting easier for clients.
- **Efficiency and Speed:** Productized services are designed to streamline legal processes, allowing for faster turnaround times. Communicate how automation and standardized procedures enable quicker delivery of legal services, saving clients time and reducing the stress associated with prolonged legal matters.
- **Specialization and Expertise:** If your productized services cater to specific legal needs or industries, highlight your firm's expertise in those areas. Clients value working with professionals who understand their particular challenges and can offer tailored solutions.
- **Transparency and Simplicity:** Explain how productized services simplify the legal process. Clients often find traditional legal services complex and opaque, so emphasizing the straightforward nature of productized services—where each step is clear and understandable—can be a significant selling point.

Example: In client communications, a law firm offering productized intellectual property services might emphasize: "Our flat-fee IP protection services ensure you know exactly what you're paying for—no hidden costs or surprise bills. With our streamlined process, your trademarks and patents are secured quickly and efficiently by experts who specialize in protecting creative and technological innovations."

Educate Clients on How Productized Services Work

Clients may need education on how productized legal services operate, especially if they are used to more traditional models. Providing clear, straightforward explanations of how these services work can help demystify the process and make clients more comfortable with their decision to use them.

Key Educational Points:

- **Step-by-Step Process:** Break down the process of using your productized services into clear, manageable steps. Whether it's how to get started, what to expect during the service, or how deliverables will be provided, clients should understand each stage of the service.
- **Technology Integration:** If your productized services involve the use of technology—such as online portals, automated document drafting, or virtual consultations—explain how these tools enhance the client experience. Assure clients that these technologies are secure, user-friendly, and designed to make their interaction with legal services more efficient and accessible.
- **Client Responsibilities:** Clearly outline what is expected of the client during the process, such as providing necessary documentation or attending virtual meetings. Setting expectations helps clients feel prepared and reduces the likelihood of misunderstandings or delays.
- **Post-Service Support:** Explain what kind of support clients can expect after the service is delivered. This could include follow-up consultations, access to additional resources, or customer service for any questions or concerns that arise. Knowing that support is available can reassure clients and build long-term relationships.

Example: A firm offering productized estate planning services could create an infographic or video that walks clients through the process: "Start by completing our simple online questionnaire. Next, our automated system will generate a draft of your estate plan, which our legal team will review. Finally, you'll receive your completed documents within a week, with the option for a follow-up consultation to discuss any questions."

Use Clear and Accessible Language

Legal jargon can be intimidating and confusing for clients, especially those unfamiliar with the law. When communicating the value of productized services, it's important to use clear, accessible language that resonates with clients and makes the benefits of your services easy to understand.

Key Strategies:

- **Avoid Legalese:** Simplify complex legal terms and concepts whenever possible. Instead of using technical language, explain legal processes in plain English. This approach not only makes your communication more accessible but also builds trust by making clients feel informed and in control.
- **Focus on Client Outcomes:** Rather than getting bogged down in the details of how the service works, emphasize the outcomes clients can expect. For example, instead of explaining the technical aspects of an automated document review process, focus on how it ensures accuracy and saves time.
- **Personalize Communication:** Tailor your messaging to the client's specific needs and concerns. Personalized communication, whether in emails, consultations, or marketing materials, shows that you understand the client's situation and are offering a solution that directly addresses their needs.

Example: When explaining a productized legal service for business formation, a firm might say: "We'll help you start your business quickly and easily. Our service takes care of all the legal paperwork, so you can focus on getting your business up and running. And with our flat-fee pricing, you'll know exactly what to expect—no surprises."

Build Trust Through Transparency

Transparency is key to building trust with clients, particularly when introducing them to a new service model like productized legal services. By being open and honest about what your services entail, how they are priced, and what clients can expect, you can alleviate concerns and foster a strong, trusting relationship.

Key Strategies:

- **Provide Detailed Service Descriptions:** Offer comprehensive descriptions of each productized service, including what is included, what is not, and any potential additional costs. Clients should have a clear understanding of what they are purchasing and what they can expect to receive.
- **Share Case Studies and Testimonials:** Use case studies and client testimonials to demonstrate the effectiveness and reliability of your productized services. Real-world examples of how your services have helped other clients can be a powerful tool for building credibility and trust.
- **Offer Transparent Pricing:** Make your pricing as transparent as possible, with no hidden fees or unexpected costs. If there are variables that could affect the price, explain these clearly so that clients understand how their final cost will be determined.

Example: A firm offering productized employment contract services might include a detailed pricing page on their website, with a breakdown of what's included at each price point: "Our standard employment contract service includes drafting, two rounds of revisions, and final review, all for a flat fee of $500. Need additional customization? We offer add-ons like non-compete clauses for an additional $100."

Engage Clients Through Multiple Channels

Effective client communication involves reaching out to clients through multiple channels to ensure they receive and understand the information you're providing. Different clients may prefer different communication methods, so offering a variety of options increases the likelihood of successfully conveying your message.

Key Channels:

- **Email Marketing:** Use email campaigns to educate clients about your productized services, share success stories, and provide updates or special offers. Emails can be personalized and segmented to target specific client groups with relevant information.
- **Social Media:** Leverage social media platforms to engage with clients, share educational content, and promote your productized services. Social media offers an interactive way to

communicate with clients and can help build a community around your brand.
- **Webinars and Online Workshops:** Host webinars or online workshops to educate clients about your productized services and how they can benefit from them. These events provide an opportunity for clients to ask questions and interact directly with your legal team.
- **Content Marketing:** Create and distribute content that addresses common client concerns and questions about productized services. Blog posts, videos, and FAQs can be valuable resources that help clients make informed decisions.

Example: A firm offering productized family law services might host a free webinar on "Understanding Child Custody Agreements" to educate potential clients about the legal process and how their productized service can simplify it. The webinar would be promoted through email, social media, and the firm's website, with a follow-up email offering attendees a discount on the service.

Communicating the value of productized legal services effectively is essential for building client trust and ensuring successful engagement. By emphasizing the benefits, educating clients on how these services work, using clear and accessible language, and maintaining transparency, law firms can help clients understand and appreciate the value of productized services. Engaging clients through multiple channels further reinforces this communication, ensuring that your message reaches its intended audience and resonates with them.

Digital Marketing

Digital marketing is a powerful tool for reaching new clients and promoting productized legal services. By leveraging online platforms, law firms can increase their visibility, attract potential clients, and build a strong online presence. For legal professionals with little to no experience in digital marketing, understanding the basics of SEO (Search Engine Optimization), content marketing, and social media can make a significant difference in how effectively they can market and sell their services. This section provides a straightforward introduction to these key aspects of digital marketing, focusing on how they can be applied to promote productized legal services.

Search Engine Optimization (SEO)

SEO is the practice of optimizing your website and online content so that it appears higher in search engine results when potential clients search for relevant legal services. A strong SEO strategy can help your law firm attract more visitors to your website, increasing the likelihood of converting them into clients.

Key Concepts:

- **Keywords:** Keywords are the words and phrases that potential clients use when searching for legal services online. For example, if you offer productized estate planning services, relevant keywords might include "affordable estate planning," "flat-fee will preparation," or "online legal services." Incorporating these keywords into your website's content, such as on service pages, blogs, and metadata, can help your site rank higher in search results.
- **On-Page SEO:** On-page SEO involves optimizing the content on your website to make it more search-engine-friendly. This includes using relevant keywords, creating high-quality content that answers common client questions, and ensuring that your site is easy to navigate. On-page SEO also involves optimizing title tags, meta descriptions, and headers, which are key elements that search engines consider when ranking pages.
- **Local SEO:** Local SEO is particularly important for law firms that serve clients in specific geographic areas. This involves optimizing your website to appear in search results for location-based queries, such as "estate planning lawyer in Los Angeles." Key strategies for local SEO include creating a Google My Business profile, listing your firm in local directories, and including location-specific keywords on your website.

Getting Started with SEO:

- **Identify Keywords:** Start by brainstorming a list of keywords that are relevant to your productized services. Think about the terms your potential clients might use when searching for legal help. You can use free tools like Google Keyword Planner or Ubersuggest to find additional keyword ideas.
- **Optimize Your Website:** Incorporate these keywords into the content on your website, focusing on areas like service pages, blog posts, and meta descriptions. Ensure that your

website is easy to navigate and that all pages load quickly, as user experience is also a factor in SEO rankings.
- **Monitor and Adjust:** SEO is an ongoing process. Use tools like Google Analytics and Google Search Console to monitor your website's performance in search results. Pay attention to which keywords are driving traffic to your site, and make adjustments as needed to improve your rankings.

Example: A law firm offering productized immigration services might optimize its website for keywords like "flat-fee immigration lawyer" and "online green card application help." By creating content that addresses common immigration questions and concerns, the firm can attract more potential clients who are searching for these services online.

Content Marketing

Content marketing involves creating and sharing valuable, relevant content to attract and engage potential clients. For law firms, this could include blog posts, articles, videos, or infographics that provide useful information related to the legal services you offer. Content marketing helps establish your firm as an authority in your field, builds trust with potential clients, and improves your SEO rankings.

Key Concepts:

- **Blogging:** A blog on your law firm's website is a great way to share helpful information and demonstrate your expertise. Regularly publishing blog posts on topics related to your productized services can help attract visitors to your site and keep them engaged. For example, if you offer productized contract drafting services, you might write blog posts about common contract pitfalls, tips for small business owners, or the benefits of using a lawyer for contract review.
- **Educational Resources:** Offering free educational resources, such as eBooks, guides, or checklists, can help attract potential clients. These resources should provide valuable information that addresses common legal concerns and guides clients through the process of using your services.
- **Videos and Webinars:** Videos are a highly engaging form of content that can help explain complex legal topics in an accessible way. Consider creating short videos that introduce your services, explain legal concepts, or answer frequently asked questions. Webinars are another effective tool for

engaging with potential clients and providing in-depth information on specific legal topics.

Getting Started with Content Marketing:

- **Identify Topics:** Start by identifying the topics that are most relevant to your productized services and that your potential clients are likely to be interested in. Consider the common questions and concerns your clients have and create content that addresses these issues.
- **Create a Content Calendar:** Plan your content in advance by creating a content calendar. This will help you stay organized and ensure that you're consistently publishing new content. Aim to create a mix of blog posts, videos, and other types of content that can be shared across different platforms.
- **Promote Your Content:** Once you've created content, it's important to promote it so that it reaches your target audience. Share your blog posts on social media, include links to educational resources in your email newsletters, and consider using paid advertising to reach a wider audience.

Example: A law firm specializing in productized family law services might create a blog post titled "5 Common Mistakes to Avoid in Divorce Settlements," a downloadable guide on "How to Prepare for Child Custody Mediation," and a video explaining the benefits of flat-fee divorce services. These content pieces can be shared on the firm's website and social media platforms to attract potential clients and build trust.

Social Media Marketing

Social media platforms are powerful tools for connecting with potential clients, building your brand, and promoting your productized legal services. By maintaining an active presence on platforms like LinkedIn, Facebook, Twitter, and Instagram, you can engage with a wider audience and create a community around your brand.

Key Concepts:

- **Platform Selection:** Not all social media platforms are created equal, and it's important to choose the ones that best align with your target audience. LinkedIn is ideal for connecting with other professionals and promoting business-oriented legal services, while Facebook and Instagram are better for reaching a broader consumer audience. X (formerly Twitter) is

useful for sharing timely updates and engaging in industry conversations.
- **Content Sharing:** Social media is an excellent platform for sharing the content you create through your content marketing efforts. This includes blog posts, videos, and educational resources. Sharing regularly on social media keeps your audience engaged and drives traffic back to your website.
- **Engagement:** Social media is not just about broadcasting your message; it's also about engaging with your audience. Respond to comments and messages, participate in discussions, and show that your firm is approachable and responsive. This interaction helps build trust and strengthens your brand's relationship with potential clients.

Getting Started with Social Media Marketing:

- **Create and Optimize Profiles:** Start by creating profiles on the social media platforms most relevant to your target audience. Ensure that your profiles are complete, with professional branding, clear descriptions of your services, and links to your website.
- **Develop a Content Plan:** Plan your social media content in advance, just as you would with your content marketing. Decide on a posting schedule and the types of content you'll share. This could include blog posts, client testimonials, industry news, and educational videos.
- **Monitor and Adjust:** Use social media analytics tools to monitor the performance of your posts. Pay attention to what types of content get the most engagement and adjust your strategy accordingly. Experiment with different content formats and posting times to see what works best for your audience.

Example: A law firm offering productized employment law services might use LinkedIn to share articles on labor law updates, post client testimonials on Facebook, and create Instagram stories that highlight the benefits of their flat-fee consultation services. The firm could also engage in relevant discussions on Twitter by responding to legal questions and sharing insights.

Digital marketing is an essential component of promoting productized legal services. By understanding and implementing the basics of SEO, content marketing, and social media, law firms can increase their visibility, attract new clients, and build a strong online presence. For those new to digital marketing, starting with these foundational strategies can provide significant returns, helping to differentiate your services in a competitive market and effectively communicate the value of your offerings.

Case Study - Atrium

Atrium was a law firm and legal technology company founded in 2017 by entrepreneur Justin Kan, co-founder video streaming app Twitch, and a team of Silicon Valley veterans. Atrium sought to disrupt the traditional legal industry by offering productized legal services, particularly targeting startups and fast-growing tech companies. The firm's innovative approach combined technology, transparency, and a client-centered focus, which allowed it to rapidly gain traction in a competitive market.

Although Atrium eventually closed its doors in early 2020 due to internal challenges and the complexity of scaling a hybrid legal-tech firm, the strategies it employed in marketing and selling productized services offer valuable insights for other law firms.

Branding and Market Positioning

Strategy: Atrium positioned itself as a tech-savvy, innovative law firm that understood the needs of startups and entrepreneurs. The firm's branding was modern, approachable, and distinctly different from traditional law firms. Atrium emphasized its understanding of the startup ecosystem, presenting itself not just as a legal service provider but as a partner in business growth.

Implementation:

- **Tech-Forward Identity:** Atrium's branding was rooted in the tech world, with a sleek website, modern design elements, and a clear focus on technology-driven solutions. The firm's name, logo, and overall aesthetic were designed to appeal to the tech community, reinforcing the message that Atrium was different from conventional law firms.
- **Value Proposition:** Atrium's unique value proposition was centered on providing predictable, transparent pricing and efficient service delivery, which resonated with startups wary of the traditional billable hour model. The firm offered subscription-based legal services, where clients could access a suite of legal solutions for a flat monthly fee, ensuring cost predictability.

Outcome: Atrium's branding and market positioning helped the firm quickly establish itself as a leader in the productized legal services space, particularly among startups looking for modern, cost-effective legal solutions. The firm attracted high-profile clients, including many venture-backed tech companies.

Digital Marketing and Client Acquisition

Strategy: Atrium leveraged digital marketing strategies to reach its target audience of tech startups and entrepreneurs. The firm utilized content marketing, social media, and SEO to build its online presence and attract potential clients.

Implementation:

- **Content Marketing:** Atrium produced a range of content aimed at educating startups on legal issues. This included blog posts, webinars, and downloadable guides covering topics like fundraising, intellectual property, and startup formation. This content was designed to address the specific legal needs of startups and establish Atrium as a trusted resource.
- **SEO and Online Visibility:** Atrium invested in SEO to ensure that its content ranked highly on search engines. The firm identified key search terms relevant to its target audience, such as "startup legal services" and "venture capital legal advice," and optimized its website and content accordingly. Atrium's digital presence was further enhanced by a well-maintained blog and active social media channels.
- **Social Media Engagement:** Atrium used platforms like LinkedIn, Twitter, and Facebook to engage with its audience, share content, and promote its services. The firm's social media strategy focused on providing value through educational content and engaging with the startup community through discussions and events.

Outcome: Atrium's digital marketing efforts successfully attracted a steady stream of clients. The firm's focus on content marketing and SEO helped it dominate search results for relevant legal queries, driving traffic to its website and converting visitors into clients. Social media engagement further amplified its reach, connecting Atrium with a broader audience of potential clients.

Productization of Legal Services

Strategy: Atrium's core innovation was the productization of legal services, offering standardized, subscription-based packages that provided startups with a range of legal solutions for a flat fee. This approach was designed to simplify legal services and make them more accessible to startups with limited budgets and a need for predictable costs.

Implementation:

- **Subscription Model:** Atrium offered a subscription service called "Atrium Counsel," where clients paid a flat monthly fee for ongoing access to legal advice and services. This package included services like corporate governance, employment law, and contract review, all bundled into a single, predictable payment.
- **Automated Processes:** To streamline service delivery, Atrium developed proprietary technology that automated many routine legal tasks, such as document drafting and compliance monitoring. This allowed the firm to deliver services more efficiently and at a lower cost, which was passed on to clients through competitive pricing.
- **Client Portal:** Atrium provided clients with an online portal where they could access their legal documents, communicate with their legal team, and manage their legal needs. This transparency and accessibility were key selling points for clients who valued convenience and real-time access to information.

Outcome: Atrium's productized legal services were well-received by the startup community, which valued the simplicity, transparency, and cost-effectiveness of the subscription model. The firm's ability to deliver high-quality legal services at a predictable price point made it an attractive option for fast-growing companies.

Client Communication and Education

Strategy: Atrium placed a strong emphasis on client communication and education, ensuring that clients understood the value of its productized services and felt confident in their decision to use them. The firm used a combination of personalized communication, educational resources, and responsive customer service to build strong client relationships.

Implementation:

- **Onboarding Process:** Atrium developed a streamlined onboarding process for new clients, which included an initial consultation to understand the client's needs and a walkthrough of how the subscription service worked. This process was designed to set clear expectations and ensure that clients knew exactly what they were getting.
- **Educational Resources:** Atrium provided clients with access to a wealth of educational resources, including articles, webinars, and tutorials on common legal issues faced by startups. These resources were available through the client portal and were designed to help clients navigate the legal aspects of growing their business.
- **Ongoing Support:** Atrium's legal team maintained regular communication with clients, offering ongoing support and advice as part of the subscription service. Clients could easily reach their attorneys through the portal, ensuring that they received timely responses to their questions and concerns.

Outcome: Atrium's focus on client communication and education helped build trust and loyalty among its clients. By providing clear, accessible information and maintaining open lines of communication, the firm was able to differentiate itself from more traditional law firms and create a strong, client-centered brand.

Atrium's approach to marketing and selling productized legal services offers valuable lessons for law firms looking to innovate and reach new clients. By combining a strong brand identity with effective digital marketing strategies, a client-focused productization model, and a commitment to communication and education, Atrium was able to carve out a niche in the competitive legal market. While the firm ultimately faced challenges in scaling its model, its initial success demonstrates the potential of productized legal services to meet the needs of modern clients in an increasingly digital world.

Playbook: Marketing and Selling Productized Legal Services for Law Firms

This playbook provides a structured approach for law firms to effectively market and sell productized legal services. By following these steps, firms can establish a strong brand identity, communicate the value of their services, and reach potential clients through strategic digital marketing efforts. A sample 12-month timeline is included to guide implementation.

Step 1: Defining the Unique Value Proposition (UVP) (Weeks 1-2)

Goal: Develop a clear and compelling UVP that distinguishes your productized legal services from traditional legal offerings.

Research Client Pain Points:

- Conduct surveys, interviews, or research to identify your clients' most pressing needs. Focus on what they value most: affordability, efficiency, or specialization.

Develop UVP:

- Create a UVP that emphasizes how your productized services solve specific client problems. Examples of key selling points include:
  - Transparency (clear, fixed pricing),
  - Efficiency (faster turnaround times),
  - Expertise (industry-specific legal advice).

Example: A firm offering productized startup legal services could have the UVP: "Legal solutions designed to launch your startup quickly, with flat-fee pricing and specialized advice from expert startup attorneys."

Step 2: Building Brand Identity

Goal: Establish a cohesive brand that resonates with your target audience and clearly reflects the values of your productized legal services.

Create Visual Branding:

- Hire professional designers to create a logo, color palette, and website that align with your brand values. Keep the design simple, professional, and trustworthy.

Craft Messaging:

- Develop consistent messaging across all touchpoints. Your tone should match your target clients—whether it's authoritative, approachable, or innovative.

Storytelling:

- Craft a brand story that explains your passion for creating productized services and how they benefit clients.

Example: A compliance-focused firm might brand itself around "efficiency and simplicity," using a clean design and messaging like, "We make compliance easy and hassle-free, so you can focus on growing your business."

Step 3: Implement E-Commerce Principles

Goal: Make your productized services accessible and easy to understand, using e-commerce principles to drive conversion.

User-Centric Design:

- Build a user-friendly website with intuitive navigation and clear calls-to-action (CTAs) like "Buy Now" or "Get Started." Ensure clients can quickly find service descriptions, pricing, and FAQs.

Clear Product Descriptions:

- Break down each productized service with straightforward descriptions of what's included, pricing, and benefits. Be transparent about what the client will receive.

Client Reviews and Testimonials:

- Display client reviews prominently on your website. Positive testimonials build trust and credibility.

Example: A firm offering flat-fee estate planning services could have dedicated pages for each service, complete with testimonials, FAQ sections, and a simple checkout process.

Step 4: Personalize Client Experience

Goal: Differentiate your services through personalization to enhance client engagement and satisfaction.

Tailor Communications:

- Use CRM tools to segment your email lists based on client needs, sending personalized follow-up messages and offers that resonate with each group.

Customizable Service Options:

- Allow clients to select from different service tiers or add-ons. Customization gives clients a sense of control over their legal service experience.

Client Onboarding:

- Develop a personalized onboarding process that welcomes new clients and sets clear expectations. This could include a welcome email series or an introductory call.

Example: A firm offering productized business formation services could provide clients with an onboarding consultation where they discuss business goals and how the service will be tailored to meet those needs.

Step 5: Educate Clients on Productized Services

Goal: Demystify productized services by educating clients about how they work, what to expect, and their specific benefits.

Create Educational Content:

- Develop videos, infographics, and blogs that explain how your services work and what the client's role will be during the process.

Step-by-Step Process:

- Offer clear, visual guides or videos that walk clients through the legal service delivery process, from onboarding to completion.

Post-Service Support:

- Clearly outline what support is available after service completion, whether through follow-up consultations or customer service.

Example: A firm offering automated document review services might create a video explaining the process: "Complete our online questionnaire, and receive a custom-reviewed document in 24 hours."

Step 6: Launch a Digital Marketing Strategy

Goal: Use SEO, content marketing, and social media to attract and engage potential clients.

SEO:

- Optimize your website for relevant keywords like "flat-fee estate planning" or "online business formation services." Implement on-page SEO tactics like optimized metadata and user-friendly design.

Content Marketing:

- Create blog posts, videos, and educational resources that address common client pain points and explain the benefits of productized legal services. Regularly update your content to keep it relevant.

Social Media:

- Build a presence on LinkedIn, Facebook, and Instagram. Share educational content, client testimonials, and promotional offers to drive traffic to your website.

Example: A firm specializing in employment law might write blogs on "5 Common Employment Contract Mistakes" and share them on LinkedIn and Twitter, leading readers to explore their flat-fee services.

Sample Timeline for Marketing Productized Legal Services

Week	Milestone	Actions
1-2	Define Unique Value Proposition (UVP)	Research client needs, develop clear UVP.
2-4	Build Brand Identity	Design logos, websites, create brand messaging and storytelling.
4-6	Implement E-Commerce Principles	Design website with clear product descriptions, testimonials, and easy CTAs.
6-8	Personalize Client Experience	Create tailored communications, customizable options, and onboarding plans.
8-10	Educate Clients	Develop educational content, step-by-step guides, and client support systems.
10-12	Launch Digital Marketing Strategy	Implement SEO changes, post content and social marketing posts.

Continuous Improvement (Post Launch)

Monitor Results: Track metrics like website traffic, client conversion rates, and client satisfaction scores.

Refine Marketing Strategy: Based on client feedback and analytics, tweak your messaging, service offerings, or digital marketing efforts to maximize impact.

Scale Marketing Efforts: After a successful launch, consider expanding your marketing budget or launching targeted advertising campaigns to reach new audiences.

By following this playbook, law firms can successfully market and sell their productized legal services, using a strategic approach that combines branding, education, and digital marketing to drive client engagement and growth

Chapter 15: Measuring Success and Scaling Automation

Successfully implementing workflow automation in a law firm is only the first step. To ensure that these initiatives deliver the desired outcomes, it is crucial to measure their success through key metrics, gather client feedback, and strategically scale automation across the firm. This section focuses on the key metrics that law firms can use to assess the effectiveness of their automation efforts, helping them make data-driven decisions and continuously improve their processes.

Key Metrics for Success

Measuring the success of workflow automation requires a clear understanding of which metrics best capture the value and impact of these initiatives. The right metrics will vary depending on the firm's goals, but generally, they should include financial performance, operational efficiency, and client satisfaction. This section outlines the key metrics that law firms should track to evaluate the success of their automation initiatives.

Return on Investment (ROI)

ROI is a critical metric for assessing the financial success of automation projects. It measures the financial return generated by the automation investment relative to the cost of implementation. A positive ROI indicates that the automation initiative is delivering more value than it costs, making it a worthwhile investment.

How to Calculate ROI:

Initial Investment: Start by calculating the total cost of implementing the automation, including software purchases, integration costs, training, and any associated expenses.

- **Financial Benefits:** Measure the financial benefits resulting from automation. These can include cost savings from reduced labor, increased revenue from handling more cases or clients, and any other financial gains directly attributable to the automation.
- **ROI Formula:** Use the following formula to calculate ROI:

$$ROI = \left(\frac{\text{Total Financial Benefits} - \text{Initial Investment}}{\text{Initial Investment}} \right) \times 100$$

Example: A law firm invests $50,000 in a document automation system that reduces the time attorneys spend on drafting by 40%. As a result, the firm can take on 20% more cases, leading to an additional $100,000 in revenue. The ROI would be calculated as:

$$ROI = \left(\frac{100{,}000 - 50{,}000}{50{,}000} \right) \times 100 = 100\%$$

This indicates that the automation project has doubled the firm's investment, making it a successful initiative.

Time Savings and Efficiency Gains

One of the primary goals of automation is to improve efficiency by reducing the time spent on routine tasks. Measuring time savings helps firms quantify these efficiency gains and assess how well automation is improving workflow processes.

Key Metrics:

- **Task Completion Time:** Track the average time it takes to complete specific tasks before and after automation. Significant reductions in time indicate that automation is working effectively.
- **Throughput:** Measure the number of tasks or cases handled within a given time frame. An increase in throughput after implementing automation suggests that the firm can handle more work without additional resources.

- **Resource Utilization:** Analyze how staff time is allocated across different activities. Automation should free up time for attorneys and staff to focus on higher-value tasks, such as client consultations and strategic planning.

Example: A firm automates its client intake process, reducing the time required to onboard a new client from 2 hours to 30 minutes. If the firm handles 100 new clients per month, this results in a time savings of 150 hours per month, which can be redirected to more productive activities.

Client Satisfaction and Experience

Client satisfaction is a crucial metric for evaluating the success of automation, as it directly impacts client retention and referrals. Automation should enhance the client experience by providing faster, more accurate, and more transparent services.

Key Metrics:

- **Client Satisfaction Scores:** Use surveys or feedback forms to gather client satisfaction scores before and after implementing automation. Look for improvements in areas such as responsiveness, accuracy, and overall service quality.
- **Net Promoter Score (NPS):** NPS measures the likelihood of clients recommending your firm to others. A higher NPS after automation indicates that clients are more satisfied with the services they received.
- **Turnaround Time:** Track the time it takes to deliver legal services to clients. Faster turnaround times, resulting from automation, are often correlated with higher client satisfaction.

Example: After automating its contract review process, a firm surveys its clients and finds that 90% are "very satisfied" with the faster service, compared to 70% before automation. The firm also sees an increase in NPS from 60 to 75, indicating a higher likelihood of client referrals.

Error Rates and Quality of Work

Automation is expected to reduce human error and improve the consistency and quality of legal work. Monitoring error rates and quality metrics helps firms ensure that automation is achieving these objectives.

Key Metrics:

- **Error Rate:** Track the frequency of errors in automated tasks compared to manual processes. A significant reduction in errors indicates that automation is improving accuracy.
- **Quality Control Audits:** Regularly audit the work produced by automated systems to ensure it meets the firm's quality standards. This includes checking for compliance with legal requirements, accuracy of documentation, and consistency in output.
- **Client Complaints:** Monitor the number and nature of client complaints related to the quality of services. A decrease in complaints after implementing automation suggests that the quality of work has improved.

Example: A firm automates its document drafting process, which reduces the error rate from 5% to 1%. This improvement leads to fewer revisions and client complaints, enhancing the overall quality of legal services.

Cost Savings

Cost savings are a direct measure of the financial efficiency gained through automation. By reducing labor costs, minimizing the need for physical resources, and improving operational efficiency, automation can significantly lower the overall costs of providing legal services.

Key Metrics:

- **Labor Cost Reduction:** Calculate the reduction in labor costs by comparing the number of hours worked before and after automation. This includes savings from reduced overtime, lower administrative costs, and potentially fewer staffing needs.
- **Operational Costs:** Measure the decrease in operational costs, such as reduced paper usage, lower office supply expenses, and decreased physical storage needs. Automation often leads to a more digital and less resource-intensive workflow.
- **Overhead Expenses:** Track changes in overhead expenses, including rent, utilities, and maintenance, particularly if automation enables more remote work or less reliance on physical office space.

Example: After implementing a cloud-based case management system, a firm reduces its reliance on physical storage, cutting its office space requirements by 25%. This reduction results in significant savings on rent and utilities, contributing to overall cost savings.

Measuring the success of workflow automation through key metrics like ROI, time savings, client satisfaction, error rates, and cost savings allows law firms to quantify the impact of their automation initiatives. These metrics provide valuable insights into how well automation is working, highlight areas for improvement, and help firms make informed decisions about future investments in technology. By tracking these metrics consistently, law firms can ensure that their automation efforts are delivering real value and driving continuous improvement.

Gathering Client Feedback

Client feedback is a crucial component of any successful legal automation initiative. Understanding how clients perceive and experience your automated services allows your firm to make informed adjustments, improve service quality, and ensure that your offerings align with client expectations. This section discusses effective methods for gathering and analyzing client feedback, focusing on how to use this information to refine and enhance your automated services.

Importance of Client Feedback

Client feedback provides direct insights into how your automated services are performing from the user's perspective. It highlights strengths, identifies areas for improvement, and uncovers potential issues that may not be immediately apparent through internal metrics alone. By actively seeking and acting on client feedback, your firm can maintain high levels of client satisfaction, improve service delivery, and strengthen client relationships.

Benefits of Gathering Client Feedback:

- **Service Improvement:** Feedback helps identify specific aspects of your automated services that may need refinement, whether it's usability, accuracy, or turnaround time.
- **Client Retention:** Regularly engaging with clients and addressing their concerns fosters loyalty and encourages long-term relationships.
- **Innovation:** Client suggestions can lead to innovative ideas for new features or services that better meet their needs.

- **Competitive Advantage:** Firms that actively gather and respond to feedback can differentiate themselves by offering a more client-centric service experience.

Methods for Gathering Client Feedback

There are various methods for collecting client feedback, each with its strengths. The most effective approach often involves using a combination of these methods to gather comprehensive insights from your client base.

Key Methods:

Surveys:

- **Post-Service Surveys:** After completing a legal service, send clients a short survey to assess their satisfaction with the process. These surveys can ask about specific aspects of the service, such as ease of use, communication, and overall satisfaction.
- **Ongoing Surveys:** For subscription-based or ongoing services, consider periodic surveys to gauge client satisfaction over time. This approach helps track changes in client perceptions and identify any emerging issues.
- **Net Promoter Score (NPS):** NPS surveys ask clients how likely they are to recommend your services to others, providing a clear metric of overall satisfaction and loyalty.

Example Questions:

"How satisfied were you with the speed of our service?"

"How would you rate the ease of use of our online platform?"

"On a scale of 1-10, how likely are you to recommend our services to a colleague?"

One-on-One Interviews:

- **In-Depth Feedback:** Conducting interviews with selected clients allows for deeper insights into their experiences. These conversations can reveal nuanced opinions and suggestions that might not surface in a survey.
- **Focus Groups:** Organize focus groups with multiple clients to discuss their experiences with your services. This method

encourages discussion and can lead to valuable insights into common client needs and expectations.

Example: After launching a new automated contract review service, a firm might conduct one-on-one interviews with a few key clients to understand how the service met their expectations and where it could be improved. The firm could then use this feedback to make targeted enhancements.

Feedback Forms:

- **Website Forms:** Incorporate feedback forms directly on your website or client portal, allowing clients to provide feedback at any time. These forms can be as simple as a single question or a more detailed survey, depending on what information you seek.
- **Service Completion Forms:** After a client completes a task, such as downloading a document or finalizing a contract, prompt them to fill out a quick feedback form. This immediate feedback is often more accurate and relevant since the experience is fresh in the client's mind.

Example: A law firm might include a feedback form at the end of an automated will preparation service, asking clients to rate their satisfaction and suggest any improvements.

Client Advisory Boards:

- **Engaged Clients:** Form a client advisory board composed of a diverse group of clients who regularly use your automated services. This board can provide ongoing feedback, participate in beta testing new features, and offer strategic advice from the client's perspective.
- **Regular Meetings:** Hold regular meetings with the advisory board to discuss new developments, gather feedback on recent changes, and explore ideas for future services.

Example: A firm specializing in productized business legal services might create an advisory board with representatives from various industries. These clients could provide valuable feedback on how the firm's services align with industry-specific needs.

Analyzing Client Feedback

Once you've gathered client feedback, the next step is to analyze it effectively to identify trends, common concerns, and areas for improvement. This analysis helps turn raw feedback into actionable insights that can drive enhancements to your automated services.

Key Steps in Analyzing Feedback:

Categorize Feedback:

- **Sort by Topic:** Organize feedback into categories based on the aspects of the service discussed, such as usability, speed, accuracy, communication, and pricing. This makes it easier to identify patterns and areas that need attention.
- **Identify Common Themes:** Look for recurring themes in the feedback. Are multiple clients mentioning the same issue or suggesting similar improvements? These common themes should be prioritized for action.

Example: A firm might find that several clients have mentioned difficulties navigating their online portal. By categorizing and analyzing this feedback, the firm can identify the specific pain points and take steps to simplify the portal's user interface.

Quantitative Analysis:

- **Survey Metrics:** Use metrics from surveys, such as average satisfaction scores or NPS, to quantify the feedback. Tracking these metrics over time can help measure the impact of any changes you make in response to client feedback.
- **Trend Analysis:** Compare feedback over different periods or after implementing changes to see how client perceptions have evolved. A positive trend indicates that your improvements are having the desired effect.

Example: If a firm's NPS score increases after making changes based on client feedback, this suggests that the changes were well-received and improved client satisfaction.

Qualitative Analysis:

- **Detailed Review:** For open-ended feedback, such as comments from interviews or feedback forms, conduct a detailed review to understand the specific issues or

suggestions being made. This qualitative analysis can provide deeper insights into client needs and expectations.
- **Sentiment Analysis:** If you have a large volume of feedback, consider using sentiment analysis tools to assess the overall tone of the feedback. This can help quickly gauge whether clients feel positively or negatively about your services.

Example: A firm might use sentiment analysis to quickly assess client comments from a survey, identifying any negative trends that require further investigation and action.

Using Feedback to Improve Services

The ultimate goal of gathering and analyzing client feedback is to use it to improve your automated services. Acting on feedback not only enhances service quality but also demonstrates to clients that you value their input and are committed to meeting their needs.

Key Strategies:

Implement Changes:

- **Prioritize Actions:** Based on the analysis, prioritize the changes that will have the most significant impact on client satisfaction. This might involve improving a specific feature, addressing a common complaint, or adding a new service that clients have requested.
- **Iterative Improvements:** Treat service improvement as an ongoing process. Implement changes incrementally, test them with clients, and gather feedback on the changes to ensure they are effective.

Example: If multiple clients suggest adding a live chat feature to your online portal, the firm could prioritize this enhancement, test it with a small group of clients, and refine it based on their feedback before rolling it out to all users.

Communicate Updates:

- **Inform Clients:** When you make improvements based on client feedback, communicate these updates to your clients. This could be through email newsletters, announcements on your website, or directly within your client portal.
- **Highlight Client Contributions:** Acknowledge the role of client feedback in driving these improvements. This not only shows

that you value their input but also encourages more clients to share their thoughts in the future.

Example: After updating its document automation system to address client concerns about ease of use, a law firm might send an email to all clients explaining the changes and thanking them for their valuable feedback.

Measure Impact:

- **Follow-Up Surveys:** After implementing changes, use follow-up surveys to measure their impact on client satisfaction. Compare these results to the initial feedback to assess whether the changes have successfully addressed the issues.
- **Client Retention:** Monitor client retention rates before and after making improvements. An increase in retention suggests that the changes have had a positive effect on client loyalty and satisfaction.

Example: A firm that improves its client onboarding process based on feedback might see an increase in repeat business from satisfied clients, indicating that the changes were successful.

Gathering and analyzing client feedback is essential for continuously improving your automated legal services. By using a combination of surveys, interviews, feedback forms, and advisory boards, law firms can gain valuable insights into client experiences and make informed decisions about how to enhance their offerings. Acting on feedback not only improves service quality but also builds stronger client relationships and fosters a culture of continuous improvement. Ultimately, this commitment to client-centric service will help your firm stand out in a competitive market and ensure long-term success.

Scaling Across the Firm

After successfully implementing workflow automation in one area of your law firm, the next step is to scale these efforts across multiple practice areas or the entire organization. Scaling automation requires a strategic approach to ensure that the benefits realized in one part of the firm can be replicated and even enhanced elsewhere. This section provides strategies for effectively scaling automation, addressing common challenges, and ensuring that the expansion of automation initiatives is smooth and successful.

Assessing Scalability of Existing Automation Solutions

Before scaling automation across the firm, it is crucial to evaluate whether the existing solutions are scalable and adaptable to other practice areas. Not all automation tools or processes will be directly transferable, so this assessment helps identify which aspects of the current system can be expanded and what modifications might be needed.

Key Considerations:

- **Tool Compatibility:** Determine whether the automation tools currently in use are compatible with the workflows and requirements of other practice areas. This includes assessing the flexibility of the software, its ability to handle different types of legal work, and whether it can integrate with other systems used in the firm.
- **Process Adaptability:** Evaluate how easily the automated processes can be adapted to new practice areas. Consider whether the workflows, document templates, and automated tasks are specific to one area of law or if they can be modified to fit the needs of other departments.
- **Resource Requirements:** Assess the resources needed to scale the automation, including additional software licenses, training, and IT support. Ensure that the firm has the capacity to handle these requirements without disrupting ongoing operations.

Example: A firm that has successfully automated its contract review process in the corporate law department might assess whether the same tools and processes can be adapted for use in real estate law, where contract review is also a common task. This assessment would include evaluating the specific needs of real estate contracts and determining if the existing automation tools can accommodate them.

Building a Scalable Automation Framework

Creating a scalable automation framework involves establishing standardized processes, tools, and guidelines that can be applied across multiple practice areas. This framework ensures consistency in how automation is implemented and managed throughout the firm, making it easier to expand efforts without starting from scratch each time.

Key Components:

- **Standardized Processes:** Develop standardized workflows that can be customized for different practice areas. This might include common steps such as document drafting, client communication, and case management. Standardization helps maintain consistency and quality across the firm while allowing for flexibility where needed.
- **Centralized Automation Tools:** Use centralized automation tools that can be accessed and utilized by multiple departments. A unified platform for document management, case tracking, and client intake ensures that all practice areas benefit from the same technological advantages, and it simplifies training and support.
- **Automation Governance:** Establish a governance structure for managing automation initiatives across the firm. This includes creating policies for how automation tools are selected, implemented, and maintained, as well as defining roles and responsibilities for overseeing these efforts.

Example: A law firm might implement a centralized document automation platform that all departments use for generating legal documents. While each department might have specific templates and requirements, the underlying technology and processes are consistent, ensuring that all areas of the firm benefit from the efficiencies of automation.

Pilot Projects and Gradual Rollout

Scaling automation across a firm is best done incrementally, starting with pilot projects in new practice areas before a full-scale rollout. This approach allows the firm to test the scalability of automation solutions, gather feedback, and make necessary adjustments before broader implementation.

Key Steps:

- **Identify Pilot Areas:** Select practice areas where automation is likely to have the most significant impact or where there is a strong need for process improvement. These areas should also be open to adopting new technologies and have the resources to support a pilot project.
- **Customize and Test:** Customize the existing automation tools and workflows for the selected practice area, and run a

pilot project to test their effectiveness. Monitor key metrics, such as time savings, error rates, and client satisfaction, to evaluate the success of the pilot.
- **Gather Feedback:** Collect feedback from the teams involved in the pilot project to understand what worked well and what challenges were encountered. Use this feedback to refine the automation processes and tools before rolling them out to additional practice areas.
- **Plan the Rollout:** Based on the results of the pilot, develop a plan for gradually rolling out the automation across the firm. This plan should include timelines, resource allocation, and training programs to ensure that each practice area is fully prepared for the transition.

Example: A firm might start by piloting its new automated litigation support tools in the employment law department, where document-heavy cases are common. After a successful pilot, the firm could then roll out the tools to the commercial litigation department, using lessons learned from the pilot to refine the implementation process.

Training and Support for Scaling

As automation is scaled across the firm, providing comprehensive training and ongoing support is essential to ensure that all staff members are comfortable with the new tools and processes. Effective training programs help minimize resistance to change, increase adoption rates, and ensure that automation delivers its full potential benefits.

Key Strategies:

- **Tailored Training Programs:** Develop training programs tailored to the specific needs of each practice area. This might include hands-on workshops, online tutorials, and one-on-one coaching sessions. The training should cover both the technical aspects of using the automation tools and the practical application in the context of each department's work.
- **Change Management:** Implement change management strategies to help staff transition to the new automated processes. This includes clear communication about the benefits of automation, addressing any concerns or resistance, and providing support throughout the transition.
- **Ongoing Support:** Establish a dedicated support team to assist with technical issues, provide refresher training, and help

staff optimize their use of automation tools. Regular check-ins and follow-up sessions can help ensure that the automation is being used effectively and that any issues are promptly addressed.

Example: When scaling automation to the firm's family law department, the firm might develop a specialized training program that focuses on how to use the automated case management system for handling sensitive client information and managing court deadlines. The program would include both in-person workshops and online resources that staff can access as needed.

Monitoring and Continuous Improvement

Even after automation has been successfully scaled across the firm, it's important to continually monitor its performance and make ongoing improvements. Regularly reviewing key metrics, gathering feedback, and staying informed about new technologies will help the firm maintain high levels of efficiency and service quality.

Key Activities:

- **Regular Performance Reviews:** Schedule regular reviews of the automation initiatives across all practice areas. These reviews should include an analysis of key metrics, such as efficiency gains, cost savings, and client satisfaction, as well as an assessment of any challenges or areas for improvement.
- **Feedback Loops:** Continue to gather feedback from staff and clients on how the automated services are performing. Use this feedback to identify opportunities for further enhancements and to address any ongoing issues.
- **Stay Updated on Technology:** Keep abreast of new developments in legal technology and automation tools. Regularly assess whether new tools or updates to existing systems could provide additional benefits to the firm.
- **Iterative Improvements:** Treat automation as an evolving process. Continuously implement small, incremental improvements based on performance data and feedback, rather than waiting for major overhauls. This approach ensures that the firm stays agile and can quickly adapt to changing needs.

Example: A firm that has scaled its automated client intake system across all departments might conduct quarterly performance reviews to assess how well the system is meeting client needs and improving efficiency. Based on these reviews, the firm could make adjustments, such as streamlining the intake questionnaire or integrating additional client communication features.

Scaling automation across a law firm requires a thoughtful and strategic approach to ensure that the benefits are fully realized in each practice area. By assessing the scalability of existing solutions, building a standardized framework, conducting pilot projects, and providing comprehensive training and support, firms can successfully expand their automation efforts. Continuous monitoring and iterative improvements will ensure that the scaled automation initiatives continue to deliver value and drive the firm's success.

Continuous Improvement

In the fast-evolving landscape of legal services, continuous improvement is essential to maintaining the effectiveness and relevance of your automation initiatives. Adapting to new technologies and changing client needs ensures that your firm remains competitive and delivers the highest level of service. This section emphasizes the importance of a culture of continuous improvement, providing strategies for staying ahead of technological advances and evolving client expectations.

The Philosophy of Continuous Improvement

Continuous improvement, often associated with methodologies like Kaizen[55], involves an ongoing commitment to enhancing processes, tools, and services. Rather than seeing automation as a one-time project, firms should view it as an evolving component of their operations that requires regular attention and refinement. This philosophy encourages a proactive approach to identifying opportunities for improvement and making incremental changes that collectively lead to significant advancements.

Key Principles:

- **Incremental Changes:** Focus on making small, incremental improvements over time rather than waiting for major overhauls. This approach allows for more flexibility, less

---

[55] Imai, Masaaki. Kaizen: The Key to Japan's Competitive Success. McGraw-Hill, 1986

disruption, and the ability to quickly adapt to new challenges or opportunities.
- **Employee Involvement:** Encourage all staff members to contribute ideas for improvements. Those who work directly with automated systems are often best positioned to identify inefficiencies or potential enhancements.
- **Client Feedback Integration:** Continuously seek and integrate client feedback into your improvement processes. Clients' needs and expectations evolve, and incorporating their insights ensures that your services remain aligned with their priorities.

Example: A firm might implement a monthly review meeting where staff members discuss their experiences with the firm's automated tools and propose small changes to improve workflow efficiency or client satisfaction. This continuous feedback loop ensures that the firm's automation efforts are always evolving and improving.

Staying Updated with Technological Advances

Legal technology is advancing rapidly, and new tools and updates are frequently released that can enhance or replace existing systems. Staying informed about these developments and being willing to adopt new technologies as they become available is crucial for maintaining a competitive edge.

Key Strategies:

- **Technology Watch:** Assign a team or individual to monitor developments in legal technology regularly. This could include attending conferences, subscribing to industry publications, and participating in online forums or webinars. The goal is to stay informed about emerging technologies and trends that could benefit the firm.
- **Pilot New Technologies:** Before fully integrating new tools, conduct pilot projects to assess their effectiveness and suitability for your firm's needs. This allows you to test new technologies in a controlled environment and make adjustments before a broader rollout.
- **Regular Updates and Upgrades:** Ensure that your existing tools are regularly updated to take advantage of new features, security enhancements, and performance improvements. Working closely with technology vendors can help you stay on

top of updates and ensure that your systems remain cutting-edge.

Example: A firm that uses an AI-driven document review tool might periodically explore new AI technologies or updates to existing software that offer improved accuracy, speed, or user interfaces. By piloting these advancements, the firm can maintain its position at the forefront of legal automation.

Adapting to Changing Client Needs

As client needs and expectations evolve, so too must your firm's services. Continuous improvement involves regularly reassessing how well your automated services meet client needs and making adjustments to ensure that you continue to provide value

Key Strategies:

- **Client Needs Assessment:** Conduct regular assessments of your clients' needs, preferences, and pain points. This could involve surveys, interviews, or analysis of client behavior data. Understanding what clients value most will guide your efforts to improve and adapt your services.
- **Service Personalization:** As automation tools become more advanced, the ability to offer personalized services at scale is increasing. Explore how you can use automation to tailor your offerings to individual clients' needs, providing a more customized experience.
- **Responsive Service Development**: Be responsive to client feedback by developing new automated services or features that address emerging needs. For example, if clients express a desire for more real-time communication, consider integrating chatbots or live chat features into your client portal.

Example: If a firm's clients begin to express a need for more flexibility in legal service delivery, the firm might respond by developing automated services that offer varying levels of service, from basic document review to full legal representation, all accessible through an online platform.

Fostering a Culture of Continuous Improvement

For continuous improvement to be successful, it must be ingrained in the firm's culture. This involves fostering an environment where innovation is encouraged, feedback is valued, and all staff members are empowered to contribute to the firm's ongoing success.

Key Strategies:

- **Leadership Commitment:** Ensure that firm leadership is fully committed to continuous improvement and sets the tone for the rest of the organization. Leaders should actively participate in improvement initiatives and recognize the contributions of staff members who drive positive change.
- **Encourage Innovation:** Create opportunities for employees at all levels to suggest improvements or new ideas. This could be through regular brainstorming sessions, an idea submission portal, or innovation-focused workshops. Recognizing and rewarding innovative thinking helps to sustain momentum.
- **Training and Development:** Provide ongoing training and development opportunities to help staff stay current with new technologies and best practices. A well-informed and skilled workforce is more likely to identify areas for improvement and implement effective changes.
- **Celebrating Successes:** Celebrate the successes of continuous improvement efforts, no matter how small. Acknowledging progress reinforces the value of ongoing improvement and motivates the team to continue striving for excellence.

Example: A firm might establish an "Innovation Award" that recognizes employees who contribute significant improvements to the firm's automated services. This award could be given quarterly and highlight both the impact of the improvement and the creative process behind it.

Monitoring and Evaluating Improvements

To ensure that continuous improvement efforts are effective, it's important to monitor and evaluate the changes made over time. This involves tracking key metrics, reviewing feedback, and assessing whether the improvements have delivered the intended benefits.

Key Strategies:

- **Track Key Metrics:** Continuously track the metrics identified earlier in the automation process, such as ROI, time savings, client satisfaction, and error rates. Use these metrics to evaluate the impact of each improvement and adjust your approach as needed.
- **Periodic Reviews:** Schedule periodic reviews to evaluate the overall effectiveness of your continuous improvement efforts. This could involve revisiting strategic goals, analyzing performance data, and making adjustments to your improvement processes.
- **Feedback Integration:** Regularly incorporate feedback from both clients and staff into your evaluation process. This helps ensure that your improvements are aligned with actual needs and that any unforeseen issues are quickly addressed.

Example: After implementing a series of improvements based on client feedback, a firm might conduct a six-month review to assess how these changes have impacted client satisfaction and service efficiency. The review would analyze feedback, track metrics, and determine whether further adjustments are needed.

Continuous improvement is a critical component of successful automation in the legal industry. By embracing a culture of ongoing enhancement, staying current with technological advances, adapting to changing client needs, and rigorously monitoring progress, law firms can ensure that their automated services remain effective, competitive, and client-focused. This commitment to continuous improvement not only drives operational excellence but also positions the firm as a leader in the ever-evolving legal landscape.

Playbook: Scaling Workflow Automation in Law Firms

This playbook outlines a strategic, phased approach to implementing and scaling automation in a law firm. It offers a timeline for gradual rollout, focusing on key metrics, training, and continuous improvement. By following this playbook, law firms can measure success, optimize processes, and scale automation across various departments.

Step 1: Initial Automation Pilot (0-3 Months)

Goal: Identify a manageable area to pilot automation and measure its impact.

Select Pilot Area:

- Choose a single process that is repetitive, time-consuming, and will have a measurable impact. Examples include client intake, document drafting, or contract review.

Define Success Metrics:

- **ROI:** Compare the initial investment in automation (software, training, etc.) against the financial returns (e.g., time saved, additional revenue).
- **Time Savings:** Measure time spent on tasks before and after automation.
- **Client Satisfaction:** Survey clients for feedback on the efficiency and quality of services.
- **Error Rates:** Track the rate of human errors before and after automation.

Customize Automation Tools:

- Ensure tools align with the specific needs of the chosen process.

Example: Use a document automation tool to standardize contracts across departments.

Run Pilot:

- Begin the pilot project and gather real-time data on task completion, client feedback, and overall efficiency.

- Track weekly progress to monitor issues and immediate improvements.

Step 2: Initial Review and Adjustments (3-6 Months)

Goal: Analyze results from the pilot and make necessary adjustments before scaling.

Evaluate Pilot Results:

- **ROI:** Calculate ROI based on time and cost savings versus the initial investment.
- **Efficiency Gains:** Compare the number of cases handled or tasks completed before and after automation.
- **Client Feedback:** Conduct surveys or interviews with clients to assess their satisfaction with automated services.

Refine Automation Process:

- Based on feedback, refine the automation tools or processes.

Example: If feedback indicates confusion in using the automated portal, update the user interface for simplicity.

Training and Support:

- Develop targeted training programs for staff involved in the pilot.
- Provide ongoing support and open feedback channels to troubleshoot any issues.

Decision Point: Decide whether the pilot met expectations and is ready to scale. If needed, run a second iteration to fine-tune further.

Step 3: Scaling Across Practice Areas (6-12 Months)

Goal: Gradually introduce automation to additional departments while maintaining quality.

Identify Next Practice Area:

- Select a department that can benefit similarly from automation, such as real estate, litigation, or corporate law. Prioritize areas with high document volumes or repetitive tasks.

Standardize Automation Framework:

- Develop a standardized framework (templates, processes, checklists) to ensure consistency in how automation is implemented across different departments.

Example: A centralized case management system with customizable workflows for each department.

Pilot Rollout in New Departments:

- Customize the automation for each department based on its specific needs, but keep the core platform and metrics uniform.
- Launch Gradual Rollout:
    - Begin with 1-2 additional departments, assess progress, and make any necessary adjustments.
    - Train staff using tailored programs for each practice area, ensuring everyone understands both the technical and practical implications of automation.

Step 4: Full-Firm Rollout (12-24 Months)

Goal: Expand automation firm-wide, ensuring seamless integration and high user adoption.

Finalize Full-Scale Rollout:

- Use insights from previous phases to guide full-scale implementation across all departments.
- Create a structured timeline for each department's integration with the automation system.

Provide Firm-Wide Training:

- Offer firm-wide training, supplemented with department-specific tutorials to address unique workflows.
- Provide self-paced learning modules, video tutorials, and one-on-one coaching to ensure comprehensive understanding.

Maintain Feedback Loops:

- Continue to gather feedback from all departments. Use this data to make continuous improvements in the automation process.

Monitor Success Metrics Firm-Wide:

- **Time Savings:** Track aggregate time savings across departments.
- **Cost Savings:** Measure reduction in overhead, administrative costs, and resource usage (e.g., office supplies).
- **Client Satisfaction:** Regularly survey clients to ensure their experience with the firm's services continues to improve.
- **Error Rates:** Monitor error rates across all departments, aiming for consistent reductions in human errors.

Step 5: Continuous Improvement and Adaptation (24+ Months)

Goal: Foster a culture of continuous improvement, making incremental changes to enhance automation.

Iterative Improvements:

- Revisit each department's automation tools regularly and implement incremental changes based on feedback and evolving needs.

Example: Add features to the automated client portal based on recurring client requests for more real-time communication options.

Monitor Key Metrics Quarterly:

- Conduct quarterly reviews to evaluate the impact of automation on efficiency, costs, client satisfaction, and quality.
- Adjust processes as needed to stay aligned with firm goals.

Stay Updated on New Technology:

- Keep an eye on advancements in legal tech. New AI-driven solutions or upgrades to existing platforms can further enhance efficiency.

Example: Integrating a machine learning tool that predicts case outcomes based on data, which can help with strategic decision-making.

Create a Culture of Innovation:

- Encourage all employees to propose ideas for further automation or process improvement.
- Establish an innovation task force to regularly assess the firm's technological needs and explore new ways to stay competitive.

Example Timeline for Automation Rollout

Time Period	Milestone	Action
0-3 Months	Pilot Project	Select process, define metrics, launch pilot, track data.
3-6 Months	Review Pilot Results	Evaluate metrics, refine tools, provide training.
6-9 Months	Pilot in New Departments	Identify new areas for automation, test in 1-2 departments.
9-12 Months	Incremental Scaling	Roll out in more departments, ensure consistency.
12-18 Months	Firm-Wide Scaling	Expand automation to all departments, monitor performance.
18-24 Months	Full-Firm Automation	Finalize rollout, provide firm-wide training.
24+ Months	Continuous Improvement	Conduct quarterly reviews, track metrics, make adjustments.

By following this structured playbook and timeline, law firms can gradually implement and scale automation while ensuring it delivers measurable improvements in efficiency, cost savings, and client satisfaction. This approach minimizes disruption, encourages firm-wide buy-in, and sets the foundation for ongoing success.

Chapter 17: Building a Culture of Continuous Improvement

Role of Leadership

Leadership plays a pivotal role in fostering a culture of continuous improvement and innovation within a law firm. The attitudes, behaviors, and decisions of the firm's leaders set the tone for the entire organization, influencing how staff approach change, innovation, and professional growth. This section explores the critical role of leadership in driving continuous improvement, outlining the strategies and practices that leaders can adopt to build and sustain an environment where innovation thrives.

Setting the Vision and Strategy

Leaders are responsible for articulating a clear vision and strategy for continuous improvement. This vision should align with the firm's broader goals and communicate the importance of innovation and adaptability in achieving long-term success. By setting a compelling vision, leaders can inspire and motivate the entire firm to embrace continuous improvement as a core organizational value.

Key Strategies:

- **Articulate a Clear Vision:** Leaders should clearly define what continuous improvement means for the firm and how it aligns with the firm's mission, values, and strategic objectives. This vision should emphasize the importance of innovation in maintaining competitiveness and delivering exceptional client service.
- **Communicate the Vision:** Regularly communicate the vision for continuous improvement to all levels of the firm. This can be done through meetings, internal communications, and

strategic planning sessions. The goal is to ensure that every employee understands the importance of continuous improvement and how their role contributes to it.
- **Integrate Continuous Improvement into Strategic Planning:** Continuous improvement should be a key component of the firm's strategic planning process. Leaders should set specific, measurable goals related to innovation and improvement and ensure that these goals are integrated into the firm's overall strategy.

Example: A law firm's leadership team might articulate a vision of becoming the most client-responsive firm in their market by continuously improving their use of legal technology. This vision would be communicated through a series of town hall meetings, where leaders explain how each department can contribute to achieving this goal by embracing new tools and practices.

Leading by Example

Leaders must model the behaviors they wish to see throughout the firm. By actively participating in continuous improvement initiatives and demonstrating a commitment to innovation, leaders can inspire similar behaviors among their staff. Leading by example also involves being open to change, taking calculated risks, and showing a willingness to learn and adapt.

Key Strategies:

- **Participate in Improvement Initiatives:** Leaders should be directly involved in continuous improvement projects, whether by championing specific initiatives, participating in workshops, or being part of pilot programs. This hands-on involvement demonstrates a commitment to the process and reinforces its importance.
- **Embrace Change:** Leaders should visibly embrace change and encourage others to do the same. This includes being open to new ideas, adapting to new technologies, and supporting changes to established processes when they offer clear benefits.
- **Promote a Growth Mindset:** Encourage a growth mindset within the firm by viewing challenges as opportunities to learn and improve. Leaders should openly discuss their own experiences with change and innovation, including any challenges they've faced and how they've overcome them.

Example: A managing partner might lead by example by personally using a new case management system and sharing their experiences with the rest of the firm. They might discuss the benefits they've observed, such as increased efficiency or better client communication, and encourage others to adopt the system as well.

Creating an Inclusive Environment

An inclusive environment where all employees feel valued and heard is essential for fostering continuous improvement. Leaders must ensure that everyone in the firm, regardless of their role, has the opportunity to contribute ideas and participate in improvement initiatives. Inclusivity encourages a broader range of perspectives, leading to more innovative solutions and stronger buy-in from staff.

Key Strategies:

- **Encourage Open Communication:** Create channels for open communication where employees can share their ideas, feedback, and concerns without fear of judgment or retribution. This could include suggestion boxes, regular team meetings, or anonymous feedback platforms.
- **Involve All Levels:** Ensure that continuous improvement efforts involve employees at all levels of the firm, from junior staff to senior partners. Leaders should actively seek input from those who work directly with clients and systems, as they often have valuable insights into where improvements are needed.
- **Recognize and Reward Contributions:** Publicly recognize and reward employees who contribute to continuous improvement initiatives. This not only motivates the individuals involved but also signals to the rest of the firm that their contributions are valued and appreciated.

Example: A law firm might establish a monthly "Innovation Forum" where employees from all departments can present ideas for improving firm processes or client services. Leaders would attend these forums, listen to the presentations, and provide feedback or support for implementing promising ideas.

Supporting Risk-Taking and Innovation

Innovation often requires taking risks and trying new approaches, some of which may not succeed. Leaders play a crucial role in creating a safe environment where employees feel empowered to experiment, knowing that they have the support of the firm even if their ideas don't always work out. This approach encourages creative thinking and helps the firm stay ahead of industry changes.

Key Strategies:

- **Promote Experimentation:** Encourage teams to experiment with new ideas and approaches, even if they involve some level of risk. Leaders should provide the necessary resources and support to help these experiments succeed.
- **Accept and Learn from Failure:** Normalize failure as part of the innovation process. Leaders should openly discuss the lessons learned from unsuccessful initiatives and use these experiences to guide future efforts. This approach helps reduce the fear of failure and fosters a more innovative culture.
- **Allocate Resources for Innovation:** Dedicate specific resources, such as time, budget, and personnel, to continuous improvement and innovation projects. This could include funding for pilot programs, time allocated for employees to work on improvement projects, or a dedicated team focused on driving innovation.

Example: A law firm might set aside a portion of its annual budget for an "Innovation Fund," which employees can apply to for resources to test new ideas or technologies. Leaders would review applications, provide feedback, and approve funding for promising projects, encouraging a culture of experimentation.

Leadership is the cornerstone of building a culture of continuous improvement in a law firm. By setting a clear vision, leading by example, creating an inclusive environment, and supporting risk-taking and innovation, leaders can inspire their teams to embrace ongoing improvement and drive the firm's success. When leaders are actively engaged in and committed to continuous improvement, the entire firm is more likely to adopt a mindset of innovation, adaptability, and excellence.

Ongoing Education

In an industry as dynamic as law, where new technologies and evolving legal trends constantly reshape the landscape, ongoing education and professional development are essential. For a law firm to maintain its competitive edge and continue to deliver high-quality services, its staff must stay informed and skilled in the latest tools, practices, and legal developments. This section emphasizes the importance of ongoing education and offers strategies for fostering a culture of continuous learning within a law firm.

The Necessity of Continuous Learning

The legal profession is not static; it is subject to frequent changes in laws, regulations, and technologies that impact how legal services are delivered. Continuous learning ensures that lawyers and staff are equipped to navigate these changes effectively, providing clients with the most current and relevant advice. In addition, as automation and other technological innovations increasingly influence legal practice, staying educated about these developments is critical for leveraging new tools and maintaining service excellence.

Key Benefits of Continuous Learning:

- **Adapting to Technological Advances:** As new technologies emerge, ongoing education helps ensure that all members of the firm are proficient in using the latest tools and platforms. This knowledge enhances efficiency, improves service delivery, and keeps the firm competitive.
- **Staying Current with Legal Developments:** Laws and regulations evolve over time, and continuous learning is necessary to keep up with these changes. Regular updates and training sessions help legal professionals stay informed about new legislation, case law, and regulatory shifts that could affect their practice areas.
- **Enhancing Professional Skills:** Continuous education also supports the development of broader professional skills, such as legal writing, negotiation, and client communication. These skills are crucial for providing high-quality legal services and maintaining strong client relationships.
- **Fostering Innovation:** A commitment to continuous learning encourages curiosity and creativity, empowering staff to explore new ideas and approaches that can lead to innovation within the firm.

Example: A law firm that specializes in data privacy might regularly offer training sessions on the latest developments in data protection laws, such as updates to the General Data Protection Regulation (GDPR) or emerging trends in cybersecurity. These sessions ensure that the firm's lawyers can provide clients with the most up-to-date advice and strategies for compliance.

Implementing a Structured Professional Development Program

To fully realize the benefits of ongoing education, law firms should implement a structured professional development program that provides regular opportunities for learning and skill enhancement. This program should be tailored to the needs of the firm and its employees, offering a variety of educational formats to suit different learning preferences and professional goals.

Key Components of a Professional Development Program:

- **Continuing Legal Education (CLE):** Ensure that all lawyers meet their mandatory CLE requirements by offering in-house CLE courses or providing access to external programs. These courses should cover both core legal topics and emerging areas of law that are relevant to the firm's practice.
- **Technology Training:** Regularly schedule training sessions on new legal technologies, such as document automation tools, AI-driven research platforms, and case management systems. Training should be hands-on and focused on practical applications to ensure that staff can effectively use these tools in their daily work.
- **Soft Skills Workshops:** Offer workshops focused on developing soft skills, such as leadership, communication, and client management. These skills are essential for building strong client relationships and leading teams effectively within the firm.
- **Mentorship Programs:** Establish mentorship programs where more experienced lawyers and staff members can share their knowledge and insights with newer employees. Mentorship fosters a culture of learning and helps junior staff develop their skills more quickly.
- **Personalized Learning Plans:** Develop personalized learning plans for each employee, based on their role, career goals, and areas for improvement. These plans should include specific educational milestones and opportunities for progression within the firm.

Example: A mid-sized law firm might implement a professional development program that includes a combination of monthly CLE seminars, quarterly technology workshops, and ongoing mentorship for junior associates. Each lawyer would have a personalized learning plan that tracks their progress and ensures they are meeting both mandatory and voluntary educational goals.

Leveraging Online Learning and Resources

In today's digital age, a wealth of online resources is available to support continuous learning. Online platforms offer flexibility and convenience, allowing legal professionals to access educational content anytime and anywhere. By leveraging online learning resources, law firms can provide their staff with more opportunities to stay informed and develop their skills.

Key Strategies for Online Learning:

- **E-Learning Platforms:** Utilize e-learning platforms that offer courses in various areas of law, technology, and professional skills. These platforms often provide certifications and can be integrated into the firm's professional development program.
- **Webinars and Virtual Workshops:** Encourage participation in webinars and virtual workshops on relevant legal and technological topics. These events often feature industry experts and provide opportunities for real-time interaction and learning.
- **Online Libraries and Research Tools:** Provide access to online legal libraries and research tools that offer up-to-date information on case law, statutes, and legal commentary. Encourage lawyers to use these resources regularly to stay current with legal developments.
- **Podcasts and Blogs:** Recommend relevant legal podcasts and blogs that offer insights into industry trends, case studies, and expert opinions. These resources can be a valuable complement to more formal education, providing quick and accessible updates on the go.

Example: A law firm might subscribe to an e-learning platform like Coursera or LinkedIn Learning, offering its staff access to a curated selection of courses on legal technology, data analysis, and client communication. Additionally, the firm could organize monthly "webinar lunch-and-learns" where staff can participate in a virtual workshop while enjoying a catered lunch.

Encouraging a Culture of Lifelong Learning

For ongoing education to be truly effective, it must be ingrained in the firm's culture. Leaders should promote a mindset of lifelong learning, where continuous education is seen as a fundamental part of professional growth and success. By fostering this culture, firms can ensure that all employees are motivated to keep learning and improving throughout their careers.

Key Strategies:

- **Lead by Example:** Firm leaders should demonstrate their commitment to lifelong learning by actively participating in educational opportunities and sharing their experiences with the team. This sets a positive example and reinforces the importance of continuous learning.
- **Incentivize Learning:** Offer incentives for completing educational milestones, such as bonuses, promotions, or public recognition. These incentives can motivate employees to take their professional development seriously and strive for excellence.
- **Create Learning Communities:** Encourage the formation of learning communities within the firm, where employees can share knowledge, discuss new ideas, and collaborate on educational projects. These communities foster a sense of camaraderie and make learning a more social and enjoyable experience.
- **Regularly Update Learning Goals:** Encourage employees to regularly update their learning goals based on new developments in their practice areas and personal interests. This ensures that their education remains relevant and aligned with their career aspirations.

Example: A law firm might implement a "Learning Leaders" program, where employees who complete a certain number of educational courses or achieve specific certifications are recognized at firm-wide meetings and given the opportunity to lead internal training sessions. This program not only incentivizes learning but also builds a community of knowledge-sharing within the firm.

Ongoing education is a critical component of a law firm's success in today's rapidly changing legal landscape. By implementing structured professional development programs, leveraging online learning resources, and fostering a culture of lifelong learning, law firms can ensure that their employees remain at the forefront of legal practice and technology. This commitment to continuous learning not only enhances the firm's ability to adapt to new challenges but also strengthens its overall service delivery and client satisfaction.

Encouraging Experimentation

Experimentation is the engine of innovation. For a law firm to truly embrace continuous improvement and stay ahead in a competitive industry, it must foster an environment where experimentation is not only encouraged but also seen as an essential part of growth. This involves creating a culture where trying new approaches is valued, and failure is viewed as a learning opportunity rather than a setback. This section outlines strategies for cultivating an environment that supports experimentation, drives innovation, and turns potential failures into valuable insights.

Building a Safe-to-Fail Culture

Creating a safe-to-fail culture means establishing an environment where employees feel comfortable taking risks and trying new ideas without fear of negative consequences. This culture is essential for encouraging experimentation, as it allows staff to explore innovative solutions and push boundaries without the pressure of always being successful.

Key Strategies:

- **Normalize Failure:** Leaders should openly discuss the importance of failure in the innovation process. By sharing their own experiences with failure and how they turned those experiences into growth opportunities, leaders can help reduce the stigma associated with not succeeding on the first try.
- **Reward Effort and Learning:** Instead of solely rewarding successful outcomes, recognize and reward the effort put into experimentation and the lessons learned from it. This can include public recognition, bonuses, or other incentives that highlight the value of taking risks and learning from them.
- **Create a No-Blame Culture:** Establish a no-blame culture where mistakes are seen as part of the learning process rather than reasons for punishment. Encourage team members to openly discuss what went wrong in an experiment and what they can do differently next time. This approach helps build trust and fosters a collaborative environment focused on continuous improvement.

Example: A law firm might implement an "Innovation of the Month" award, where employees can nominate a colleague who attempted a new approach, regardless of whether it succeeded. The winner could be recognized at a firm-wide meeting, with a focus on what was learned from the experience.

Allocating Time and Resources for Experimentation

For experimentation to be viable, employees need the time and resources to explore new ideas without it interfering with their regular responsibilities. By dedicating specific resources to experimentation, law firms can ensure that innovation is a continuous, structured part of their operations.

Key Strategies:

- **Innovation Time Allocation:** Allow employees to dedicate a certain percentage of their work hours to experimentation and innovation. This "innovation time" can be used for exploring new technologies, developing new processes, or working on passion projects that could benefit the firm.
- **Innovation Budget:** Set aside a specific budget for experimentation, which can be used to fund pilot projects, test new tools, or hire external consultants with specialized expertise. This financial support demonstrates the firm's commitment to innovation and provides the resources needed to pursue new ideas.
- **Dedicated Innovation Teams:** Create small, cross-functional teams tasked with experimenting and innovating within the firm. These teams should have the autonomy to explore new ideas and the support of leadership to implement their findings on a larger scale.

Example: A firm might allocate 10% of each employee's time to work on "Innovation Fridays," where they can pursue new ideas or projects related to improving firm processes or client services. This dedicated time ensures that employees have the opportunity to experiment without the pressure of their day-to-day tasks.

Encouraging Collaborative Experimentation

Collaboration is key to successful experimentation. By bringing together diverse perspectives and expertise, law firms can generate more creative ideas and develop more robust solutions. Collaborative experimentation also helps build a sense of shared ownership and accountability for the outcomes, whether successful or not.

Key Strategies:

- **Cross-Departmental Collaboration:** Encourage collaboration across different practice areas and departments. Diverse teams bring varied perspectives that can lead to more innovative ideas and solutions. This cross-pollination of ideas can be particularly effective in developing new products or improving processes.
- **Innovation Workshops:** Host regular workshops or hackathons where employees from different parts of the firm come together to brainstorm and develop new ideas. These sessions should be structured to encourage creativity and free thinking, with a focus on generating actionable ideas that can be tested and refined.
- **Peer Review of Experiments:** Implement a peer review process for experiments, where colleagues provide feedback and suggestions before a new idea is tested. This collaborative approach can help refine ideas, identify potential challenges, and increase the likelihood of success.

Example: A law firm might organize a quarterly "Innovation Hackathon," where teams made up of lawyers, paralegals, IT staff, and administrative personnel work together to develop new tools or processes. At the end of the hackathon, teams present their ideas, and the best ones are selected for further development and testing.

Implementing a Structured Experimentation Process

While experimentation should be encouraged, it is important to approach it systematically to maximize learning and minimize wasted effort. A structured experimentation process helps ensure that new ideas are tested rigorously, results are analyzed objectively, and successful innovations are scaled effectively.

Key Strategies:

- **Define Clear Objectives:** Before starting an experiment, clearly define what you hope to achieve. This includes setting specific goals, such as improving efficiency, enhancing client satisfaction, or reducing costs. Clear objectives help focus the experiment and provide a benchmark for success.
- **Develop Hypotheses:** Based on the objectives, develop hypotheses that can be tested through experimentation. For example, "Implementing a new AI-driven research tool will

reduce the time spent on legal research by 30%." Hypotheses provide a clear direction for the experiment and a basis for measuring its success.
- **Design Small-Scale Pilots:** Start with small-scale pilots to test your hypotheses before rolling out changes on a larger scale. These pilots should be designed to gather data quickly and efficiently, allowing for rapid iteration and improvement.
- **Measure and Analyze Results:** After the pilot, carefully measure the results against the objectives and hypotheses. Use data-driven analysis to determine whether the experiment was successful and what can be learned from it. Document both the successes and failures, as this information will be valuable for future experiments.

Example: If a law firm wants to experiment with a new automated billing system, it might start by implementing the system in one practice area and comparing the results with a similar area that continues to use the traditional system. The firm would track metrics like time saved, error rates, and client feedback to determine whether the new system should be adopted more broadly.

Scaling Successful Experiments

Once an experiment proves successful, the next step is to scale it across the firm. Scaling involves refining the process, ensuring that it is sustainable, and gradually implementing it in other areas. A systematic approach to scaling ensures that the benefits of successful experiments are realized across the entire organization.

Key Strategies:

- **Refine the Process:** Before scaling, refine the experimental process based on feedback and results from the pilot. Address any issues or inefficiencies to ensure that the process is as effective and streamlined as possible.
- **Create Implementation Guidelines:** Develop clear guidelines and training materials to support the broader implementation of the new process or tool. These guidelines should be easy to follow and provide step-by-step instructions for adoption in other practice areas or departments.
- **Gradual Rollout:** Implement the new process or tool gradually, starting with departments or teams that are most likely to benefit or that have the capacity to adopt it quickly.

Monitor the rollout closely, gather feedback, and make adjustments as needed before full-scale implementation.
- **Continuous Monitoring:** Even after scaling, continue to monitor the process or tool to ensure that it remains effective and delivers the intended benefits. Regularly review performance metrics and gather feedback to make further improvements as necessary.

Example: After successfully piloting a new client intake process that uses automation to reduce data entry errors, a law firm might refine the process and then roll it out to other practice areas. The firm would provide training sessions and implementation guides to ensure a smooth transition and continue to monitor the process for any issues that arise during the broader rollout.

Encouraging experimentation is essential for fostering a culture of continuous improvement and innovation within a law firm. By building a safe-to-fail culture, allocating time and resources for experimentation, encouraging collaboration, and implementing a structured process for testing and scaling new ideas, firms can create an environment where innovation thrives. This approach not only drives ongoing improvement but also positions the firm as a forward-thinking leader in the legal industry.

Case Study: Seyfarth Shaw LLP - Building a Culture of Continuous Improvement

Seyfarth Shaw LLP, a global law firm with over 900 attorneys, is widely recognized for its innovative approach to legal service delivery. The firm has successfully built a culture of continuous improvement through its SeyfarthLean[56] initiative, which combines Lean Six Sigma principles with legal practice to enhance efficiency, improve client service, and foster a mindset of ongoing innovation. This case study explores how Seyfarth Shaw established this culture, the practices and policies that have driven its success, and the lessons that other law firms can learn from their experience.

---

[56] Rohrer, Lisa, and DeHoratius, Nicole. "SeyfarthLean: Transforming Legal Service Delivery at Seyfarth Shaw." Harvard Law School Case Studies, May 2015

The SeyfarthLean Initiative

Background: In 2005, Seyfarth Shaw launched SeyfarthLean, a comprehensive initiative aimed at transforming the way legal services were delivered. Inspired by Lean Six Sigma, a methodology used in manufacturing to improve efficiency and reduce waste, SeyfarthLean was tailored to meet the specific needs of legal practice. The initiative focused on streamlining processes, enhancing collaboration, and delivering greater value to clients. Over the years, SeyfarthLean has become a cornerstone of the firm's culture, driving continuous improvement across all practice areas.

Key Components of SeyfarthLean:

- **Process Improvement:** SeyfarthLean applies Lean Six Sigma principles to legal processes, identifying inefficiencies and implementing solutions to streamline workflows. This includes mapping out processes, identifying bottlenecks, and eliminating steps that do not add value to the client.
- **Client Collaboration:** The initiative emphasizes close collaboration with clients to understand their needs and expectations. By involving clients in the process improvement journey, Seyfarth Shaw ensures that the changes made align with client priorities and deliver tangible benefits.
- **Data-Driven Decision Making:** SeyfarthLean relies heavily on data to inform decisions and measure success. The firm uses metrics to track performance, identify areas for improvement, and assess the impact of changes. This data-driven approach ensures that continuous improvement efforts are focused on the areas that will have the most significant impact.

Outcome: Since its inception, SeyfarthLean has led to significant improvements in efficiency, client satisfaction, and profitability. The initiative has helped Seyfarth Shaw differentiate itself in a competitive market by consistently delivering high-quality legal services that meet clients' evolving needs.

Leadership Commitment and Vision

Leadership at Seyfarth Shaw played a critical role in the success of SeyfarthLean. Firm leaders recognized the need for innovation in legal service delivery and were committed to driving this transformation. Their active involvement in the initiative set the tone for the entire organization and ensured that continuous improvement became a core part of the firm's culture.

Key Practices:

- **Articulating a Clear Vision:** Seyfarth Shaw's leadership articulated a clear vision for SeyfarthLean, emphasizing the importance of efficiency, client value, and innovation. This vision was communicated consistently across the firm, helping to align all employees with the goals of the initiative.
- **Leading by Example:** Leaders at Seyfarth Shaw led by example, actively participating in Lean Six Sigma[57] training and process improvement projects. Their hands-on involvement demonstrated their commitment to the initiative and encouraged others to embrace continuous improvement.
- **Resource Allocation:** The firm's leadership allocated significant resources to SeyfarthLean, including time, budget, and personnel. This investment signaled the importance of the initiative and provided the necessary support for its success.

Outcome: The strong commitment of Seyfarth Shaw's leadership to SeyfarthLean was instrumental in embedding continuous improvement into the firm's DNA. By setting a clear vision and leading by example, leaders created a culture where innovation and efficiency are prioritized and celebrated.

Training and Development

To ensure that all employees were equipped to contribute to SeyfarthLean, Seyfarth Shaw implemented a robust training and development program. This program provided staff with the skills and knowledge needed to apply Lean Six Sigma principles to their work, fostering a culture of continuous learning and improvement.

Key Practices:

- **Lean Six Sigma Training:** Seyfarth Shaw provided Lean Six Sigma training to attorneys, paralegals, and administrative staff across the firm. This training covered the fundamentals of process improvement, data analysis, and project management,

---

[57] George, Michael L., et al. Lean Six Sigma: Combining Six Sigma Quality with Lean Production Speed. McGraw-Hill, 2002

enabling employees to participate actively in SeyfarthLean initiatives.
- **Ongoing Education:** The firm encouraged ongoing education by offering advanced training opportunities, workshops, and seminars. These programs helped employees stay current with new tools, techniques, and best practices in continuous improvement.
- **Mentorship and Coaching:** Seyfarth Shaw established a mentorship and coaching program to support employees as they applied Lean Six Sigma principles to their work. Experienced mentors provided guidance and feedback, helping employees develop their skills and confidence in leading process improvement projects.

Outcome: Seyfarth Shaw's commitment to training and development ensured that all employees were empowered to contribute to continuous improvement efforts. The widespread adoption of Lean Six Sigma principles across the firm led to more efficient processes, higher-quality work, and greater client satisfaction.

Encouraging Experimentation and Innovation

Seyfarth Shaw's culture of continuous improvement is also characterized by a strong emphasis on experimentation and innovation. The firm created an environment where employees are encouraged to try new ideas, take calculated risks, and learn from their experiences.

Key Practices:

- **Pilot Projects:** Seyfarth Shaw frequently uses pilot projects to test new ideas and approaches before rolling them out firm-wide. These small-scale experiments allow the firm to gather data, refine processes, and assess the feasibility of innovations in a controlled setting.
- **Innovation Lab:** The firm established an Innovation Lab, a dedicated space where employees can collaborate on developing new tools, processes, and services. The lab provides the resources and support needed to turn innovative ideas into actionable projects.
- **Celebrating Success and Learning from Failure:** Seyfarth Shaw recognizes and celebrates both successful innovations and the lessons learned from less successful experiments. This

approach fosters a culture where experimentation is valued and failure is seen as an opportunity for growth.

Outcome: The emphasis on experimentation and innovation has enabled Seyfarth Shaw to stay at the forefront of the legal industry. The firm's willingness to try new approaches and learn from experience has resulted in a continuous stream of improvements and innovations that benefit both the firm and its clients.

Measuring Success and Continuous Feedback

Seyfarth Shaw's commitment to continuous improvement is reinforced by a rigorous approach to measuring success and gathering feedback. The firm uses a variety of metrics and feedback mechanisms to assess the impact of SeyfarthLean and identify opportunities for further improvement.

Key Practices:

- **Performance Metrics:** Seyfarth Shaw tracks a wide range of performance metrics related to efficiency, client satisfaction, and profitability. These metrics provide a clear picture of how well the firm's processes are functioning and where improvements can be made.
- **Client Feedback:** The firm regularly solicits feedback from clients to understand their needs and expectations. This feedback is used to refine processes, enhance service delivery, and ensure that SeyfarthLean continues to deliver value to clients.
- **Continuous Improvement Reviews:** Seyfarth Shaw conducts regular reviews of its continuous improvement efforts, analyzing the results of process improvements and identifying areas for further innovation. These reviews ensure that the firm's culture of continuous improvement remains dynamic and responsive to changing conditions.

Outcome: The use of performance metrics and continuous feedback has allowed Seyfarth Shaw to sustain and build upon the success of SeyfarthLean. By constantly measuring and refining its processes, the firm has maintained its position as a leader in legal innovation and efficiency.

Seyfarth Shaw LLP's SeyfarthLean initiative provides a powerful example of how a law firm can successfully build a culture of continuous improvement. Through strong leadership, comprehensive training, a commitment to experimentation, and a focus on measurable results, Seyfarth Shaw has transformed its approach to legal service delivery. The firm's experience demonstrates that with the right practices and policies in place, any law firm can foster a culture of innovation and continuous improvement that drives lasting success.

Chapter 18: Legal Automation and the Global Market

Cross-Border Legal Services

"Time zones, languages, laws—pick two, and you're already behind."

That's how it can feel when navigating the intricate web of cross-border legal work. For many law firms, handling international cases means balancing the demands of multiple jurisdictions, cultural expectations, and vast amounts of documentation—all while clients expect answers faster than ever. As businesses operate on a global scale, the pressure to deliver efficient, accurate, and timely legal services is unrelenting. The stakes are high, and the margin for error is thin.

Consider this scenario:

A client comes to you with a high-profile international arbitration involving parties from Europe, North America, and Asia. The legal questions themselves are complex, but the real challenge lies in managing thousands of documents spread across multiple languages, ensuring that the case complies with varying regulations, and predicting potential outcomes based on unfamiliar precedents. It's an all-too-common reality in today's global legal market: you have the expertise, but not enough hours in the day.

Enter legal automation—the key to navigating this complexity without compromising quality. Automation tools are rapidly changing the game by handling routine tasks like document review, cross-jurisdictional research, and compliance monitoring. What once took weeks or months of manual work can now be done in hours, with greater accuracy. Automation isn't about replacing the expertise you've spent years building; it's about amplifying it, enabling you to focus on the strategic decisions that truly matter.

In this chapter, we'll dive into the transformative role legal automation plays in cross-border legal services. From streamlining international arbitration to ensuring compliance in multiple jurisdictions, we'll explore how these tools are reshaping the future of global legal practice. For those prepared to embrace this shift, the opportunity to serve clients faster, more accurately, and more cost-effectively has never been greater.

Streamlining International Arbitration

International arbitration, a preferred method for resolving cross-border disputes, often involves navigating complex legal issues across multiple jurisdictions. Automation enhances the efficiency and accuracy of the arbitration process by taking over routine administrative tasks, managing large volumes of documentation, and providing advanced analytical tools that offer strategic insights.

Key Applications:

Document Management and Review:

Automation tools can efficiently manage the large volumes of documentation typically involved in international arbitration. AI-powered document review systems can sift through thousands of contracts, communications, and evidence, identifying key information, and flagging inconsistencies. This not only reduces the time and costs associated with manual document review but also minimizes human error.

Practical takeaway: Invest in an AI-driven document review platform to enhance your firm's efficiency in international cases, enabling faster identification of crucial details.

Case Analytics:

Predictive analytics tools can review past arbitration cases to identify patterns and likely outcomes based on specific legal arguments, jurisdictions, or arbitrators. This data helps legal teams develop more effective strategies, offering clients insights that are rooted in data rather than just experience.

Practical takeaway: Use predictive analytics to gain a competitive advantage by analyzing trends in arbitration outcomes.

Cross-Jurisdictional Research:

Automated research tools can scan legal databases across multiple jurisdictions, offering up-to-date information on relevant laws, regulations, and case precedents. This is especially important in arbitration, where a firm understanding of the legal frameworks in different countries is essential.

Practical takeaway: Incorporate cross-jurisdictional research tools to expand your firm's ability to handle complex international cases without increasing the workload on junior lawyers.

Example: Consider a law firm handling an international arbitration case involving parties from Europe, Asia, and North America. By using an AI-driven document review platform, the firm processes thousands of pages of documents in multiple languages. The platform's multilingual capabilities and advanced search functions enable the legal team to quickly identify key documents, thus improving both the accuracy of their case preparation and the speed at which they work, giving them an edge in negotiation and case strategy.

Enhancing Compliance with Global Regulations

Compliance with global regulations is one of the most significant challenges for multinational corporations. These companies must navigate a complex web of legal requirements across multiple jurisdictions. Legal automation simplifies this process by automating routine compliance tasks, continuously monitoring regulatory changes, and providing real-time updates that keep companies in line with evolving standards.

Case Study: HSBC and HighQ[58]

Challenge: HSBC's legal team, spread across 46 countries and with over 1,300 legal professionals, struggled to efficiently manage legal knowledge sharing and ensure compliance with ever-changing global regulations. They needed a platform that could consolidate knowledge, foster collaboration, and maintain up-to-date regulatory compliance across jurisdictions.

---

[58] HSBC Case Study, Thomson Reuters HighQ Customer Stories, available at https://legalsolutions.thomsonreuters.co.uk/en/products-services/highq/customer-stories/hsbc.html (last accessed Sept. 5, 2024).

Solution: HSBC implemented Thomson Reuters HighQ, a cloud-based platform that centralizes legal knowledge, tracks compliance changes, and automates routine legal processes. The legal team collaborated on building a global knowledge hub, where lawyers could quickly access relevant legal updates, compliance rules, and external training programs.

Result: By using HighQ, HSBC significantly improved compliance monitoring and internal knowledge sharing. The platform streamlined the way the legal team tracked global regulatory changes, allowing them to manage risks and ensure compliance across multiple regions. The centralized system also facilitated collaboration with external counsel and helped with ongoing training programs.

Key Applications:

Automated Compliance Monitoring:

Automation tools can continuously monitor legal and regulatory changes across various jurisdictions and alert legal teams to updates that may impact their clients. This proactive approach ensures companies remain compliant with the latest regulations, thus reducing the risk of fines or legal disputes.

Practical takeaway: Implement automated compliance monitoring systems to track jurisdiction-specific regulations, ensuring that your clients are always up to date on compliance obligations.

Cross-Border Contract Management:

Legal automation tools streamline the management of cross-border contracts by automating drafting, review, and approval processes. These tools can ensure that contract templates comply with local laws and allow for electronic signatures, making it easier to manage contracts in multiple countries.

Case Study: OpMentors—Streamlining Cross-Border Contract Management with PandaDoc

Company Overview: OpMentors is a technology consulting firm specializing in solutions for Salesforce and FinancialForce clients. With operations spanning multiple regions, the company manages complex contracts and Statements of Work (SOWs) for its customers across industries and locations. This heavy reliance on contract documentation created challenges in maintaining efficiency, especially as OpMentors expanded its business globally.

Challenges: Before implementing PandaDoc, OpMentors struggled with a manual, time-consuming process for creating and approving documents. The team often found itself spending hours drafting SOWs and contracts, resulting in significant delays and inefficiencies, particularly when managing cross-border contracts. This inefficiency became a bottleneck as the company scaled its operations, leading to lost time and resources.

Key challenges included:

- **Time-Intensive Document Creation:** Generating contracts and proposals manually took up to several hours.
- **Lack of Real-Time Collaboration:** Editing and approving documents involved multiple parties, often resulting in delayed responses.
- **Inconsistent Workflow Management:** Managing various versions of contracts across regions led to confusion and extended approval timelines.

Solution: OpMentors adopted PandaDoc, an AI-powered contract management platform, to automate its document creation, review, and approval processes. This transition allowed the firm to create and send complex proposals, contracts, and SOWs to clients in minutes rather than hours. PandaDoc's integration with Salesforce enabled seamless collaboration and real-time tracking of document progress, ensuring that OpMentors could manage global contracts efficiently across all regions.

Key Features Used:

- **Automated Document Creation:** Using pre-built templates to automate contract and SOW generation.
- **Real-Time Collaboration:** Multiple team members could edit, approve, and sign documents simultaneously, reducing back-and-forth delays.
- **Compliance and Tracking:** Integrated tracking allowed OpMentors to monitor document status, ensuring all regional requirements were met.

Results

The implementation of PandaDoc delivered significant improvements to OpMentors' cross-border contract management processes:

- **90% Reduction in Document Creation Time:** What once took hours to create was now done in minutes, allowing the team to focus on core business tasks.
- **24% Increase in Revenue:** The faster turnaround time for proposals and contracts improved client acquisition and retention, directly boosting revenue.
- **27% Decrease in Sales Cycle Time:** PandaDoc helped shorten the time from proposal to contract signing, making it easier to close deals with clients globally.

By leveraging PandaDoc's automation capabilities, OpMentors streamlined its operations and improved its ability to handle complex, cross-border contracts efficiently, all while maintaining compliance with regional regulations.

Practical takeaway: Adopt contract automation systems that support electronic signatures and compliance checks, simplifying the management of international contracts.

Risk Assessment and Reporting:

AI-powered risk assessment tools can analyze a company's operations across jurisdictions to identify potential compliance risks. These tools provide detailed reports, which highlight areas that may require corrective action, enabling companies to take a proactive approach to risk management.

Practical takeaway: Incorporate AI-powered risk assessment tools to provide clients with in-depth analyses of their global operations, identifying potential risks before they escalate into legal problems.

Example: A global technology company with operations in Europe, Asia, and North America uses an automated compliance monitoring tool to track regulations such as the GDPR in Europe and the CCPA in California. The tool continuously updates the company's legal team on new regulatory developments, ensuring that the company's data handling practices remain compliant across all jurisdictions. This not only protects the company from potential legal exposure but also strengthens its reputation for compliance.

Facilitating Cross-Border Mergers and Acquisitions

Cross-border mergers and acquisitions (M&A) are among the most complex legal transactions, involving intricate legal, financial, and regulatory considerations across multiple jurisdictions. Legal automation can streamline these transactions by automating the due diligence process, managing contract drafting, and providing advanced data analysis.

Key Applications:

Due Diligence Automation:

Due diligence is one of the most time-consuming aspects of M&A, often involving extensive reviews of financial records, contracts, and intellectual property. Automation tools can expedite this process by automating the collection, organization, and analysis of relevant data. AI-powered platforms can quickly flag potential compliance risks and other red flags, allowing legal teams to focus on higher-level strategy.

Practical takeaway: Use AI-driven due diligence platforms to manage document-intensive M&A processes, reducing both time and the potential for human error.

Automated Contract Drafting and Review:

Legal automation tools can ensure that contracts related to cross-border M&A transactions comply with the specific legal requirements of each jurisdiction. Automated contract drafting systems help avoid errors, ensuring that each document meets the necessary legal standards for all parties involved.

Practical takeaway: Streamline your M&A processes with automated contract management tools that ensure multi-jurisdictional compliance.

Example: A U.S. law firm advising on a cross-border merger between companies in the U.S. and Germany might use an AI-driven due diligence platform to analyze the target company's financial records. The platform identifies potential compliance risks related to German employment laws, allowing the firm to address these issues early in the transaction. By leveraging automation, the firm can complete due diligence faster and with greater accuracy, giving the client confidence in their legal strategy.

Overcoming Language and Cultural Barriers

Language and cultural differences pose significant challenges in cross-border legal services. Legal automation helps overcome these barriers by offering multilingual support, cultural context analysis, and tools for managing international client relationships.

Key Applications:

Multilingual Document Processing:

Automation tools with natural language processing (NLP) capabilities can translate legal documents, contracts, and correspondence into multiple languages. This ensures that all parties involved in cross-border transactions fully understand the content, regardless of their native language.

Practical takeaway: Leverage NLP-powered translation tools to ensure accuracy and clarity when working with international clients.

Cultural Context Analysis:

AI-driven tools can analyze cultural norms and legal traditions in various jurisdictions, providing insights into how these factors might influence negotiations or case strategy. This allows legal teams to navigate cross-cultural negotiations more effectively.

Practical takeaway: Integrate cultural analysis tools into your practice to improve client relations and negotiation strategies across jurisdictions.

Example: A law firm negotiating a cross-border licensing agreement between a U.S. company and a Japanese company could use NLP-powered translation tools to ensure all contracts are accurately translated into both English and Japanese. Additionally, the firm could use cultural analysis tools to advise the U.S. team on Japan's negotiating styles and legal customs, helping the team to navigate cultural differences more effectively.

Opportunities in Emerging Markets

Emerging markets offer significant opportunities for legal automation, allowing regions to leapfrog traditional legal models and adopt advanced technologies from the outset. In many of these regions, legal infrastructure is still developing, making them ripe for transformation through automation.

Leapfrogging Traditional Legal Models

In emerging markets, where legal resources are often limited, slow judicial processes and inconsistent access to services are common challenges. However, these challenges create opportunities to bypass traditional legal models and adopt more innovative, automated solutions that offer greater efficiency and accessibility.

Key Opportunities:

Adopting Advanced Technologies:

Emerging markets can implement AI-driven legal research, document automation, and online dispute resolution platforms without being held back by legacy systems.

Practical takeaway: Law firms in emerging markets should prioritize adopting legal automation tools that allow them to streamline services and improve access to justice for underserved populations.

Improving Access to Legal Services:

Legal automation can provide self-service tools for basic legal needs, such as drafting contracts or resolving disputes. This allows individuals and small businesses to access legal services that were previously out of reach.

Practical takeaway: Develop automated self-service platforms to make legal assistance more accessible and affordable for clients in emerging markets.

Example: In Rwanda, where there is a shortage of legal professionals, legal automation offers a solution by providing self-service legal assistance through AI-driven platforms. These platforms help individuals and small businesses draft contracts, file documents, and resolve disputes without the need for expensive legal representation.[59]

Globalization and Innovation

Globalization is reshaping the legal industry, breaking down geographic barriers and enabling the flow of legal services across borders. Legal technology plays a central role in this transformation,

---

[59] ICT in Rwandan Justice Service Delivery, Ministry of Justice Rwanda, available at https://www.minijust.gov.rw (last accessed Sept. 5, 2024).

allowing legal professionals to collaborate internationally, access global resources, and deliver services more efficiently.

Facilitating Global Collaboration

As businesses continue to operate on a global scale, the demand for legal services that span multiple jurisdictions is growing. Legal professionals from different countries can now collaborate seamlessly, overcoming challenges such as time zones and language barriers.

Key Opportunities:

Virtual Collaboration Tools:

Cloud-based platforms allow legal teams from different parts of the world to work together in real-time. These tools support document sharing, video conferencing, and project management, making it easier to coordinate complex international cases or transactions.

Practical takeaway: Adopt secure virtual collaboration platforms to manage cross-border legal teams more effectively.

Recap of Key Themes

As we conclude this book, it's important to reflect on the key themes discussed throughout. We began by examining the historical development of legal services and highlighted how traditional models—especially the billable hour—are giving way to more innovative, client-focused approaches. Workflow automation and productized services are fundamental shifts that will shape the future of the legal profession.

Call to Action

The legal profession stands at the cusp of profound transformation. The time to act is now, and everyone—whether senior partner, associate, or support staff—has a role to play. By embracing workflow automation, productized services, and continuous innovation, you can be part of the evolution shaping the legal industry.

Concrete Steps for Action:

- **Embrace Lifelong Learning:** Commit to ongoing education in legal technology and automation.
- **Advocate for Change:** Don't wait for permission—advocate for tools that improve efficiency and client service.
- **Experiment and Iterate:** Continuously test new approaches to legal work. Even small innovations can lead to big improvements.
- **Collaborate Across Roles:** Work together with colleagues across departments and roles to implement change.
- **Focus on Client Value:** Automation and productization aren't just about efficiency—they're about delivering better, more predictable, and more valuable services to clients.

The path ahead is clear: the future of the legal profession will be shaped by those who are willing to embrace transformation. As we've explored, the rise of automation, productized services, and global collaboration signals a new era, one that demands forward-thinking legal professionals ready to redefine their roles. **Whether you are a senior partner, an associate, or support staff, you are equipped with the tools to create meaningful change—not just for your firm, but for the entire legal industry.**

This is not just about keeping pace with change; it's about leading it. To be truly *future-ready*, you must take bold steps, collaborate across roles, and commit to continuous learning. **The opportunity to innovate, elevate client service, and reshape the legal landscape is right in front of you. The time for action is now. The future is yours to shape—so embrace it and become the future-ready lawyer you are meant to be.**

Appendix A: Glossary of Terms Related to Workflow Automation and Legal Technology

Artificial Intelligence (AI):

A branch of computer science focused on creating machines capable of performing tasks that typically require human intelligence, such as decision-making, language understanding, and visual perception. In the legal field, AI is often used for tasks like document review, legal research, and predictive analytics.

Automation:

The use of technology to perform tasks with minimal human intervention. In the legal context, automation can streamline processes such as document drafting, client intake, and case management, reducing time and increasing efficiency.

Blockchain:

A decentralized digital ledger that records transactions across multiple computers in such a way that the registered transactions cannot be altered retroactively. In law, blockchain can be used for smart contracts, secure transactions, and maintaining transparent records.

Cloud Computing:

A technology that allows data and applications to be stored and accessed over the internet instead of on a local computer or server. Cloud computing facilitates collaboration, data storage, and the use of software applications without the need for extensive on-premises infrastructure.

Client Relationship Management (CRM) Software:

A type of software that helps law firms manage and analyze client interactions and data throughout the client lifecycle. CRM systems support client retention, improve client service, and enhance client communication.

Compliance Monitoring:

The process of ensuring that a company or law firm adheres to legal, regulatory, and ethical standards. Automation tools can monitor changes in regulations and ensure that the firm's practices remain compliant.

Continuous Improvement:

An ongoing effort to improve products, services, or processes over time. In a legal context, continuous improvement often involves regularly updating workflows, adopting new technologies, and refining service delivery methods.

Contract Lifecycle Management (CLM):

A systematic approach to managing contracts from their creation through execution, performance, and renewal or expiration. CLM software automates and streamlines the contracting process, ensuring consistency, compliance, and efficiency.

Document Automation:

The use of software to automatically generate legal documents based on templates and inputted data. Document automation reduces the time required for drafting, minimizes errors, and ensures consistency in legal documents.

E-Discovery:

The process of identifying, collecting, and producing electronically stored information (ESI) in response to a legal request or litigation. E-Discovery tools automate and streamline the review and analysis of large volumes of digital data.

Electronic Signature (E-Signature):

A digital version of a handwritten signature used to sign documents electronically. E-Signatures are legally binding in many jurisdictions and are commonly used in automated workflows to expedite contract execution.

Innovation Lab:

A dedicated space or program within a law firm that focuses on developing new legal technologies, processes, and services.

Innovation labs encourage experimentation and foster a culture of innovation within the firm.

Lean Six Sigma:

A methodology that combines Lean manufacturing principles and Six Sigma quality control to improve efficiency and reduce waste. In the legal industry, Lean Six Sigma is used to streamline workflows, improve service delivery, and enhance client satisfaction.

Legal Process Outsourcing (LPO):

The practice of a law firm or corporation outsourcing legal work to external service providers. LPO often involves routine tasks such as document review, legal research, and contract management, which can be enhanced by automation.

Machine Learning:

A subset of AI that involves training algorithms to learn from and make predictions based on data. In the legal field, machine learning is used to improve predictive analytics, automate legal research, and enhance the accuracy of document review.

Natural Language Processing (NLP):

A field of AI that focuses on the interaction between computers and human language. NLP enables machines to understand, interpret, and generate human language, making it a powerful tool for legal research, document review, and contract analysis.

Predictive Analytics:

The use of statistical algorithms and machine learning techniques to identify the likelihood of future outcomes based on historical data. In law, predictive analytics can forecast case outcomes, assess risks, and guide legal strategies.

Productized Services:

Legal services that are standardized, scalable, and offered at a fixed price. Productized services are designed to be repeatable and efficient, providing clients with clear value and predictability in legal costs.

Project Management Software:

Tools that help legal teams plan, execute, and manage projects more efficiently. Project management software can track deadlines, allocate resources, and monitor progress, ensuring that legal projects are completed on time and within budget.

Return on Investment (ROI):

A measure of the profitability of an investment, calculated as the ratio of the net profit to the initial investment cost. In the context of legal automation, ROI is used to assess the financial benefits of adopting new technologies.

Robotic Process Automation (RPA):

A technology that uses software robots to automate repetitive, rule-based tasks. In the legal industry, RPA can be applied to tasks such as data entry, billing, and compliance monitoring, freeing up time for more complex work.

Smart Contract:

A self-executing contract with the terms of the agreement directly written into code. Smart contracts automatically enforce the terms when predefined conditions are met, reducing the need for intermediaries and increasing the efficiency of transactions.

Software-as-a-Service (SaaS):

A software delivery model where applications are hosted by a service provider and accessed by users over the internet. SaaS platforms are commonly used in legal automation for case management, document storage, and client communication.

Virtual Law Firm:

A law firm that operates without a traditional physical office, using technology to deliver legal services online. Virtual law firms leverage cloud computing, video conferencing, and other digital tools to provide flexible and cost-effective services to clients.

Workflow Automation:

The use of technology to automate a sequence of tasks or processes in a legal workflow. Workflow automation streamlines operations, reduces manual work, and ensures consistency and accuracy in legal tasks.

Appendix B: Resources for Further Reading and Tools for Automation

This appendix provides a curated list of recommended books, articles, and tools that can help you delve deeper into the world of workflow automation and legal technology. These resources are valuable for legal professionals who want to expand their knowledge, explore practical applications, and stay updated with the latest developments in the industry.

Books

1. **"Tomorrow's Lawyers: An Introduction to Your Future" by Richard Susskind**
   - This book offers a forward-looking perspective on the legal profession, exploring how technology will reshape the practice of law. Susskind discusses the impact of automation, artificial intelligence, and the changing expectations of clients.
   - *Why Read:* It provides a comprehensive overview of the future of legal services and prepares lawyers for the changes ahead.

2. **"Artificial Intelligence: A Guide for Thinking Humans" by Melanie Mitchell**
   - While not specifically focused on law, this book offers a clear and accessible introduction to artificial intelligence, its capabilities, and its limitations.
   - *Why Read:* Understanding AI is crucial for legal professionals who want to harness its potential in automating legal tasks and improving decision-making processes.

3. **"The Future of the Professions: How Technology Will Transform the Work of Human Experts" by Richard Susskind and Daniel Susskind**
   - This book explores how technology, including automation and AI, is transforming various professions, including law, and what this means for the future of professional services.
   - *Why Read:* It provides insights into how legal professionals can adapt to the changing landscape and the role technology will play in their future careers.

4. **"The Legal Tech Book: The Legal Technology Handbook for Investors, Entrepreneurs and FinTech Visionaries" edited by Sophia Adams Bhatti, Susanne Chishti, Akber Datoo, and Drago Indjic**
    - This book is a comprehensive guide to legal technology, covering various topics from legal AI and blockchain to cybersecurity and regulatory technology.
    - *Why Read:* It's a great resource for those looking to understand the full spectrum of legal tech innovations and their practical applications.

5. **"Law Is a Buyer's Market: Building a Client-First Law Firm" by Jordan Furlong**
    - Furlong argues that the legal market has shifted from being supply-driven to demand-driven, with clients taking control. He discusses how law firms can adapt to this new reality by focusing on efficiency, client service, and innovation.
    - *Why Read:* This book offers practical advice on how to build a law firm that is responsive to client needs and positioned for success in a competitive market.

Articles and Reports

1. **"Law Firm Automation: Transforming Legal Services with AI and Automation" by McKinsey & Company**
    - This report explores the impact of AI and automation on law firms, providing insights into how these technologies are transforming legal services.
    - *Link:* Law Firm Automation by McKinsey
    - *Why Read:* It offers detailed analysis and case studies on how automation is reshaping the legal industry.

2. **"The Future of Legal Services: Global Research Study" by Thomson Reuters**
    - This global research study examines the trends driving change in the legal services market, including the adoption of legal technology and automation.
    - *Link:* The Future of Legal Services
    - *Why Read:* Provides data-driven insights into how the legal industry is evolving and what law firms can do to stay competitive.

3. **"Artificial Intelligence and the Legal Profession" by The Law Society of England and Wales**
    - This report examines the current and potential future uses of AI in the legal profession, highlighting ethical considerations and practical applications.
    - *Link:* AI and the Legal Profession
    - *Why Read:* It offers a comprehensive overview of AI's impact on the legal sector and practical guidance on its implementation.

4. **"Legal Technology: The Rise of Lawtech" by PwC**
    - This article discusses the rapid growth of legal technology, its impact on the legal profession, and how law firms can leverage it to gain a competitive advantage.
    - *Link:* Legal Technology by PwC
    - *Why Read:* Provides an overview of the latest trends in legal tech and offers strategies for law firms to incorporate these technologies into their practices.

5. **"The Impact of Automation on the Legal Profession" by Harvard Law School Center on the Legal Profession**
    - This article discusses how automation is changing the practice of law, the roles within law firms, and the future of legal work.
    - *Link:* Impact of Automation on the Legal Profession
    - *Why Read:* Offers insights from leading legal scholars and practitioners on how automation will shape the future of the legal profession.

Tools for Automation

1. **Clio**
    - Clio is a cloud-based legal practice management software that offers tools for case management, document automation, billing, and client communication.
    - *Link:* Clio
    - *Why Use:* Clio is widely used by law firms of all sizes to streamline their operations and improve efficiency.

2. **Lawyaw**
    - Lawyaw provides document automation software that allows law firms to create customized legal documents quickly and accurately.
    - Link: Lawyaw
    - Why Use: It's a powerful tool for reducing the time spent on drafting and ensuring consistency across legal documents.

3. **PracticePanther**
    - PracticePanther is a legal practice management software that offers features such as task automation, time tracking, billing, and document management.
    - Link: PracticePanther
    - Why Use: This tool helps law firms automate routine tasks and manage their practice more effectively.

4. **Neota Logic**
    - Neota Logic is an AI-driven platform that enables the automation of legal processes and decision-making workflows.
    - Link: Neota Logic
    - Why Use: Ideal for firms looking to implement more advanced automation solutions, particularly for complex legal reasoning and compliance tasks.

5. **DocuSign**
    - DocuSign is an electronic signature platform that allows for secure and legally binding signatures on digital documents.
    - Link: DocuSign
    - Why Use: DocuSign is essential for firms looking to streamline contract execution and reduce the turnaround time for signed documents.

6. **Kira Systems**
    - Kira Systems is an AI-powered contract analysis software that automates the extraction and analysis of key information from contracts.
    - Link: Kira Systems
    - Why Use: This tool enhances due diligence, contract review, and regulatory compliance by speeding up document analysis and improving accuracy.

7. **Relativity**
    - Relativity is a leading e-discovery platform that automates the collection, processing, and review of electronic documents in legal cases.
    - *Link:* Relativity
    - *Why Use:* Relativity is essential for law firms handling large-scale litigation and regulatory investigations, providing powerful tools for managing e-discovery processes.

Appendix C: Legal Automation Tools by Function

1. Document Management and Review

These tools help manage large volumes of documents, automatically review and extract key information, and streamline document-related tasks in litigation, arbitration, and contract management.

Relativity

E-discovery, AI-powered document review, predictive coding, multilingual support.

Kira Systems

AI-driven document analysis, contract clause extraction, customizable templates, multilingual support.

Everlaw

Cloud-based document review, e-discovery, collaborative case preparation.

2. Contract Management

Automating the drafting, reviewing, and approval of contracts across different jurisdictions, these tools help ensure compliance with local laws and reduce manual work.

Ironclad

End-to-end contract lifecycle management, customizable workflows, AI-powered contract analysis.

DocuSign CLM (Contract Lifecycle Management)

Contract automation, secure e-signatures, compliance monitoring.

ContractPodAi

Contract automation, AI-powered contract analysis, risk management.

3. Case Analytics

These tools use predictive analytics to analyze past legal cases, helping legal teams forecast outcomes and strategize more effectively.

Lex Machina

Predictive legal analytics, historical case analysis, outcome prediction.

Premonition AI

Arbitrator and judge analytics, case outcome predictions, jurisdiction-specific data analysis.

DISCO AI

AI-driven litigation insights, document review, and case predictions.

4. Cross-Jurisdictional Research

These platforms help legal professionals access and analyze laws, regulations, and case precedents across multiple jurisdictions.

Thomson Reuters Westlaw Edge

AI-powered legal research, cross-jurisdictional case law access, global legal commentary.

vLex

Multijurisdictional legal research, AI assistant (Vincent), real-time global updates on laws and cases.

LexisNexis

Comprehensive legal research, global case law access, analytics.

5. Compliance Monitoring

These tools monitor regulatory changes and ensure that businesses and clients comply with laws across multiple jurisdictions.

Thomson Reuters HighQ

Compliance tracking, real-time updates on legal changes, workflow automation.

ClauseMatch

Compliance management, automated policy review, regulatory monitoring.

Compliance.ai

Continuous monitoring of regulatory changes, AI-driven compliance updates, multi-jurisdictional tracking.

6. Workflow Automation

These tools help automate routine legal tasks, improving efficiency and freeing up lawyers to focus on higher-value work.

Clio

Legal practice management, workflow automation, client intake, billing.

ZyLAB

Document review, AI-powered e-discovery, automation of litigation workflows.

Smokeball

Workflow automation, document management, legal practice management.

7. Risk Assessment and Reporting

AI-powered tools for analyzing legal risks and generating detailed reports to help businesses and law firms identify potential compliance issues.

LawGeex

AI-powered contract review, risk assessment, automated report generation.

Onit

AI-driven contract lifecycle management, risk assessment, compliance tracking.

Compliance.ai

Risk management, automated regulatory tracking, real-time reporting.

8. Virtual Collaboration and Client Management

These platforms enable law firms to collaborate across borders, manage client relationships, and handle case files digitally.

Microsoft Teams (Legal Edition)

Secure collaboration, integrated case management, real-time document sharing.

HighQ

Collaborative project management, secure document sharing, client portals.

Slack (Legal Integrations)

Team collaboration, legal-specific integrations for case and document management.

9. Legal Research and AI Assistants

These AI tools assist lawyers in legal research, helping them quickly access relevant information and precedents.

Casetext

AI-powered research assistant (CARA), legal research, brief analysis.

Blue J Legal

Predictive legal analytics, tax and employment law focus, jurisdiction-specific insights.

Alexi

On-demand legal research assistant, provides detailed legal memos and summaries across various practice areas.

The Future-Proof Lawyer

This book was created using a blend of traditional research, document drafting, and modern technologies, including AI-driven tools for writing, editing, and research. These tools helped streamline the process and allowed for greater efficiency in producing high-quality content. If the use of AI or other technology in the creation of this book gives you pause, perhaps consider reading it again— you may have missed the point about how embracing innovation can enhance, rather than detract from, the quality and delivery of legal services.